NEVER-ENDING WONDER

BODIES, MOVEMENTS, AND TIME IN CONTEMPORARY FILM

NEVER-ENDING WONDER

BODIES, MOVEMENTS, AND TIME IN CONTEMPORARY FILM

JULIO BEZERRA

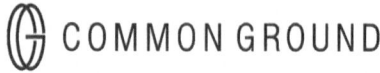

First published in 2025
As part of **The Image Book Imprint**
Common Ground Research Networks
University of Illinois Research Park
2001 South First St, Suite 201 L
Champaign, IL 61820 USA

Library of Congress Cataloging-in-Publication Data
Names: Bezerra, Julio author
Title: Never-ending wonder : bodies, movements, and time in contemporary film / Julio Bezerra.
Description: Chicago, IL : Common Ground Research Networks, 2025. |

Includes index. | Summary: "In Never Ending Wonder, Julio Bezerra embarks on a lyrical and rigorous journey through the sensorial, philosophical, and affective territories of a certain contemporary cinema. With a keen eye for nuance and an expansive intellectual grounding, Bezerra draws connections between film and phenomenology, threading together thinkers like Merleau-Ponty, Deleuze, Bazin, and Ayfre with filmmakers such as Claire Denis, Pedro Costa, Tsai Ming-Liang, and Apichatpong Weerasethakul. This is not a conventional film theory book. It is an evocative meditation on how cinema can transform perception, dissolve dualities, and bring forth new ways of being in the world. Moving beyond narrative and representation, Bezerra explores a cinema of atmosphere, bodies, and affect-a cinema that touches, confuses, and embraces, inviting the viewer into an experience that is both intimate and open-ended. Written with poetic clarity and philosophical depth, Never Ending Wonder is an invitation to reimagine how we watch, think, and feel cinema. It speaks not only to scholars and cinephiles, but to anyone who believes in the power of film to challenge, comfort, and awaken. This book is a passionate, personal, and intellectually generous exploration of a cinema that does not seek to explain the world-but to encounter it, feel it, and remain in awe of its infinite becoming"-- Provided by publisher.

Identifiers: LCCN 2025015335 (print) | LCCN 2025015336 (ebook) | ISBN 9781966214533 hardback | ISBN 9781966214540 paperback | ISBN 9781966214557 adobe pdf
Subjects: LCSH: Motion pictures--Philosophy | LCGFT: Film criticism
Classification: LCC PN1995 .B436 2025 (print) | LCC PN1995 (ebook) | DDC 791.4301--dc23/eng/20250424
LC record available at https://lccn.loc.gov/2025015335
LC ebook record available at https://lccn.loc.gov/2025015336

CONTENTS

To my beautiful Polola,
whose presence makes everything suddenly lighter

I want the unfinished: the deep organic disorder
which, however, suggests an underlying order.
The great power of potentiality.

Clarice Lispector

INTRODUCTION

It is night. Tong and Keng ride a motorcycle. Tong urinates on the side of a deserted road. When he returns to his partner, he mentions something about the following day. Keng interrupts to sniff Tong's hand and gently rubs it over his own face. Tong says he did not wash his hands. Reverse shot. Tong smiles broadly. The smile gives way to a longing gaze. In a medium shot, and shortly afterward, in a close-up, Tong reciprocates the affection. But now he not only smells Keng's hand but also licks it intensely. After another exchange of shots, they both smile. Tong turns his back on Keng and inexplicably walks alone into the pitch-black darkness of the night. Reverse shot. Keng remains where he was and looks directly into the pitch blackness. A few seconds pass. A pop song ("Straight," by the Thai band Fashion Show) invades the diegesis, disrupting the previously somewhat bucolic setting of the soundtrack. Lulled by the song, Keng smiles as he rides his motorcycle through the streets of a small town. Traveling shots, combined with the music, show us cars circulating along an avenue, crowded markets, and a fight. One of the bullies throws a bottle at Keng, toward the camera, toward us, as if he was being filmed without his consent. These are spontaneous fragments, stolen from reality without its knowledge. They appear intimate, amateurish, sticky, and genuine to me. Night gives way to day. We are now in the back of a pickup truck with Keng, his army buddies and the song. There follows a succession of close-ups and a shot filled with a mixture of road dust and white smoke coming out of the vehicle's exhaust.

This is one of the most famous sequences from *Tropical Malady* (*Sud Pralad*, 2004), by Apichatpong Weerasethakul. I could, however, have chosen other scenes, from other films made in various regions of the world. *Good Work* (*Beau Travail*, 1999), by Claire Denis, for example, begins with a frontal tracking shot of an uneven wall, deteriorated by time. In faded inks, there is a drawing of soldiers in black on a red background. In the soundtrack, the anthem of the Foreign Legion — a military unit created in the nineteenth century to defend the interests of France with its colonies. Cut. Credits. Cut. A nightclub. Colorful lights. A woman blows a kiss outside the frame, introducing the song "Kiss Kiss," from Tarkan. She dances with a haughty look in her eyes, exuding a certain confidence in her being in the world, like a sensitive presence that imposes itself. The camera walks between bodies on the dance floor. Some soldiers appear. Only two of them remain still. A soldier, accompanying the chorus of the song, blows a kiss to his companion. Cut. Movie title. Cut. A telephone station. On the phone, a gentleman says: "Hello, Djibouti." We are in Africa. From the window of a moving train we see the desert, and then the passengers. Montage takes us back to the desert, whose substance, as if by osmosis, takes all the bodies for itself. One shadow, two, three…Legion soldiers appear shirtless with their arms stretched to the sky. "Billy Budd" (the song has the same name as the book by Herman Melville, in which Denis was inspired to make the feature), by Benjamin Britten, grows in the soundtrack. The bodies scribble the space, cut the wind, fill the frame, from earth to sky. Cut to the blue sea. A superposition shows us a letter being written. We are now on a boat. A close-up. A sequence of close-ups.

Something different happens in these films. A different kind of time is privileged, a wandering, fragile, brief, and indeterminate kind of time. These movies are sensitive to the slightest movement, but they seem unwilling to prioritize the impressions and elements in the scene. Scene? Maybe the term does not make sense. *Tropical Malady* and *Good Work* are deliberately "on hold" features: The characters, the plot, and the narrative are stripped of their most conventional anchorages. Nothing is apprehended. Nothing beyond what we see and feel. And I feel at the same time abandoned and uplifted, by the music, by the atmosphere, by affections and emotions. It is difficult to say exactly where the filmmakers want to go, but, on the other hand, it is evident that something, some meaning, lies ahead. An enigma, without a doubt—but an intimate enigma.

Instead of establishing an informative context, giving us the necessary elements for us to orient ourselves in the middle of a story, these sequences focus on fundamental qualities of cinema that tend to be annulled by its representative, discursive, and narrative functions: the variations of movement and light, colors and sounds, a process of constant figuration, of constitution of atmospheres, tones, tonalities, and rhythms. A kind of hypnosis is taking place. The images and sounds create an impression of volume and density, and seem to undergo several mutations, as if they were being sculpted. The screen becomes a sort of partially open portal to the time and space of each shot.

A cinema that bets on a sensory experience that is no longer connected, as underlined by Erly Monteiro Vieira Jr. (2012), to a decantation/condensation or, on the contrary, to a deconstruction/denial of the narrative thread "but rather to a logic of narrative dilution"[1] in the landscape, in the bodies. The image is no longer subordinated to the action, to the plastic and dramatic organization of the elements of a film, or to a specific discourse or ideology. Apichatpong and Denis are far from the mannerism, the hyper-realism, or the blurring of technology frontiers, which marked the 1980s and 1990s. They are also far from the predominant paradigm of the modern cinema of the 1960s and 1970s, which also prioritizes bodies and a certain idea of sensoriality, although in the midst of an insistent and varied attack on the notions of fiction and representation. Tatian Monassa (2004) elaborates:

> If modern cinema broke the pact of trust between the spectator and the image, leading to a generation that needed to reflect on language in order to reflect on the world, some paths of the vast and polyform 'contemporary cinema' indicate a return to the belief in the image. As a statement of belief in the world. The cinematographic image serves as a privileged mediator between the spectator, who is immersed in the pleasure of experiencing it, and the physical and living world. Surrendering to the pulsating images, we can also pulsate along with them and feel them in all their intensity.[2]

Apichatpong and Denis play with the ability of vision to evoke the other senses in a way that blurs and confuses them, without completely erasing their distinctions. A certain tactility is regained. A haptic gaze is established, not only in the sense of a two-dimensionality and/or a lack of visual depth, which would cause us to explore the surface of the cinematographic image, as well as the bodies on stage, but also in terms of vision, which starts to be conceived, summoned, and perceived as an organ of touch. Although I am discussing an entirely different set of films, Laura U. Marks (2000) helps me out:

> Haptic images can give the impression of seeing for the first time, gradually discovering what is in the image rather than coming to the image already knowing what it is. Several such works represent the point of view of a disoriented traveler unsure how to read the world in which he finds himself.[3]

---

[1] Vieira Jr. (2012, 16).

[2] Monassa (2004).

[3] Marks (2000, 178).

This sense of being adrift is something that often accompanies me throughout a certain contemporary cinema. Apichatpong and Denis are not alone. What about the scene of a focused young man who listens and records sounds in a subway station while multiple trains pass through the frame and the camera appears to be a living thing (*Café Lumière* [Kohi Jiko, 2003], by Hou Hsiao-Hsien)? Characters, such as *Colossal Youth*'s Ventura (*Juventude em Marcha* [2006], by Pedro Costa) can be seen as fable-like figures who assert themselves by the desired imagination and narrativity? Gus Van Sant's Gerrys, abandoned in a meaningless world, running the dazzling and threatening risk of becoming abstract blotches on the canvas? The fabric of routine and the "real as a miracle"[4] in *Shara* (*Sharasojyu*, 2003), by Naomi Kawase. The rain, idleness, heat, Mecha and her guests, drunk on wine, stretched out on beach chairs by an inoperable swimming pool in *The Swamp* (*La Ciénaga*, 2001), by Lucrecia Martel. Or even Hsiao-Kang, Tsai Ming-Liang's fetish character/actor, who makes each shot a field of experimentation in the world?

A kind of "new transnational wave," unique since the mid-1960s, has asserted itself by the end of the 1990s and beginning of the 2000s. It is intriguing to pay attention to the fact that directors as different as Costa, Denis, Hsiao-Hsien, Tsai, and Apichatpong,[5] in addition to many others, such as Edward Yang, Karim Aïnouz, Kawase, Martel, and Van Sant, have affinities in their views of the world and cinema. It is something that undoubtedly brings them closer to the great names of modern cinema, reaffirming traditional issues in different terms. It is a process of radicalization of the project of emptying the notion of representation in the name of other forms of apprehending reality. *Tropical Malady*, *Good Work*, *Café Lumière*, *Shara*, *The Swamp*, *Gerry* (2002), and *The River* (*He Liu*, 1997), among many others, narrate a state of affairs at the surface of the skin, calling the spectator closer and demanding from us the ability to be fascinated by moving images. It must be said that these films are not in an oppositional mode. This contemporary cinema is not made in a movement of antagonism in relation to the so-called modern and classic cinema. Quite the opposite. This is a cinema that combines the ability to listen and observe the present with a rare plastic sensitivity to the image and its material. It is a cinema in which the

---

[4] This is the title of an interview with Naomi Kawase conducted by Felipe Bragança for *Cinética* magazine in 2007: http://www.revistacinetica.com.br/kawase.html.

[5] Tsai Ming-Liang and Apichatpong Weerasethakul are very particular cases of filmmakers who, in general, are more likely to be cited with their first names. I, for absolutely idiosyncratic reasons, follow the trend. Hereafter I will refer to them as Tsai and Apichatpong—the latter, in fact, even adopted a Western name (Joe) that never really caught on.

body functions as a catalyst. It is political but not exactly militant. At the same time, conceptual and sensory, narrative and disnarrative. A cinema that seems to demand a certain cinematographic virginity and operates in the shattering of the borders and dualisms that mark film's history and theory.

It was in the mid-1980s, through the work of Hsiao-Hsien, that this cinema came to the fore. Alongside the mannerist[6] cinema of Brian De Palma, Wim Wenders, and many others, the fetishized body of Hollywood (from successful and paradigmatic films such as *9½ Weeks* [1986], by Adrian Lyne), the technological intervention in the organic body (Paul Verhoeven), and the conception of the body as an electronic system, originated with the power of computational engineering (as in much of David Cronenberg's cinema), the Taiwanese filmmaker embarked on his first feature films (*Cute Girl* [*Jiu shi liuliu de ta*, 1980], *The Green, Green Grass of Home* [*Zai na he pan qing cao qing*, 1982], and *The Sandwich Man* [*Er zi de da wan'ou*, 1983]). What we see, however, especially from *The Boys from Fengkuei* (*Fengkuei-lai-te jen*, 1983), reaching a kind of peak of no return in *Goodbye South, Goodbye* (*Zaijian, nanguo, zaijian*, 1996), is a mise-en-scène of ephemerality, fascinated by movement, by any and all forms of movement (train, motorcycle, car, people). Movement as what makes the world visible.

These films oscillate between the banality of certain situations and the superficiality of the most varied rituals, between audiovisual landscapes and empty characters and the epiphanic emergence of a wide range of feelings. It is a cinema of sketches, silhouettes, suggestions, and, at the same time, the singular presence of things. A form of cinema "sustained between contemplation and composition."[7] Hsiao-Hsien completely transforms the traditional notion of a shot and delicately experiments with a certain distance as a condition for a gaze, for a cinema, in which things can reappear, in which the spectator's feelings and affections are engulfed in contemplation. It is something truly paradoxical: from the emptiness, the insipidity of meaning, from the failure of my eager rush for meanings, to the conscious and embodied realization of an experience pregnant with possibilities, as "an initiation to Taoist cosmogony."[8] In an interview, Hsiao-Hsien, a central

---

[6.] The term "Mannerist," which indicates an artistic ideal of refinement and sophistication, was first used to refer to a school of painting in the second half of the sixteenth century that favored form over content. It is the art of complex forms, arabesque and elegance with a taste for asymmetries. The so-called great Mannerist painters are Pontormo and Rosso. In April 1985, *Cahiers du Cinéma* published a dossier that tried to account for that period. The hypothesis behind this undertaking had already been discussed in previous editions of the magazine and was based on the idea that cinema, like the visual arts after the Renaissance, was going through a "mannerist moment."

[7.] Baecque (2011, 34).

[8.] Ibid., 35.

reference for filmmakers who will be investigated further ahead, sets the tone of his cinema:

> *I was influenced by an old Chinese proverb attributed to Confucius: 'Look and don't intervene,' 'Observe and don't judge.' The important thing is not to intervene in things, modify them or criticize them. Every thing, every person is different. Each person has his own environment. So to judge is vain and useless. What I want is to be in the middle, and simply see what happens inside each environment, without trying to create judgments. I know that I am nothing more than a subjectivity, but I can, despite everything, try to place myself in the middle of things without imprinting the mark of my subjectivity on that of others. Until now, it was always in this direction that I worked.*[9]

French critics were the first to highlight and speculate about this cinema. Several perspectives emerged in the early 2000s. One of the initial milestones in this regard was Stéphane Bouquet's essay, "Plan contre flux" ("Shot Against Flux"), published by *Cahiers du Cinéma* in March 2002. In it, the critic proposes a distinction between what he calls "shot aesthetics" and "flow aesthetics," both sharing space in the contemporary scenario. This distinction goes back to a debate that, in the seventeenth century, opposed the defenders of design and the advocates of color. Drawing was not exactly copying reality but rather applying knowledge, logic, and a certain order into work. Lovers of color, on the contrary, allow themselves to be captivated by a sense of vertigo, which is evident in Baroque art. Bouquet mentions Poussin's anger toward Caravaggio, who was accused of "destroying painting" by renouncing "beautiful ideas," drawing, in the name of the "seductive charms of color." One believed in resisting the physical character of color in order to pursue a more analytical investigation of things. The other privileged the notion of consistency and volume, emphasizing the need to keep the formal construction of figures open. On the one hand, there is the sharpness of the contour. On the other, the dash.

The painters close to drawing would be for shot filmmakers what lovers of color would be for flow filmmakers. The French François Ozon would belong to the first group. His films are made in a brick-by-brick construction, in an exercise of the frame, as a sum of speeches composed at different levels. In features such as *8 Women* (*8 Femmes*, 2002) and *Sitcom* (1998), Bouquet identifies the belief in the possibility of a transcendent order that shapes reality. For the author, by

---

[9.] Frodon (1999, 68, 69).

making his work in a "void," no longer in a story, but in its construction, Ozon would be a kind of "limit representative" of a cinematographic line centered on a law of mental organization that goes back especially to Alfred Hitchcock. Flow aesthetes, on the other hand, would plunge into the empirical disorder of appearances, into a certain sensory confusion, in the indistinctness of things captured by the camera. Bouquet mentions filmmakers such as Hsiao-Hsien and Denis, who are more interested in exploring the body–space relationship within an experience of time as atmosphere. He explains:

> *Flow aesthetes' mission is not to create a well-defined form to turn it into a discourse, but to intensify zones of reality and concretize certain powers, leaving everything to the account of the real and its uncertain, undecided, moving status. This consists of creating rhythm while others generate meaning.*[10]

This notion of a cinema or aesthetics of flow took root in the magazine. Jean-Marc Lalanne would return to the concept in the midst of the 2002 Cannes Film Festival coverage. In search of a lowest common denominator among the films that intrigued him the most that year, Lalane outlines a behavior of the gaze that challenges the more traditional elements that circumscribe the concept of mise-en-scène.[11] He redefines the equation between flow and shot, no longer in terms of a distinction, and points to an aesthetic horizon that would take the form of a flow, redescribing the notion of shot. Olivier Joyard echoes Lalane's question, "C'est quoi ce plan? (La suite)" ["What Shot is That? (the continuation)"], the following year, in the midst of yet another Cannes Film Festival. Joyard begins by acknowledging cinema's integration into the broader realm of visual imagery. He proposes a distinction between two approaches: "eternal mannerism" (recycling of forms, restoration of myths) and what he calls "cinema-karaoke" (the history of cinema as a "picture jukebox" that filmmakers can tap into). When walking between these two options, the critic makes use of the expression "sentimental-concept-shot." Bouquet himself would return to the concept of flow in a text from that same year. In it, the critic claims that perhaps what brings filmmakers as diverse as Denis and Wong Kar-wai closer is their depiction of a world as a kind of ripple or "generalized fluctuation." Flow, for him, implies a world that is always changing, as an accumulation of temporalities, no

---

[10] Bouquet (2002, 46).

[11] To learn more about this, which is one of the richest and most passionate terms in the history of film criticism, see Oliveira Jr. (2014).

longer organized according to the demands of a drama, an ideology, a discourse, or even a mise-en-scène.

Although they had a significant impact on film criticism (including the Brazilian one, especially in online magazines such as *Contracampo* and *Cinética*), these discussions were not duly deepened, and would only timidly reach the academy, whether on this or the other side of the Atlantic. The critics' effort, in close contact with the films, was able to identify and explore a series of common elements and interests with regard to contemporary cinema. However, the need to single them out as something new and group them under a name, be it "aesthetics of flow," "subtle cinema," or "sentimental-concept-shot," perhaps even due to the heat of the moment, amid coverage of a festival such as Cannes, it reveals a work that does not stand up to a more rigorous review.

The notion of flow, for example, has been around since at least the French Impressionists of the 1920s.[12] Jean Epstein, poet, filmmaker, and philosopher of cinema, is a notable example. In his writings, Epstein observes that the fundamental energies that sustain cinema are balanced between rapt attention (associated with stillness) and ceaseless flow (associated with movement), and he gives privileged emphasis to the latter. For him, cinema does not simply reproduce things when they are offered to my gaze. It registers them as the human eye cannot see them, as they arise, in a state of waves and vibrations, before they can be classified as intelligible objects, people, or events. In *The Tempest* (*Le Tempestaire*, 1947), Epstein experiments with various variations of speed, exploring ideas about time in film as a set of simultaneous temporalities. He allows the wind, the sea, the coast, and humans inform and interact with each other, granting each other different perspectives. These entities are continuously filmed in slow motion, with an equally unique manipulation of sound. What I see and hear is something between solid and liquid, the ocean alive in viscous movements. Cinema is not just a reproduction of movement but rather a new form of movement, created through variations in the audiovisual material of image and sound.

And what about Maya Deren's cinema? Watching her films is like undressing little by little. She does not think of the seventh art in terms of its uses or conventions but of its sensitive powers and potentials. *Meshes of the Afternoon* (1943), her first and most famous film, assimilates the most diverse materials and transforms them into elements of her cinema: space-time discontinuities, flashbacks, ellipses, speed variations, different angles, etc. Deren never made the

---

[12.] The collections of French criticisms and theories organized by Richard Abel (1988, 1993) reveal the recurrence of both the term and the themes associated with it.

use or mixture of these procedures an issue. Most importantly: they operate as an anagram in which all elements exist in a simultaneous and non-hierarchical relationship. *A Study Choreography for Camera* (1945), for example, is a film-thesis about the infinite possibilities of articulations between the filmic space and the movements of a dancer. The character keeps moving, fulfilling an internal logic, jumping from one space-time to another, unaffected by the constraints of time and gravity, in a compilation of floating images. This is a cinema that transcends bodies, obstacles, and the laws of nature, where any body can connect with any other, without limitations of space-time.

The distinction made by Bouquet between the shot and the flow filmmakers — as well as his diagnosis of an indisposition among flow aesthetes concerning all forms of otherness[13] — also sounds inappropriate to me. It does not seem to me that an approach that operates according to divisions and dichotomies does justice to the cinema of Hsiao-Hsien, Denis, Costa, Tsai, and Apichatpong. This cinema defies the borders and dualisms (between concept and feeling, between body and character, between the "real" and its spectral extensions, between mise-en-scène and the exercise of the gaze) that have traditionally defined film history and theory. These are filmmakers who believe in the image as a way of believing in reality — breaking once and for all with the distinction made by André Bazin between those "who believe in the image" and those who "believe in reality." There are not, on the one hand, directors who start from a saturated history of cinema, and on the other, those who seek a reunion with a kind of indeterminate access to the world. There are not those who inform the real and those who open up to the real. The question is no longer there. Perhaps this was never the issue. When watching films like *Colossal Youth* or *The River* "suspicion" and "fascination" seem to be more appropriate terms. Perhaps a fascination questioned by suspicion and a suspicion interdicted by fascination. Nor do I yield to thought in the name of sensation. On the contrary, films like *Tropical Malady* and *Good Work* serve as fluid and embodied forms of thought, helping me to imagine ways out of the dead ends that dual thinking inevitably leads us to.

It is, therefore, necessary to look for other ways, other references, to constitute another look. Films like *Colossal Youth*, *The River*, *Tropical Malady*, and *Good*

[13.] In 2003, when he resumes the concept, Bouquet makes the following caveat:
On the one hand, the flow is a folding of the filmmaker over the heart of his desire outside the fearsome reality that is necessarily rupture. From this point of view, it is not guaranteed that Tsui Hark or Hou Hsiao-Hsien, Wong Kar-wai, Claire Denis are less reactionary filmmakers than Sokourov, that is, less haunted by the reconstitution of a paradise lost or even never possessed; on the other hand, the flow does not offer the Other any possibility of remaining at the edge of the film, or at the side. It is a world without difference, without otherness. It is necessary to dive into the common movement, to give up thought for sensation. (2003, 53)

Work intuitively shape a certain cinema. A cinema interested in broadening notions of cinematographic corporeality, emphasizing the tangible presence of the image and exceeding the limits of representation. A cinema that privileges the primary identification with the film as an event rather than identification with characters captured in plot developments. These characters are presented to us not as spirits, symbols, or metaphors, not even as "psychisms," but, as I see them, in the experience of some sensation. These bodies are present no longer just according to their projective appearance or referencing to the demands of a drama. Instead, they stand insistently, bothering and seducing the eye with their edges and fluency. These bodies claim an absolute, almost exclusive presence. They never let themselves be fully grasped.

The world described in films such as *The Swamp* and *Madame Satã* (2002), by Karim Aïnouz, is, above all, a physical realm, in its interstices, in its microscopic and permanent movement. It is a promiscuous world that identifies itself with the sensorial aspect of the characters; bodies that interact with the landscape, with the bodies of nature, animated or inanimate, integrated, in an always reversible process of reciprocal constitution. These are films that are situated in a kind of naive dimension of the world, which express or denote an immediate, perceptual, non-conceptual (but not for that reason chaotic or disjointed) dimension of experience. A feature film like *Goodbye South, Goodbye* gropes around an intention to express something for which we have no model. It is the film itself, in action, in its ebb and flow, that opens an access route to the images that make possible an experience that is loaded with meaning—but that does not seek to anchor it in pre-established meanings.

The cinematographic experience is a creative experience that not only enables us to think what has already been thought but compels us to feel what still has no name: the capture of the instituting as creation or the dawn of the world. This power, which fuels the seventh art and seems to me to be exploited to the last consequences in this contemporary cinema, is seen especially in the way in which contemporary filmmakers venture under the skin, for a more sensorial realism centered on the phenomenon of experience. One of the greatest impulses of this cinema is the physical enchantment of the body. The bodies take on a different look. They are, once again, fascinating. They are thrown into my lap. We become intimate. These bodies, however, are opaque, resistant, and unpredictable. These bodies serve as a reflection, as a metaphor, as an experimental place of representation and expression, between their materiality, their impenetrable thickness, and their sense or significance.

This contemporary cinema that interests me finds in phenomenology a certain support, an inspiration, methodological subsidies, and/or a strong dialogue partner. The major hypothesis that drives this book is precisely that phenomenology, which can be explored as a valuable tool in this encounter with a certain contemporary cinema. By seeking a reunion with a more naive contact between shapes, colors, planes, movements, and what they express to us; by deconstructing these layers of meanings in order to reconstitute them, in the film itself, in its ebb and flow; by inviting and/or imposing on us the experience of an experience, a sort of shared perspective on the characters' experiences created through film, phenomenology, in short, proves to be able to make me envision a different way of approaching and expanding these features.

Although the term "phenomenon" comes directly from Kantian philosophy, and Hegel was the first to use the word phenomenology to indicate the knowledge that consciousness has of itself through the other phenomena that appear to it, it is with Edmund Husserl that it perpetuates itself as a philosophical current that aims to clarify how the possibility of knowing worldly events and objects is based on the structures of consciousness. An investigation centered on the concept of "intentionality," tying consciousness to the world: "to be aware is to always be aware of something," says the Husserlian maxim. This motto, this desire to speak about things as they were touched, resounded throughout Europe, inspiring the most diverse thinkers toward the possibility of a more concrete philosophy of everyday life, which did not deny the existence of the outside world (on the contrary, it affirmed that it is already there before any reflection) nor the existence of the "inner world."

Maurice Merleau-Ponty is one of them. In the French thinker's theory, the problem of the relationship between the soul and the body is exposed in new terms. Merleau-Ponty founds a particular phenomenology that does not start from consciousness, as in Husserl, who, taking the Cartesian separation between the corporeal and the psychic to its ultimate consequences, ended up affirming that subjectivity would constitute reality or conceive the world from itself. In *Phenomenology of Perception*, the author undertakes a bodily turn within phenomenology, making the body defined in another way the central foundation of his initial thought. Merleau-Ponty distinguishes the "objective body," taken as a thing, extensive matter situated in space, and the "phenomenal body," also called the "proper body." One is the body I observe, governed by biological laws. The other is my body or the body that I am. It is what gives me the first-person experience, which opens the doors of perception, the point of reference that situates me in time and space, thereby engendering the world I inhabit.

It is important to stress that, for Merleau-Ponty, these are not exactly two different bodies, one objective and the other subjective, but two different inscriptions of the body in experience. The center of gravity of my experience shifts as well. When I touch my left hand, I experience it as an object of touch rather than as part of the touching subject. The right hand, in turn, is perceived as the subject of touch, and not as an object. This experience, however, is changeable. After all, I can perfectly invert the equation. The general sensitive layer in which body and things participate and which legitimizes the naive pretension of reaching the world itself in immediate experience is called "flesh," while the interweaving and always possible inversion between subject and object positions is called "reversibility" — concepts that will accompany the phenomenologist in a second moment of his philosophy, when he reviews the role of the body and the notion of sensitive, moving toward an ontology.

In this movement to recover a pre-logical or pre-predicative dimension of experience, along with its ambiguity and indeterminacy, Merleau-Ponty, at the beginning of his trajectory, would find a maximum convergence with cinema: the common intention of making us relearn how to see the world. In "The Cinema and the New Psychology", published in 1945, the same year as his most famous work, *Phenomenology of Perception*, the phenomenologist sees in cinema the celebration of an inherence of the being to the world and to the next, an active dialectic between interior and exterior, between sensitive and intelligible, between shown and hidden, between world and narrative. Cinema would be an art particularly apt "to make manifest the union of mind and body, mind and world, and the expression of one in the other."[14]

Phenomenology, in fact, proved to be a rich foundation from which various analyses of cinema developed throughout the 1940s and 1950s. In a more elementary sense, phenomenology is not just a current of thought that prioritizes certain ideas and principles but a way of restructuring the way we position theoretical problems as a whole, not placing the entity in its being but seeking to accompany it in its own field of manifestation. Phenomenology would initially attract names like Bazin and Amédée Ayfre, who, inspired by the emergence of Italian neorealism, would turn to the realistic half of the cinematographic image. Michel Mourlet, Roger Munier, and, later, Jean Mitry, based on other filmographies, drew upon their discussion about the image within its relationships with

---

[14.] Merleau-Ponty (1991, 58).

the object of which it is an image, about what this relationship would be able to manifest and what meanings it would radiate.

Although squeezed between two periods of strong and disparate ideological charges (post-war realism and deconstructive ruptures), having been pushed to the sidelines amid the transition from the film club era to the university era, the phenomenological tradition in cinema built a field consistent enough to stand on its own two feet. When going to the cinema, the phenomenologically inspired authors move in an attempt to describe the value and "importance which all of us have sensed within certain moments of cinema."[15] They share a certain primacy granted to the immediate plane of life, considered as founding and originating. This common point is expressed in the very structure of the experience, seen as containing a pre-reflective or non-discursive dimension that has a particular richness and complexity, which are not overcome by the linguistic ordering of meanings. Andrew continues:

> *Instead of systematic grammars they write chapters on 'Emotion in the Cinema' and on 'Our Experience of Movement in the Cinema,' because for them such experiences, both private and societal, must be the starting point and the ultimate goal of research. Grammars, lexicons, and structural studies in general can only remove us from the cinema and force us to focus on a second-level system (a logical system), which itself rests on a metaphysics or an epistemology masking a metaphysics.*[16]

The objective of the first chapter is precisely to explore this tradition, beginning with Merleau-Ponty, an author who believed that cinema had the ability to give us with a tacit understanding of the human being in the world, but also to imbricate us in an ontological proposition by the act of vision. Then I go to Ayfre, Bazin, Mourlet, Munier, and Mitry. These are some of the names who nourished this dialogue between cinema and phenomenology—although, it must be said, this is an absolutely personal approach, influenced by preferences that are mine, and that, in no way, accounts for the richness that marks this association. I will, however, cover a wide range of investigations into the essence of cinema, the way in which thought and thing, exterior and interior, are captured in the same texture, the ontological proposition that the images set in motion, the role of the spectator, the ability to record everyday life, the contingent, the

---

[15.] Andrew (1976, 253).

[16.] Andrew (1978, 46).

world in its incessant becoming…I walk among these authors as if looking for artifacts, tools, and hypotheses. With these findings, I will navigate more and better through a certain contemporary cinema.

Despite his harsh criticism of phenomenologically inspired film theory, in particular, and phenomenology, in general, Gilles Deleuze is also extremely important to me—beyond his movement-images and time-images. Deleuze left aside epistemological questions around the image, the subject, language and knowledge, and definitely put ontology back on the agenda. Instead of thinking of cinema as a (misleading) epistemological practice, opposing true/false, appearance/being, body/spirit, Deleuze imagined the seventh art not in opposition to life or as a double of it, but part of it, open to the Bergsonian universe of energies, processes, becomings, and intensities. What is at stake is considering cinematographic images as critical acts, analyzing them through the questions that emerge from them.

Deleuze interests me, as we will see in the second chapter, because he was able to describe, like few others, the primordial dialectic between what is thought and what is not thought that constitutes cinema. He speaks of a "the birth of the visible which is still hidden from view."[17] Cinema as an art that makes the space and light that are there speak, that captures the look of things, which is not an appreciation, nor a judgment of the world, but belief and faith in its continued rebirth. Cinema being able to raise the faculty of feeling to a certain threshold of intensity that frees it from the schemes that engender it, and makes me envision new forms of life, a new type of relationship between things in the world.

Deleuze had several criticisms of phenomenology—including Merleau-Ponty's cinematographic approach. According to him, by raising "natural perception" as a norm, phenomenology would constitute a static focus, based on an intentional awareness in a situation. If Deleuze is right in alerting to the foundational aspect that embarrasses Merleau-Ponty's initial phenomenology, it is necessary to recognize the transformation that the phenomenologist's thought was going through at the moment of his death, when he understood that his first works had not been able to conceive the unity of the phenomenal body and the objective body, since the transcendental field was thought, ultimately, as depending on the act of a subject, of an "existence," of a "spirit."

In *The Visible and the Invisible*, the experience is described as dehiscence. It is no longer seen as a coupling between subject and object but as a fission that, from the primordial unity of the flesh, gives rise, one to the other, body and

---

[17.] Deleuze (1989, 201).

world, observer and observed, I and other. It is the very statute of the body that changes as Merleau-Ponty advances in a redescription of the sensible. I do not understand myself while I understand myself. This non-coincidence is insurmountable. Totality is always present as an absence. The self cannot coincide with itself in pure interiority. It can only be found and reached within the thickness of the world to which it is open. The philosopher discovers in this description a subversion of current ideas of things and the world, which lead to an ontological rehabilitation of the sensitive. For Merleau-Ponty, the ontological problem is the one that takes precedence over all others. For this very reason, ontology could not be a theism, a naturalism or a humanism.

My bet, therefore, is not on an opposition but rather on a sort of communion between Deleuze, Merleau-Ponty and a theory and criticism of phenomenological inspiration. I believe that each work has a certain unthought—that is, that which, through it, and only it—that comes to us as not yet thought. This thoughtless does not belong to Merleau-Ponty, Bazin or Deleuze, much less to their fervent and respective followers.

Cinema enters philosophy through a specific scrutiny of the question of the meaning of the world without referring to anything other than the experience of this world. Cinema makes me recognize that my relationship with the world and the meanings that emerge from it are a possibility, they are my responsibility, and that they always remain inadequate, filled with bifurcations, orders, units and hierarchies. It is not, therefore, a philosophy that dominates cinema. Nor is it a philosophy that lends cinema an authority it lacks. Cinematic thinking must be able to resist being absorbed into a specific worldview and be seen as an opportunity to think beyond that. Daniele Rugo helps me: "This irreducibility, the lack of an essence, the pressure that brings thinking to the outside."[18] So what interests me is an engagement with what cinema can show us about the world and ourselves in the world. Let me be clear: This is not about giving up my ability to critically analyze and evaluate what is presented to me but about affirming varied, diverse ways of expanding the experience of a film.

Following the views of the main thinkers mentioned and discussed throughout this book, I will consider film both as representation—in the more general sense of providing us with symbolically constructed models of experience—and as presentation, inseparably linked to aesthetic perception and appreciation. Aesthetics here not only refer to the formal and sensory properties of works as conceived and experienced apart from their represented and interpreted (or interpretable)

[18.] Rugo (2016, 124).

"content" but will be understood more broadly as applied to potentially all forms, meanings, experiences, and values. distinctly artistic features of a cinematographic work. Aesthetics is, in this effort, ontology — and vice versa.

Merleau-Ponty and Deleuze help me understand that the cinematic image perceives and expresses itself before articulating its meanings. That is, a film must be thought of in virtue of its aesthetic and ontological proposal. What is envisioned then is a way of seeing and venturing through cinema in its continued renaissance. This is a way that differs significantly from analyses more centered on notions such as narrative or mise-en-scène. I envision a cinema that pivots on a new look at the body, which does not "reproduce" bodies, but "compose" them, shot by shot, sequence by sequence, from a line to a luminous volume, and then to a character, a concept, a speech. With the teachings gathered in the dialogue with the authors investigated in the previous chapters, I go hand by hand with the films of Denis, Costa, Tsai, and Apichatpong. I investigate the bodies and what they reveal, tracing differentiated genealogies, identifying the particularity of each of these directors, and investing in a different vision of cinema. In the third chapter, what will guide me through the works of these filmmakers is something like the capture of the instituting: the transgression through feeling of Denis, the political and aesthetic power of a body in Costa, the carnal exploration of the world in Tsai, and the indeterminate openness of Apichatpong.

What appears to be of the utmost importance is to remain at a certain point in the experience, when everything is still possible. That is the demand that sets this book in motion: to recognize that my "immediate instinctive attitude," to use the expression of the philosopher George Santayana (2012), irresistibly exceeds the limits assigned by any theory. This is my challenge in the face of this "a certain contemporary cinema": to resist theories that, in one way or another, make nature bifurcate, that slip into divisions and dualisms that violate the cinematographic experience, simplifying and fixing it in restricting categories. And then, the success of a film theory should not be judged by its ability to dodge objections made to its norms and concepts but rather by making us more fully aware of how reality and cinema always escape and disturb these norms and concepts.

Before proceeding, some clarifications are necessary. I do not intend to exhaust the theme, nor to propose an introduction to contemporary cinema that addresses all its aspects and all the relevant filmmakers that have emerged in the last two decades. By the way, when talking about filmmakers, I am referring not only to the director but also to the others involved in the production of a film. I give the final word to the filmmakers because we have good reason to assume that they were in charge of the whole process. I will also be attentive to the existing differences between these filmmakers, taking care not to generalize works that manifest different procedures. The selection of filmmakers discussed in this book does not correspond to a "movement." His films tend to be best defined as "unclassified." Nor am I willing to carry out a kind of exegesis of the most important filmmakers and films in contemporary cinema. The intention is definitely not to institutionalize a particular look at contemporary cinema, which should be defended in place of another. On the contrary, the idea is to keep the interrogation open and moving.

Let us go.

1.

Film and Phenomenology

How is knowledge possible? How can I access transcendence? How is the subject able to refer to the world? Phenomenology was born through the formulation of these questions. The term "phenomenology" comes directly from Kantian philosophy. Immanuel Kant uses two Greek terms to refer to reality: noumenon, which means reality in itself, rational in itself, intelligible in itself; and phainomenon, or phenomenon, which indicates reality as it appears or manifests itself to my reason or conscience. For Kant, I can only know the phenomenon, which refers to that which presents itself to consciousness based on the a priori structure of consciousness itself. The world exists. I simply cannot know it as it is.

GWF Hegel, in his reinterpretation of the relationships between being, the absolute, and the phenomenon, broadened the scope of the latter. He would argue that everything that appears can only appear to a consciousness and that consciousness itself shows itself in the knowledge of itself, being itself a phenomenon. For Hegel, it is not a question of constituting a philosophy in which the truth of the absolute would be enunciated independently of human experience. On the contrary, Hegel wants to demonstrate how the absolute is present in each moment of this experience, regardless of what it may be.

However, while it is with Hegel that the notion of phenomenology begins to indicate the knowledge that consciousness has of itself through the other phenomena that appear to it, it is with Edmund Husserl that phenomenology perpetuates itself as a philosophical movement. If Kantian phenomenology understands being as that which limits the claim of the phenomenon while remaining out of reach, and if Hegel reabsorbs the phenomenon into a systematic knowledge of being, Husserl, unlike Kant, stresses that the meaning of being and the phenomenon cannot be dissociated. Unlike Hegel, Husserl also emphasizes that consciousness has an essence different from the essences of phenomena, as it gives meaning to things.

In its Greek origin, "phenomenon" means light or brightness. For Husserl, the phenomenon does not only concern the material things that I perceive, imagine, or remember on a daily basis. Nor is it restricted to natural things researched by the natural sciences (chemistry, physics, biology, etc.). It encompasses purely ideal things or idealities, which exist only in thought, such as the entities studied by mathematics and logic, as well as everything created by human action and practice, such as art, technique, and religion. The phenomenon is the presentation of an object to consciousness, the way things appear in my experience, and the way I directly experience them through the senses and attribute meanings to them. That is, knowing phenomena and knowing the structure and necessary functioning of consciousness are one and the same thing, for it is consciousness itself that constitutes the phenomenon.

In *The Idea of Phenomenology*, composed of five lectures given in 1907, Husserl presents phenomenology as a philosophical inquiry that seeks to elucidate how the ability to know worldly events and objects is grounded in the structures of consciousness. His is an investigation centered on the concept of "intentionality":

> *Conscious processes are also called intentional; but then the word intentionality signifies nothing else than this universal fundamental property of consciousness: to be consciousness of something; as a cogito, to bear within itself its cogitatum.*[1]

Coming from Brentano, of whom Husserl was a student, the concept of intentionality suggests that the essential characteristic of consciousness is its quality of always referring to something other than itself. To be conscious is to always be aware of something. In other words, consciousness is an activity constituted by various acts (perception, imagination, speculation, volition, passion, etc.), through which it aims at something. For Husserl, as for Brentano, mental or subjective phenomena are intentional. Perception is the perception of what is perceived, desire is the desire for what is desired, and imagination is the imagination of an imagined object. There is no distinction between the role of the knowing subject and the influence of the known object. This does not mean that the object is contained within consciousness but rather that it only holds its sense of object for a consciousness. Consciousness is consciousness only when it is directed toward an object. Just as an object can only be defined in its relation to consciousness.

The adoption of this perspective calls into question the dualistic assumptions inherent in the formulation of the Cartesian cogito, revealing an interconnection

---

[1] Husserl (1982, 33).

between mind and world that is absent in the relationship between the *res cogitans* and *res extenso* of the philosopher of the *Meditations*. Interestingly, Husserl considered himself a neo-Cartesian and found in the work of the French philosopher the revelation of an undeniable truth, an unshakable foundation on which it would be possible to philosophize "rigorously." For the phenomenologist, as well as for Descartes, the "I think," with which the "I am" is inseparably given, is the first certainty, what Husserl calls the "original intuition." The cogito, or, why not, subjectivity, becomes the necessary starting point for knowledge. This is because the cogito remains identical under the multiplicity of experiences, and this permanence allows him to reach the identity of things through the meaning he attributes to them. However, Husserl regrets that Descartes not only resorted to the theological argument, placing the cogito in dependence on the divine will but also conceived "the ego becomes a substantia cogitans, a separate human 'mens sive animus,' and the point of departure for inferences according to the principle of causality."[2]

Thanks to the concept of intentionality, Husserl glimpses a more original correlation between subject and object, or consciousness and world, than the Cartesian subject–object duality. To better clarify the issue, I can resort to the concrete example mentioned by Husserl: the feeling of pleasure I experience when observing an apple tree blooming in a garden. Common sense dictates that this perception would take into account two factors: first, the presence of the apple tree in the garden; second, the connection between this actual apple tree and the consciousness of the thinking subject. This connection would result in the formation of a mental representation of the apple tree in consciousness. So, there would be two apple trees. Husserl calls this conception, derived from common sense, as "natural attitude," and suggests that we should not begin from the apple tree itself or from the represented apple tree but rather from the apple-tree-as-perceived.

What is at stake here is a method of cognition that, while maintaining the analysis "immanent" to the contents of consciousness, can still lead to an "absolute" and "universal" knowledge. Husserl aimed to identify the essential elements of the world of experience through the act of perception: the "thought-act" in its "pure" form. Thoughts were always "about something," but their contents could be conceived, he insists, as data-in-themselves, without recourse to objects in the natural world, "out there." The phenomenological world is composed of the modes of donation of objects in correlation with acts of consciousness. This is

---

[2] Ibid., 24.

why Husserl shares transcendental idealism. The attempt, however, to place us, before all reasoning, on the same plane as reality, on the level of "things themselves," as Husserl says, marks his far-reaching project.

Access to this primordial dimension is only possible if we suspend our belief in the reality of the outside world and consider transcendental consciousness as a prerequisite for the appearance of this world and the source of its meaning. It is in this way that intentional analysis leads to what Husserl refers to as phenomeno-logical reduction. The phenomenological reduction circumscribes a phenomenon within a realm of pure evidence, setting aside — in parentheses — anything beyond the evident data. This reduction does not make the world doubtful, as it happens in Descartes, but rather it remains unchanged, only "phenomenalized," that is, stripped of the "natural attitude." The Husserlian description foresees the apprehension of the thing itself, beyond all predication. Hence, the supreme motto of phenomenology: the "return to things themselves."

That motto echoed in a cafe on Rue Montparnasse in Paris. Raymond Aron had spent a year at the French Institute in Berlin and, back in the French capital, he met the couple Jean-Paul Sartre and Simone de Beauvoir. It was 1933, and France was dominated by the "spiritualism" of the University of the Third Republic, a blend of positivism and neo-Kantianism. Friends ordered the specialty of the house: apricot cocktails. Aron then spoke enthusiastically about Husserl's ideas. "You see, my little fellow," he says to Sartre, pointing to his glass, "if you are a phenomenologist, you can talk about this cocktail, and it is philosophy."[3]

Talking about things the way he touched them. It was precisely this possibility of a philosophy of concrete everyday life that the French generation of the 1930s desired greatly. The generation of the "discontented" or the "3 H" (referring to the initials of the names of three German philosophers, Husserl, Heidegger, and Hegel), as it was known, already questioned the philosophy taught in traditional high schools and universities, whose courses followed until Immanuel Kant. Philosophy needed to address the challenges of its era: the new discoveries of psychology and psychoanalysis, the imminence of war, the class struggle, the surrealist movement and impressionist painting. This was the promise of phe-nomenology, a current that neither denied the existence of the external world (on the contrary, it affirmed that it is already there before any reflection) nor that of the "internal world."

If, for Husserl, the main focus is on the phenomenological reduction, which directs attention to the act of consciousness that brings the object into the

---

[3.] de Beauvoir (1984, 138).

world for us, suspending my belief in the significance of the external world and investigating the object for what it might reveal of its essence, for Heidegger, the phenomenological reduction involves a shift from a naive understanding of individual beings to a more profound apprehension of the Being of these beings. The method of reduction and its connection to consciousness is emphasized to promote an attitude of openness toward Being, in which Being—as a final foundation—can manifest itself to us. Sartre, in turn, thought he found in phenomenology the necessary instruments for breaking with the dominant epistemology in French philosophy.[4] Husserl's notions about a conscience that is not closed in on itself but is directly related to the world were translated by Sartre into the foundations of a philosophy of action. The philosopher threw consciousness into the world, concretely, as a "being-in-the-world," to use Heidegger's expression. Merleau-Ponty undertook a corporal turn in phenomenology, expanding the notion of intentionality, rooting it in the primary, immediate, and pre-reflexive experience of the body situated in the world. My gaze is directed toward the object as a physical entity in the world, imbued with consciousness. The object enters the world—and my consciousness within it—and becomes intertwined with it. The object is not reduced but comes to my perception through a mutual act of seeing.

The scope of Husserl's philosophy would not be restricted to the field of philosophy. It was never confined to a particular science. Phenomenology simply means different things to different people. The field of phenomenology today comprises a veritable miscellany of theoretical positions: transcendental and hermeneutic phenomenology; life or existential phenomenology; structural, responsive, oenological, alien phenomenology; post-phenomenology; neurophenomenology; etc. In some cases, categorizing a certain philosopher as a phenomenologist can raise additional problems—in which I sometimes find myself entangled in some passages of this book. For in their later writings, Heidegger, Sartre, Merleau-Ponty, and Ricoeur departed from phenomenology, at least in a narrower sense of the term.

I tend to welcome this polysemy—even more complex, as we will see, when it starts to be applied in cinema—of the term phenomenology. Husserl's work pointed to the constitution of an epistemological approach and an ontology based on the very experience of the pre-reflective consciousness of the knowing subject in its intrinsic correlation with the world. And, in fact, if we stick to the

---

[4] Later, Sartre would reject what he called the idealistic and foundational character of Husserl's theories. Husserl and Heidegger would even be called "little philosophers" (1983, 67). For Sartre, Husserl and Heidegger were not radical enough and did not characterize a new era of "philosophical creation."

etymology of the word, "anyone who deals with the way in which every thing appears, anyone who describes appearances or apparitions, does phenomenology."[5] Or, as Heidegger observed, "phenomenology is not a school. It is the possibility of thinking, at times changing and only thus persisting, of corresponding to the claim of what is to be thought."[6] In this manner, several thinkers, particularly in the realm of human sciences, sought support, inspiration, methodological subsidies, or even a dialogue partner in phenomenology.

Reflection on the seventh art would develop in the post-war period in perfect harmony with the intellectual ambience of France. The sound had already been seized. The color was in the process of being conquered. The equipment was becoming lighter and lighter. Cinema entered an astonishing process of techno-logical evolution and film theory was abandoning the quarrel about the advent of sound once and for all.[7] The formative theory of Rudolf Arnheim and Sergei Eisenstein, among others—which explored the differences between cinema and not just reality but with the other arts as well, reinforcing awareness of the image as a surface effect and calling attention to the apparatus technique that made the representation possible—was facing its first decline.

The 1940s would see a renewed urgency in realism. It is not by chance, as Serge Daney pointed out, that a new cinema, apart from traditional cinematographic production, would emerge in a post-war destroyed and traumatized Europe, in a conflicting relationship with the more traditional notions of direction and scene, against the illusionism of classic cinema and the alienation of industrial series. A cinema that aims to bridge the gap between life and art, to turn reality into history, and to encourage the audience to contemplate the connection between man and society. In a country that was formerly part of the Axis powers, but which had also suffered under their yoke, Italy had lost its national identity and therefore needed to rebuild it. With *Obsession* (*Ossessione*, 1943), by Luchino Visconti, *Rome, Open City* (*Roma, città aperta*, 1945), by Roberto Rossellini, and *Bicycle Thieves* (*Ladri di biciclette*, 1948), by Vittorio De Sica, the nation regained the right to look in the mirror. Neorealism took cinema to the streets, gave birth to a new breed of characters, squandered the impression of a reality which the camera approached directly, without—apparently—relying on formal mediations.

---

[5] Ricouer (1953, 821).

[6] Heidegger (2003, 76).

[7] See the appendix of *The Film Form* (1977) which contains the manifesto against the use of sound in cinema signed by Sergei Eisenstein, Vsevolod Pudovkin, and Grigori Alexandrov, in August 1928.

Inspired by the Italian movement, film theory then turned hard to the realistic half of the cinematographic image. The spectator's intense relationship with the world captured by the camera takes center stage, highlighting the privileged notion of experience. In this scenario, phenomenology—responding to the desire for a discussion about the image within its relationships with the object of which it is an image, about what this relationship would be able to manifest and what meanings it would radiate—would serve as the basis for various approaches. Based on a strong analogy between human experience and the way in which cinema "engages" with the world, phenomenology was present at the root and in the unfolding of a varied series of questions: cinema as an expression and/or revelation of the world, the essence of cinema, its ontological dimension, the possibility of a record of everyday life, of capturing contingency itself, of the world in its incessant becoming, and so on.

Cinema registers the experience and presents itself as an object to be experienced. It is this double movement that the phenomenological approaches try to resolve. Phenomenology is an attitude toward the world and our experience, as well as a philosophical method aimed at gaining access to the essence of things. It is also a theory of being, concerned with concepts such as presence and manifestation, and an extraordinary exploration of the potential of visual expression. Rather than speculating about the nature of reality, phenomenology attempts to investigate the boundary between the self and reality. In that sense, it is a philosophy of reduction: trying to strip away everything that is not essential and leaving only the facts that we can be sure of, namely the fact of my experience. Cinema is a prime example of a medium that operates on the boundary between ourselves and the world, in a process that mutually shapes them.

Over the years, phenomenologically inspired theory developed a field that is consistent enough to stand on its own. Merleau-Ponty himself venture into cinema both at the beginning and toward the end of his career. Initially, he was interested in exploring the tension that film could create between mind and body, individual consciousness and external reality, one expressing itself in the other. Later on, Merleau-Ponty tried, albeit timidly, to incorporate the seventh art into his project of a new ontology. Other authors, drawing from their personal experiences with the cinematographic production of their time, expressed a shared perspective on cinema. This is the case of Siegfried Kracauer, André Bazin, Albert Laffay, Amédée Ayfre, Roger Munier, and, later, Jean-Pierre Meunier, Stanley Cavell, and Jean Mitry.

The phenomenological approach to cinema can be divided into two main paths: the embodied experience I have when watching a film and the relationship that the film has with the reality that serves as its foundation. When they go to the cinema, authors of phenomenological inspiration share a certain primacy granted to the immediate plane of life, considered as founding and original in relation to the reflection and intellectual understanding, which they conceive as derivative and secondary. This common point is expressed in the very structure of experience, seen as containing a pre-reflective or non-discursive dimension that possesses a unique richness and complexity, and whose linguistic ordering of meanings is incapable of overcoming. Dudley Andrew underlines a relationship of mistrust between this philosophical current and a certain notion of rationality:

> *Indeed, phenomenologists have a longstanding distrust of pure reason, viewing rationality as a single mode of consciousness among others, a mode whose un-quenchable thirst to swallow all experience must be restrained precisely because life itself tells us that experience is dearer and more trustworthy than schemes by which we seek to know and change it.*[8]

A more attentive reader might cling to what "life itself tells us" and reject this passage by Andrew on the grounds that all experience is mediated and structured by social classes, codes, systems, and so on. The argument, however, is nothing more than an evasive rebuttal. To adhere to it is to evade the confrontation with a certain moment of the experience that the linguistic ordering proves to be incapable of dealing with. It must be said that phenomenology is not foreign to notions such as "mystery," "paradox," or "ambiguity." Phenomenology considers these terms to be ineffable yet essential. It values the attempt to understand them and seeks for an aesthetic and a language that expresses and appreciates them.

Although it exerted enormous influence in many fields, phenomenology be-came, however, little visible in film theory from the 1960s onward. Squeezed between two periods of strong and disparate ideological charges (post-war realism and the deconstructive ruptures), the philosophical current of Merleau-Ponty ended up being sidelined in the midst of the transition from the film club era to the university. Furthermore, by the time film study was officially sanctioned by the French university system, the most brilliant supporters of this dialogue between film and phenomenology, Bazin in 1958, Merleau-Ponty in 1961, and Ayfre in 1963, had already died, prematurely. Even the Institute of Filmology, created in 1950 by the aesthete Etienne Souriau with the goal of uniting professors from different disciplines who shared a passion for cinema, and whose magazine

---

[8] Andrew (1978, 46).

(*La Revue Internationale de Filmologie*) had published numerous essays influenced by phenomenology, had also closed its doors in 1963.

Mitry, the first recognized professor of cinema at the University of Paris, had, as we shall see, a leading role in this transition. Despite being many years younger than Bazin, Mitry's work already announced itself as belonging to a new period of thought on the seventh art. In his work, one often gets the impression that "ideas about cinema" have taken precedence over "cinema" as the primary focus of investigation. Throughout this process, reflection on cinema distanced itself from the realistic themes that characterized the post-war period. The concept of phenomenological origin, which was still very present in Mitry, served as a reference for a few (especially Stanley Cavell and Jean-Pierre Meunier). For Fernão Ramos, this tradition would be seen with a certain disregard:

> *Jean Mitry's thought actually represents the full stop of an evolutionary line that was broken and ignored in the following decades. Although he criticizes authors who preceded him, seeking to approach the theoretical framework that he saw emerging contemporaneously with the publication of The Aesthetics and Psychology of the Cinema, Mitry's work does not break with the past. If the excessive length ends up diluting some points, the critique that Mitry elaborates on phenomenology and classical theory appears, from our point of view, more significant than the attempts to reach the film theory that succeeds him.[9]*

Bazin, especially, has become something of a position to be overcome. Soon after his death, his essays were denounced as "poor ontology," "naive," or even "religious." For Thomas Elsaesser (2011), it seems that the theoretical perspectives of Mitry and, later, Christian Metz were more scientifically grounded. They appeared more "academic" in nature and seemed to depend on a rejection, or more insidiously, a skillful erasure of Bazin. A second generation of theorists and critics (Metz, Jean-Louis Baudry, Peter Wollen, Laura Mulvey, etc.), including those who would assume the editorship of *Cahiers du Cinéma* (Jean-Louis Comolli,[10] among others), shifted the focus of film analysis from a certain notion of ontology

---

[9] Ramos (2012, 65–66).

[10] In an interview given in 2012 to the online magazine *Senses of Cinema*, Comolli stresses a sort of a mea culpa: The principal act of faith of the magazine (Cahiers du Cinéma) is that forms bear a tremendous ethical correlation. Aesthetics can not be separated from ethics. […] I must admit that we were very Bazinian […]It is an affinity which comes from an opposition, that is what is interesting. In trying to critique Bazin I ended up very close to him. But the epithet "idealist", which was a kind of bogeyman for us, took precedence. When we said, "Bazin is an idealist," it was an overly simplistic manner of distancing ourselves from his thought, of course. I am very critical about this. (Fairfax 2012)

to a more epistemological project. For them, Bazinian realism was a discourse naively based on truth claims. It was interested in the correspondences between what he saw on screen and what was out there in the world. Tom Gunning, for example, recalls a time when it was not advisable to mention Bazin:

> *Most of us can remember a time when displaying a sympathy for, or even a particular interest in, the ideas of André Bazin encountered the objection that he was an 'idealist.' The term was seldom used to open a serious discussion of the philosophical context of Bazin's thought — such as his relation to either the Hegelian or the Platonic tradition — but instead to label his writings as politically retrograde or naïve, a bit like the use of the terms 'terrorist' or 'socialist' in American politics.*[11]

Phenomenology was also, for a long time (and to some extent still is), associated with a multitude of pre-contemporary shortcomings. It came to be conceived as idealistic, essentialist, and even ahistorical. It was also seen as completely naive, interested in notions such as "direct experience," at a time when contemporary theory, more focused on the constitutive and mediating processes of language structures, emphasized the inaccessibility of a direct experience of reality. Merleau-Ponty, who died at a time when his philosophy was going through a profound process of transformation, intended to build a system and maintained the certainty that philosophy should be a constant interrogation, a "dialectics without synthesis," ended up equally, at least for a few years, relegated to a peculiar form of quarantine.

The radicalization of a critical and theoretical movement aimed at utilizing the sciences of language and psychoanalysis to demystify the dogma of the veracity of the image, marking the discontinuity between film and reality and underlining what is conventional in the film experience, culminated in a limiting operation (in its worst moments) which split image and world, form and matter. It is of no surprise that few authors along the years have shown interest in debating or developing either the phenomenology inherent in the work of Bazin and Ayfre, or even Merleau-Ponty's work in relation to cinema. In 1978, Andrew published an article in the then influential journal *Wide Angle* in which he identified, first, a neglect of the phenomenological tradition within film theory, and, second, a

---

[11.] Gunning (2011, 119).

general tendency to ignore "the peculiar way in which meaning is experienced in cinema."[12] He continues:

> *The fact that no phenomenological film theory ever self-consciously developed is a matter for regret only insofar as this lack of an opposing tradition locks us within a structuralist project and vocabulary. We can speak of codes and textual systems which are the results of signifying processes, yet we seem unable to discuss that mode of experience we call signification. More precisely, structuralism and academic film theory in general have been disinclined to deal with the 'other-side' of signification, those realms of preformulation.*[13]

This scenario is completely different today. A kind of sensitive somatic turn began to take hold in film studies in the mid-1990s. French theorists such as Raymond Bellour, Nicole Brenez, and Vincent Amiel, among others, promote a return to textual analysis, while in the Anglo-Saxon world, new approaches (Vivian Sobchack, Laura Marks, and Steven Shaviro, especially initially), heavily indebted to the writings of Merleau-Ponty and Deleuze, emerged simultaneously, focusing on an embodied cinematic experience. These authors argued that the semiotic, psychoanalytic, and Marxist theories reigning at that time could not explain the richness of the cinematic experience. They sought to address the disconnect between cinema as an intellectual object and its existence as an aesthetic and sensual entity.

Throughout this process, the established methodologies of film theory were systematically criticized for their universalist and transcendental ambitions. Shaviro, for example, dismisses the psychoanalytic approach in characteristically definitive terms, describing its methods as entirely irrelevant: "the psychoanalytic model for film theory is at this point utterly bankrupt; it needs not to be refined and reformed, but to be discarded altogether."[14] He elaborates:

> *In film viewing, there is pleasure and more than pleasure: a rising scale of seduction, delirium, fascination, and utter absorption in the image. [...] On the other hand, however, theory derives its particular form from its endeavor to separate itself from these founding impulses [...] What disturbs me in the founding texts of psychoanalytic and poststructuralist film theory is an almost reflex movement*

---

[12] Andrew (1978, 45).

[13] Ibid., 47.

[14] Shaviro (1993, VIII.I X).

of suspicion, disavowal, and phobic rejection. It seems as if theorists of the past twenty years can scarcely begin their discussions without ritualistically promising to resist the insidious seductions of film.[15]

This turn challenged the belief that distance and cold logic are the only valid method to determine the meaning of things. This challenge took the form of three key considerations: the spectator's corporeality, the temporality of the moment, and the film as an event, a meeting. As Nicole Brenez points out, pursuing the exploration of film as a material phenomenon has allowed "temporarily, at least, the film itself to take precedence over the context."[16] What is being investigated are the more immediate sensory and expressive features of films, and films as perceptual objects rather than, or in addition to, cognitive, narrative, and cultural-ideological ones.

Critical voices of this shift are also being heard. The insistence on prioritizing the work itself over its context of production and the tendency to embrace extreme eclecticism when selecting a body of work is not without its problems. On the one hand, there is the temptation to take the purely speculative path, which can be as empty as the claim to scientific objectivity professed in the most obscure of academic analyses. On the other hand, there is a risk of falling into descriptions that can be applied to all films, regardless of their genesis, which can lead to the creation of universal or universalizing evaluation methods. There is still a constant threat of a narcissistic and uncritical investigation of experience, consisting solely of impressionist and subjectivist analyses,[17] which disregard the aesthetic and formal tradition of phenomenology.

What is no longer disputed is that phenomenology is no longer on the margins of film theory but close to its center. Phenomenology in film, known for its celebrated openness to all human experience, has directed its attention not only on time but also on space, atmospheres, the act of reading, the body, emotions, affects, and, of course, on movies themselves. This diversity of supposedly phenomenological approaches is compounded by the inherent difficulty in pinpointing an exact definition for the term "phenomenology," even within its original field. There is an enormity of texts that explore the spectator's sensual and bodily experience. They mention authors or phenomenological concepts

---

[15.] Ibid., 9 e 10.

[16.] Brenez (1997, 10).

[17.] In 1978, Andrew already warned us: "As always, in the phenomenological critique of any art, casual impressionism is found alongside a decisive and revealing observation, the former disguising itself as the latter" (1978, 48).

and, most times, even appropriate the term "phenomenology." These texts often reference a highly diverse and occasionally conflicting landscape, to the extent that certain some authors, like Frank Tomasulo, suggest a reversion to a more stricter understanding of phenomenology:

> *Attention needs to be directed away from the strain of affective, intuitive, and psychological phenomenology that has become the sine qua non in film circles (Bazin, Metz, Cavell, Linden, Andrew) and redirected toward the pure phenomenology of consciousness originally posited by Husserl.*[18]

I suggest, however, a broad definition: first, because it is the one that most adequately mirrors the contemporary scenario; second, because it seems to me that my role should never be that of a judge, decreeing what is or is not phenomenology; third, because if what interests me is the conflicting richness of the cinematographic experience, the materiality, forms and aesthetics of cinema, and its insistent ontological bet, my conceptual tools must be more open, perhaps a little vague or unclear. Making my own the words of Ludwig Wittgenstein regarding his "language game":

> *One might say that the concept 'game' is a concept with blurred edges. — 'But is a blurred concept a concept at all?' — Is an indistinct photograph a picture of a person at all? Is it even always an advantage to replace an indistinct picture by a sharp one? Isn't the indistinct one often exactly what we need?*[19]

It is, therefore, necessary — in order to respond to my belief that phenomenology enables me to envision a more suitable approach to meeting the diverse demands that films like *Tropical Malady* and *Good Work* impose on me — to revisit the authors who tried to address cinema in this manner. Delineating a *corpus* and a path was more than necessary. The foregoing excerpt takes me back to the initial moments of the convergence between cinema and phenomenology, beginning with Merleau-Ponty and cinema's capacity not only to provide us with a tacit apprehension of the human being and the world but also to imbricate us in an ontological proposition by the act of vision. Then I turn to Ayfre, who argues that neorealism enables us to reorganize our perceptual field and, consequently, our behavior in the world. I will also consider Bazin, who believes cinema should be

---

[18.] Tomasulo (1988, 21).

[19.] Wittgenstein (1986, 34 § 71).

committed to the unique connection it can establish with reality, opening itself up to the expression of a sense of ambiguity. Michel Mourlet is also interested in what he refers to as the "feeling of being" that a film registers and builds. Munier advocates for the cinematographic image as nature in its nascent state, as the vibration and flash of the world before man, while Mitry, finally, already announcing another era, seems, sometimes, to see the seventh art as a celebration of the concrete mystery of visibility.

The aim of this lengthy chapter is precisely to explore this tradition in its early stages—with occasional references to more recent theorists. The idea is to walk among these authors, identifying potentialities that still need to be explored and seeking valuable tools and paths in them to sketch a different way of approaching films. Merleau-Ponty—and I believe Deleuze would endorse it—resumes this different way by saying that to think

> is not possess the objects of thought; it is to use them to mark out a real^ U think about which we therefore are not yet thinking about. Just as perceived world endures only through the reflections, shadows, leveis and horizons between things (which are not things and are not not}/ ing, but on the contrary mark out by themselves the fields of possifi} variation in the same thing and the same world), so the works ail[j thought of a philosopher are also made of certain articulations between things said. There is no dilemma of objective interpretation or arbitral}, ness with respect to these articulations, since they are not objects 0{ thought, since (like shadow and reflection) they would be destroyed by being subjected to analytic observation or taken out of context, and since we can be faithful to and find them only by thinking again.[20]

1.1 Maurice Merleau-Ponty

Tacitly Decipher the World and Men

"The Film and the New Psychology" is the title of a conference by Maurice Merleau-Ponty, presented at the IDHEC (Institut des Hautes Études Cinémato-graphiques) in Paris on March 13, 1945. *Phenomenology of Perception* was published that same year. In this essay, his interest in cinema is associated with the concept of film as an "object of perception," capable of revealing or making explicit certain fundamental characteristics that define our commerce with the

---

[20.] Merleau-Ponty (1964c, 160).

world. For Merleau-Ponty, the cinematographic image, as a "temporal Gestalt," illustrates the inherent connection between the interior and the exterior, and asserts that perception precedes intellectual understanding. In this context, the philosopher examines the parallels between the seventh art and the psychology of form (Gestalt), incorporating cinema into his critique of the classical conception of perception.

Merleau-Ponty's intellectual journey commenced in the early 1940s with an inquiry into the legacy of modern rationalism, particularly the division between the corporeal (viewed as pure exteriority, an everlasting source of disillusionment) and reflective thought (consciousness as pure interiority, transparent in and of itself). By rejecting the corporeal and favoring the role of reason, Descartes created an inevitable abstraction, simplifying our relationship with the world to a dominant consciousness. For Merleau-Ponty, the philosopher of the *Meditations* did not begin at the starting point. After all, when I think, I am a complex body, immersed in the uncertainties of the sensitive world. The unshakable belief that I perceive the world and that I live in it concretely rather than illusory is the primary level of knowledge. For the phenomenologist, this is the true origin of any reflection. His main challenge, already stated in his first book, *The Structure of Behavior*, is to provide an analysis that substantiates the validity of this belief conveyed by perception.

In *The Structure of Behavior*, Merleau-Ponty presents a thorough analysis of theories that view the living organism as a collection of cells and bones that can be analyzed separately, independent of the whole to which they belong. Merleau-Ponty criticizes the conception of linear and punctual relationships between the elements of the physical world and the organism's physiology. Instead, he aims to demonstrate that the organism responds to *stimuli* and projects itself into the environment as a totality or structure. The term "structure" is understood as the inseparable "joining of an idea and an existence."[21] The concept makes it possible to understand the living organism and human behavior as a whole, in which each part only makes sense when acting together with the others.

In *The Structure of Behavior*, Merleau-Ponty is clearly influenced by the Psychology of Form: the investigation of perception, the notion of a perceptive field, and the attempt to overcome the dualism of body–mind and man–world. The philosopher challenges the behaviorist and gestalt positions in psychology and opposes the traditional mechanistic perspective, which situates the body and mind in a universe composed of mechanical relations, establishing purely causal

---

[21.] Merleau-Ponty (1967, 206).

connections with each other. The notion of "behavior," thought of as "structure," enables him to distinguish the physical–chemical and biological (or vital), and the symbolic aspects. He also affirms that, although these are irreducible to each other, they are intertwined and interact to create the experience of self and the world.

All behavior, including instinctive behavior, is a mode of organization, a form that firmly unites the organism and the environment. In other words, all behavior is imbued with a structure that conveys meaning and intention and can never be understood as simply triggering cause-and-effect mechanisms. The "behavioral structures" of living beings are organized in levels of increasing complexity, corresponding to the organism's ability to interact with the environment. This involves not only adapting to its physical and chemical properties but also creating worlds in which life can thrive. Throughout the book, Merleau-Ponty utilizes psychological research to conduct a moderate phenomenological reduction. This reduction does not lead to a pure transcendental subject as a condition of experience, but rather to the phenomenal body intertwined in a field of concrete situations.

In the fourth chapter of the book, Merleau-Ponty thoroughly analyzes the naive experience of the world. This refers to the state in which we are fully engaged in a concrete lived situation without questioning or reflecting on its nature or meaning. In this experience, people do not feel confined to their private states of consciousness. They believe they can relate to things themselves. The perceptual-motor systems that enable this experience often go unnoticed. I am subject to the physiological and structural determination of my organs. Yet, in this thoughtless, pre-reflective experience, the body does not appear as an intermediary between a presumed soul or consciousness and the world. On the contrary, the body is precisely the means by which things can be known as they are.

While Husserl's phenomenology remained fundamentally centered on an all-powerful consciousness, with "truth" no longer being the conformity between thought and thing or the correspondence between idea and object but an event internal to my intellect, Merleau-Ponty prioritizes the question of the body in its primary, immediate, and pre-reflective experience of the world. The body is no longer seen as just a support for the mind's activity or as an object of consciousness but as the source of all possible experiences. This path was explored in his second and most influential work, *Phenomenology of Perception*, which was published three years after *The Structure of Behavior*.

Phenomenology of Perception begins insightfully with the question: What is phenomenology? Merleau-Ponty's response, still in the preface, outlines a different direction for the current initiated by Husserl. If phenomenology is the study of essences, it is also a philosophy that reestablishes essences in existence and does not believe that man and the world can be understood in any other way than through their "facticity." In other words, we are dealing with a thinking that does not deny the existence of the external world, as some idealist currents suggest, nor does it reject the "internal world," as certain empiricist perspectives do. A philosophy that posits the world as always already there, prior to any reflection. A philosophy that suspends the assumptions of the "natural attitude": "It is the search for a philosophy which shall be a 'rigorous science', but it also offers an account of space, time and the world as we 'live' them."[22]

Phenomenology is, for Merleau-Ponty, an alternative to what he understood as "the mistakes," both in scientific theories and in the grand constructions of philosophy regarding the perception and production of knowledge. His main argument is that scientists' experiments and their conclusions, as well as philosophical theories, do not take into account that their origin lies in "lived experience." Merleau-Ponty refers to an evidently pre-reflective dimension. "Lived experience," for him, is a privileged field of body–world interweaving. The author critiques the intellectualism of the philosophies of consciousness, by extending the Cartesian division between the body and mind to its ultimate consequences, claiming that subjectivity constitutes reality or projects the world from within itself. In *Phenomenology of Perception*, the invocation of an unreflected, or a "tacit cogito," before any proposition posed by the intellect, aims to discover within phenomenology itself a way to transcend the confined realm of consciousness. "The world," he says:

> is not what I think, but what I live through. I am open to the world, I have no
> doubt that I am in communication with it, but I do not possess it; it is inexhaust-
> ible. 'There is a world', or rather: 'There is the world'; I can never completely
> account for this ever-reiterated assertion in my life. This facticity of the world is
> what constitutes the Weltlichkeit der Welt, what causes the world to be the world;
> just as the facticity of the cogito is not an imperfection in itself, but rather what
> assures me of my existence.[23]

The course of Merleau-Pontian phenomenology will be guided by the search for an encounter with the "world which precedes knowledge, of which

---

[22.] Merleau-Ponty (2002, VII).

[23.] Merleau-Ponty (2002, XVIII, XIX).

knowledge always speaks."[24] This is because all reflection is a derived from this pre-reflective and original plane that is ontologically and chronologically prior to it, "as is geography in relation to the country-side."[25] To meet this challenge, it is necessary to conceive of the experience not as psychological or introspective (much less as a passive experimentation with stimuli from the environment) but as an "opening to the world." The goal is to study the way in which, through my bodily inscription in the world, an experience of interiority and external reality that compose my existential field is delineated.

This world, "which is always already 'there,'" before reflection, cannot be seen as a set of determined objects and *stimuli*. It is the latent horizon of my experience and constitutes a phenomenal realm that encompasses me not only as an object, which I perceive alongside others, but also as a subject who perceives. In this way, matter, life, and meaning, as well as the psyche, body, and world, cannot be thought outside of their relations with each other. After all, "there is, therefore, never determinism and never absolute choice, I am never a thing and never bare consciousness."[26] To be born is simultaneously to be born of and in the world.

By adopting this perspective, Merleau-Ponty redefines the traditional conception of the body as an object or mere self-regulating biological entity, simply a support for the activities of a mental instance understood as immaterial. In *Phenomenology of Perception*, the author further elaborates on the distinction made in his first book between the "objective body" and the "phenomenal body." The objective body, extensive matter located in space, is the body I observe, an object among others. It is the body in its material and physiological existence, regulated by biological laws governing its exchange with the environment. The phenomenal body is not just my body; it is also the body that I am. It is the so-called body-subject. It is what gives me the first-person experience, which opens the doors of perception and provides the point of reference that situates me in time and space, thus shaping the world I inhabit.

> The body is our general medium for having a world. Sometimes it is restricted
> to the actions necessary for the conservation of life, and accordingly it posits
> around us a biological world; at other times, elaborating upon these primary
> actions and moving from their literal to a figurative meaning, it manifests through
> them a core of new significance: this is true of motor habits such as dancing.

---

[24] Ibid., X.

[25] Ibid.

[26] Ibid., 527.

Sometimes, finally, the meaning aimed at cannot be achieved by the body's natural means; it must then build itself an instrument, and it projects thereby around itself a cultural world.[27]

For Merleau-Ponty, we are not talking about two distinct bodies, one objective and the other subjective, but two different ways in which the body is inscribed in experience. A body is both an object in the world and the perspective from which I perceive all objects in the world. When I observe my own body, I move from one perspective to another, sometimes placing myself as an observing body, and sometimes as an observed body. My body, with its properties and characteristics, is a sensitive entity that interacts with other sensitive entities, enabling me to transition from one position to another and causing the center of gravity of my experience to shift accordingly. When I touch my left hand, I experience it as an object of touch rather than as a part of the touching subject. The right hand, in turn, is perceived as the subject of touch and not as an object. However, this experience is subject to change. After all, I can perfectly reverse the equation. The general sensitive layer in which the body and things participate, and which legitimizes the naive pretension of reaching the world itself in immediate experience, is called "flesh," while the interweaving and always possible inversion between subject and object positions is called "reversibility."

"Flesh" and "reversibility" are introduced in *Phenomenology of Perception* and gain prominence in a later phase of Merleau-Ponty's philosophy, when the author realized that his initial two works had failed to grasp the unity of the phenomenal body and the objective body. In fact, Merleau-Ponty emphasized the subjective delimitation of the investigation, meaning the consideration of the world always in reference to the subject's capacities. He even goes so far as to say that "being for myself" is "the only sense that the word can have for me."[28] Merleau-Ponty's thought remained within the field of the philosophy of consciousness, although the philosopher never ceased to underline the difficulties of walking within these parameters. Only in the essays in *Signs* and the posthumous book, *The Visible and the Invisible*, will we find a radical ontology, an open "reckoning" with no end in sight.

This *detour* in Merleau-Ponty's philosophy will be further explored later. It is important, however, to underline in which stage of his intellectual trajectory he

---

[27] Ibid., 169.

[28] Ibid., IX.

was when he made his brief foray into cinema.[29] As I said, "The Film and the New Psychology" dates from the same year of publication of the *Phenomenology of Perception* (1945) and therefore shares with the first two works of the philosopher an interrogation about the legacy left by modern rationalism, about the split between corporeal and reflective thinking, and about the abandonment of seeing and feeling in the name of thinking about seeing and feeling. While these criticisms were already part of the theoretical framework opened by Husserl's phenomenology, I can identify a different notion of philosophical project as an endless questioning about the mystery of the sensitive world.

Art is one of Merleau-Ponty's great allies. It helps him fight the battle toward legitimizing the belief that I am in direct contact with the world. "The world is what we see and that, nonetheless, we must learn to see it."[30] Or, rather, we must learn to see it without disconnecting from it. It is no coincidence that Merleau-Ponty turned to the seventh art form at this period of his career. For him, phenomenology and cinema intersected, especially in relation to the themes of our connection with the world and with others. Cinema, in general terms, defines the conditions that have made it a privileged medium for expressing a "view of the world," in which notions such as contingency and ambiguity, and the conception of man as a being-in-situation are key elements. This is the argument behind "The Film and the New Psychology."

The test is divided into two parts. First, Merleau-Ponty describes what he calls "classical psychology," opposing it to the "new psychology" (Gestalt). The first one assigns a primary role to sensations, which are understood as punctual effects of local excitations that the intellect and memory would have to successively compose in a unitary framework. On the contrary, the second one indicates that what should be taken as original is perception understood as a sensitive apprehension of a phenomenon as a whole. For Merleau-Ponty, perception should not be viewed as creating a division between sensation and organizing intelligence. Instead, it should be taken as an organized activity that reflects the bodily relationship with the world, a structured decipherment that precedes intellectual understanding.

---

[29]. This was Merleau-Ponty's most direct foray into cinema, although traces of his interest in cinematographic art can be found in several other moments, especially in "Eye and Mind" (*The Primacy of Perception*, 1964c) and notes of courses he gave or would give at the Collège de France ("Nature et Logos" [1968], "L'ontologie cartésienne et l'ontologie d'aujourd'hui" [1996], and "Le monde sensible et le monde de l'expression" [2011]) before his death. These notes and other traces scattered here and there in this second moment of Merleau-Ponty's philosophy indicate that cinema would be a central part of one of the chapters of his unfinished book, *The Visible and the Invisible* (1968a).

[30]. Merleau-Ponty (1968a, 4).

That is to say, for Merleau-Ponty, what comes first to my perception are not juxtaposed individualized elements but sets. It is what enables me to see constellations in the sky, for example, to group separately spelled letters and pair the points according to each other. The aspect of the world, highlighted by the philosopher, would be tumultuous if I perceived the gaps between things as things themselves. The same applies to perceptions of hearing, although in this case, I am no longer dealing with forms in space but with forms in time.

In other words, Merleau-Ponty defends the fact that analytic perception, which provides the unique value of each element, corresponds only to a subsequent activity. The perception of forms, in a broad sense of structure, should be understood as my most spontaneous means of perception. The philosopher persists in approaching the question from a different perspective, stressing that my five senses can no longer be considered as independent worlds without communication with each other. After all, how could I explain the case of a blind person who manages to perceive colors through the sounds they hear? According to Merleau-Ponty, this should not be viewed as an exceptional occurrence, as classical psychology does, but as a universal phenomenon: "I perceive in a total way with my whole being; I grasp a unique structure of the thing, a unique way of being, which speaks to all my senses at once."[31]

It certainly seems that Merleau-Ponty's criticisms are not solely directed at what he refers to as classical psychology. In fact, at times, the author himself replaces the term "psychology" (classical) with "thought" (classical). Descartes is unquestionably one of the primary targets of this essay. The philosopher of the *Meditations* found unity in the perceptual field through intellectual reasoning. If I say that I see men walking down the street, it is because I captured, through intellectual reasoning, what I believe I saw. The objects in front of me are not really seen but rather visualized. In this way, perception becomes a kind of intellectual deciphering of sensory data.

It is against this notion of perception that Merleau-Ponty stands up. For him, perception cannot be conceived as a kind of "science in embryo" or as an "inaugural exercise of intelligence." On the contrary, it is essential to reestablish a "reversibility" with the world. Cézanne comes to the philosopher's rescue, as the French painter made the blurring of the distinctions between color and form or substance perhaps his strongest mark. How would the imposition of specific meanings on certain sensitive signs occur if the signs themselves are unnamable,

---

[31] Merleau-Ponty (1964b, 50).

"in their most immediate sensitive texture,"[32] without reference their meaning? This is the philosopher's response:

> *I do not think the world in the act of perception: it organizes itself in front of me. When I perceive a cube, it is not because my reason sets the perspectival appearances straight and thinks the geometrical definition of a cube with respect to them. I do not even notice the distortions of perspective, much less correct them; I am at the cube itself in its manifestness through what I see. The objects behind my back are likewise not represented to me by some operation of memory or judgment; they are present, they count for me, just as the ground which I do not see continues nonetheless to be present beneath the figure which partially hides it. Even the perception of movement, which at first seems to depend directly on the point of reference chosen by the intellect is in turn only one element in the global organization of the field.*[33]

The essay examines and critiques the distinction, unquestionably accepted by classical psychology, between inner and outer observation. From this perspective, feelings (like, for example, love, anger, hate, and shame) could only be known directly from within, and only by the individual experiencing them. Merleau-Ponty, however, argues that when studying feelings like love through introspective investigation, one may only find a few things to describe, such as anguish and palpitations. The most interesting observations about love only arise when we refuse to dismiss it as a mere coincidence with a feeling. It is only when they appear in their external configuration and perceived by others that feelings such as love or hate can attempt to account for and explain a situation experienced as the embodiment of a behavior.

The concept of behavior is also significant for the phenomenologist. It is the legible form of the "way of being in the world" specific to each thing, which enables us to understand the feeling of the other as an exteriority. If a feeling cannot be conceived as an internal psychic fact but as a variation of our relationships with the world, evident in our bodily attitude, then the other must also be seen as an attitude, a behavior. The new psychology, according to Merleau-Ponty, brings a new conception of how we perceive others.

In this sense, he sees a connection between cinema and the new psychology. Cinema, like the new psychology, offers a fresh perspective on the world and

---

[32.] Ibid., 51.

[33.] Ibid.

makes me see man not as an intelligence that constructs the world but as a being that finds itself thrown into it. Merleau-Ponty believed that the most intriguing insights regarding cinema intersected with the novelties brought by the new psychology. That is what he means with the idea of a film as an object to be perceived, "not a sum total of images but a temporal gestalt."[34] These ideas are related to the praise of montage, especially the Kuleshov effect[35] (referred to by Merleau-Ponty as the "Pudovkin effect"[36]).

Montage and its effects attract Merleau-Ponty as an example of a form that surpasses the mere sum of its elements. The Kuleshov effect illustrates the unity of the visual field and its systemic organization. The meaning of an image depends on those that precede it, and their sequence creates a new reality that is not simply the sum of its parts. Sound is also analyzed by the philosopher not as a phonographic reproduction of noises and words, but as a composition of a "being in the world" of its elements. For Merleau-Ponty, sound and image are inseparable. They both consummate a new and irreducible whole.

When delving into cinematographic theory, the phenomenologist is influenced by two major sources: the fundamental psychological analyses of technique and the studies on the categories of sound, image, and montage developed by André Malraux in *Esquisse d'une psychologie du cinéma* (2003) during the 1940s, and the essay "Le rythme cinématographique" written by Roger Leenhardt for *Esprit* magazine in 1936. Malraux reinforces the importance of incorporating into the process of creating meaning not only the images that precede and follow each other but also the duration of each one of them. Editing is not underlined solely for its constructive character, as was common among the avant-gardes of the 1920s and 1960s, but as evidence that cinema is a "temporal form" in which images convey meaning through their inherent way of exposing themselves in duration. In other words, cinema, as "temporal" art, can only be understood, like perception, in its belonging to the flow of the world.

I should clarify that this does not mean that Merleau-Ponty defends the possibility of a direct reproduction of the world. The phenomenologist does not believe that film is the most faithful and complete audiovisual representation of a drama. This is something that literature can only suggest with words. According to him,

---

[34.] Ibid., 54.

[35.] The same inexpressible close-up of an actor is mounted successively with different shots (a served table, a child, a naked woman, etc.). Editing leads the spectator to perceive and interpret the actor's expression differently.

[36.] Ismail Xavier, organizer of the book *The Experience of Cinema* (1983), which contains the Portuguese translation by José Lino Grünewald of Merleau-Ponty's essay, explains that Pudovkin was the one who publicized Kuleshov's work in France, where he held a conference series, hence the philosopher's mistake.

this misconception persists precisely because realism is a fundamental element of moving images. The "power of reality" in the cinema,[37] says Merleau-Ponty, quoting Leenhardt, makes even the slightest stylization jarring. The actors should perform in a natural manner. The direction should be as believable as possible. Although no film is meant to replicate the exact visual and auditory experience I would have if I were present in the narrated situations. Merleau-Ponty outlines the concept of realism in cinema, but it would be an exaggeration to speak of an anticipation of André Bazin and the idea of the ontology of the cinematographic image. The phenomenologist's explanation, in a dialogue with poetry, aims to emphasize that the art of a film lies not in didactically describing things or exposing ideas but in creating a "language machine" to evoke a specific sensitive state.

> The meaning of a film is incorporated into its rhythm just as the meaning of a gesture may immediately be read in that gesture the film does not mean anything but itself. The idea is presented in a nascent state and emerges from the temporal structure of the film as it does from the coexistence of the parts of a painting. The joy of art lies in its showing how something takes on meaning—not by referring to already established and acquired ideas but by the temporal or spatial arrangement of elements.[38]

For Merleau-Ponty, a film means the same way as a thing does. Both are not addressed to an isolated intelligence but to "our power tacitly to decipher the world or men and to coexist with them."[39] Cinema does not present me with the thoughts of a character. What I see are gestures, looks, and mimes. A character becomes visible through his behavior and the unique way of him being in the world and dealing with what surrounds him. If a director wants to show a character experiencing vertigo, he should not attempt to delve into the inner experience of vertigo but instead observe it from an external perspective, focusing on an unsteady body contorting at the edge of a precipice.

The spectator, in turn, is in an immediate relationship with the world through the film. To watch a film is not to read or even to understand, but primarily to feel something whose meaning is not immediately clear to me. That is, a film should not be viewed solely as a vehicle for certain ideas or themes, or merely as a plastic work, but as a combination of form and meaning that can only be understood

---

[37] Merleau-Ponty (1964b, 57).

[38] Ibid., 57, 58.

[39] Ibid., 58.

through the exercise of perception. Therefore, the famous Merleau-Pontian formula: "a movie is not thought; it is perceived."[40]

This is where the maximum convergence between cinema and the new psychology reappears: the shared goal of helping us re-apprehend how we perceive the world:

> *Phenomenological or existential philosophy is largely an expression of surprise at this inherence of the self in the world and in others, a description of this paradox and permeation, and an attempt to make us see the bond between subject and world, between subject and others, rather than to explain it as the classical philosophies did by resorting to absolute spirit. Well, the movies are peculiarly suited to make manifest the union of mind and body, mind and world, and the expression of one in the other.*[41]

Merleau-Ponty concludes his essay with an interesting hypothesis about the connection between cinema and the new psychology: generational affinity. In fact, phenomenology proved to be a rich foundation for developing theories and criticisms about cinema in the late 1940s and throughout the 1950s. Bazin and Aymédée Ayfre are two of the authors who emerged in this context. Like Merleau-Ponty, Bazin and Ayfre believe that meaning in film emanates from organizing appearances. They both work around the theme of the ambiguity between image and reality. Each of these authors approaches cinema in their own way. They go to the cinema as a different manner of getting closer to reality and exploring the richness of experience. However, while they do share many premises, Bazin and Ayfre would also diverge from the phenomenologist, especially concerning cinematographic aesthetics.

It is quite curious that Merleau-Ponty never comes close to criticizing classical decoupage, much less defending the use of depth of field or long shots. On the contrary, the phenomenologist embraces the alignment of his philosophy with the ideas of montage theorists, a point that will only be contested as a rejection by other important authors like Bazin, Ayfre, and Michel Mourlet. "The Film and the New Psychology" is one of the pioneering essays to initiate a conversation between cinema and phenomenology. Its originality, as noted by Fernão Ramos (2012), can be noted, curiously, by an absence: neorealism. If, on the one hand, I can say that Merleau-Ponty's essay predates the explosion of this movement

---

[40] Ibid.

[41] Ibid.

across Europe, on the other hand, it is not very difficult to see the philosopher's lack of familiarity with his contemporary cinematographic production.

In fact, Merleau-Ponty's focus was never on cinema, but rather on the new psychology, a topic that would pave the way for his most famous work, *Phenomenology of Perception*, published that same year. In this essay, cinema is always discussed in general terms, and Merleau-Ponty mentions only a few films, never really engaging in direct critiques of them. Although the notion that the seventh art tacitly deciphers the world has influenced many people, it is quite evident the "unequal balance that leads cinema to serve as a counterweight, in a brilliant analysis of contemporary psychology."[42] This is what Gilles Deleuze comments in an interview with *Cahiers du Cinéma*:

> *It's very odd. I have the feeling that modern philosophical conceptions of the imagination take no account of cinema: they either stick to movement but lose sight of the image, or they stick to the image losing sight of its movement. It's odd that Sartre, in The Imaginary, takes into account every type of image except the cinematographic image. Merleau-Ponty was interested in cinema, but only in relation to the general principles of perception and behavior.*[43]

In *Phenomenology of Perception*, Merleau-Ponty conceptualizes movement as the transition from immobile and privileged moments. However, for him, these moments are no longer essential but rather existential. He does not evoke intelligible forms but perceptible Gestalts that organize my field of perception based on my being-for-the-world so that this being-for-the-world constitutes the anchor point of perception. This is what most bothers Deleuze. For him, Merleau-Ponty can only see film as an ambiguous ally. Cinema would emerge as a counterpoint to the idea of the subject as anchor for the perception of the world. In this way, by elevating "natural perception" as a norm, phenomenology would establish a static focus centered on the intentional awareness of a situation. This is what the philosopher contests in *The Movement-Image*:

> *The cinema can, with impunity, bring us close to things or take us away from them and revolve around them, it suppresses both the anchoring of the subject and the horizon of the world. Hence it substitutes an implicit knowledge and a second intentionality for the conditions of natural perception. It is not the same*

[42.] Ramos (2012, 54).

[43.] Deleuze (1995, 47).

> *as the other arts, which aim rather at something unreal through the world, but makes the world itself something unreal or a tale [récit]. With the cinema, it is the world which becomes its own image, and not an image which becomes world.*[44]

This privileged concept of natural perception would lead the phenomenologist to perceive movement as a series of "poses" that vary depending on the perceiving subject and the situation. Deleuze argues that phenomenology is rooted in "pre-cinematographic" conditions, which may explain its embarrassment and ambiguity in relation to cinema, sometimes denouncing the cinematographic movement as unfaithful to the conditions of perception, sometimes exalting it as a new narrative, capable of bringing the perceived and the percipient, the world and perception together.

It is important to note, as I emphasized at the beginning of this chapter, that "The Film and the New Psychology" belongs to a certain moment in the phenomenologist's journey, characterized by a philosophy of transcendental consciousness that establishes "natural perception" and its conditions as a norm. In *Phenomenology of Perception*, cinema is discussed within this context. Merleau-Ponty says:

> *To see an object is either to have it on the fringe of the visual field and be able to concentrate on it, or else respond to this summons by actually concentrating upon it. When I do concentrate my eyes on it, I become anchored in it, but this coming to rest of the gaze is merely a modality of its movement: I continue inside one object the exploration which earlier hovered over them all, and in one movement I close up the landscape and open the object.*[45]

In natural perception, I focus my gaze on an area to reveal it. This revelation brings the area and its objects to life, while relegating other areas to the background or periphery, rendering them dormant. However, for Merleau-Pointy, in cinema, something else happens, and the perception offered is entirely different. In a film, when the camera turns to an object and moves closer to present it in the foreground, "we can remember that we are being shown the ash tray or an actor's hand, we do not actually identify it. This is because the screen has no horizons."[46] In other words, cinema and natural perception are markedly different. This distinction may also be the driving force behind Merleau-Ponty's emphasis

---

[44] Deleuze (1997, 57).

[45] Merleau-Ponty (2002, 78).

[46] Ibid.

on montage as the essential characteristic of cinema, rather than the cinematic image and its relation to reality.

Deleuze is right to call our attention to the foundationalist aspect that embarrasses Merleau-Ponty's early phenomenology. However, this embarrassment does not undermine the phenomenologist's claims about the kinesthetic nature of perception. Either in "The Film and the New Psychology" or in *Phenomenology of Perception*, Merleau-Ponty never expresses reservations about cinematographic art or denounces its movement as unfaithful to the conditions of perception. He does not conceive of movement in cinema as a series of poses. On the contrary, similar to Deleuze, Merleau-Ponty regards the image and movement as inseparable. The cinematographic image, says the phenomenologist, is a temporal form in movement, a "new reality" that cannot be simply reduced to a sum of its elements. It is also important to note that the idea that cinema "suppresses the anchorage of the subject as much as the horizon of the world" is derived from Deleuze. Merleau-Ponty never mentions or criticizes it. Furthermore, Deleuzian criticism and his main conclusion (phenomenology can only see cinema with ambiguity) are based on readings of Merleau-Ponty's first works.

Shortly before his death,[47] the phenomenologist was working on a book that would remain unfinished, originally titled "The Origin of Truth," but which was published under the title that Merleau-Ponty adopted in the end. *The Visible and the Invisible*, a work in which only the first part and a few notes were written, testifies to his desire of providing a new expression for his phenomenology. It is only in this book and in some of his final essays that Merleau-Ponty's thought is presented in a more comprehensive form, fulfilling what the earlier works had only hinted at. To no longer run the risk of being interpreted as a merely superficial or a "psychological anecdote," the description of what is perceived is replaced by the philosophy of expression. The philosophy of expression, viewed in all its implications, becomes an ontological endeavor.

If in *Phenomenology of Perception*, Merleau-Ponty used the analysis of the perceptive phenomenon to describe the experience by highlighting the coupling between subject and object, the body and the world. He started from the duality between these poles and reconciled them in the unity of the experiential field. In *The Visible and the Invisible*, the experience is described as dehiscence. To think of the relationship with being as dehiscence is no longer to conceive of it as a coupling, fusion, or coincidence but as a fission that, from the primordial

---

[47.] Merleau-Ponty died suddenly on May 3, 1961, aged 53, from coronary thrombosis.

unity of the flesh, gives rise to the other, the body and the world, the observer and the observed, the self and the other.

In *The Visible and the Invisible*, Merleau-Ponty revisits the world from the perspective of expression, capturing the genesis of meaning instead of immediately referring to a perceptive terrain. He wants access to the true picture of the world as a land or source of expression. The world, as the ground of expressive movement, gains an infinite depth. After all, meaning is never completely filled. "Because," explains Barbaras,

> *no expression erases itself in the face of a pure sense, because expression cannot claim to be nailed down in a full meaning, the world will be given only as withdrawal, as this 'presence' which, through its obscurity, gives birth to expression without ever being absorbed into the expressed. Considered on the basis of expression, the world can no longer be defined through presence but as that whose being consists in exceeding every presentation.*[48]

This differentiated theoretical framework would serve as the basis for a phenomenological approach to the cinematographic experience developed by Vivian Sobchack from the 1990s onward. It would deepen toward a new ontological proposal — a way of incorporating the existential and embodied experience of the spectator and rethinking his relationship with the film. This process is reversible and involves reciprocal constitution using the modes and structures of direct perceptive and reflexive experience.

In an essay in her second book *Carnal Thoughts* (2004) titled "What My Fingers Knew: The Cinesthetic Subject, or the Vision in the Flesh," Sobchack argues, amidst an analysis of the opening scene of *The Piano* (1993) by Jane Campion, about the tactile and sensory aspects of the cinematic experience. It is a point-of-view shot. The fingers in front of the camera obscure our view of what is happening behind them. We only see beams of light that escape between them. Sobchack reinforces that, before the counter-shot that shows Ada seeing the world through her fingers and identifies the previous image with the character's gaze, our own fingers already knew what was going on, to the point that this revelation reached us without surprise.

For Sobchack, there is no doubt that cinematographic images are filtered and absorbed by our senses. Sight and hearing are certainly the most prominent ones, but we do not leave the other senses out of the theater — it is, in fact, precisely our

---

[48]. Barbaras (2014, 60).

ability to smell, touch, and taste that enable us to experience events or actions that would engage these senses in the cinema in a more comprehensive manner. By the way, she adds, if we challenge the strict hierarchy of the senses, and accept, for example, that vision informs and is informed by our other senses, then cinema no longer touches us exclusively in a metaphorical sense.

However, film theory and criticism often overlook the fleshy aspects of the movie-watching experience. Although we can identify a more recent wave of researchers who each, in their own way, explore the "sensory fleshiness of the cinematic experience," Sobchack suggests that as film scholars, we still feel uneasy when faced with our physiological response to a film, confining its importance to a merely metaphorical value.

> *Contemporary film theory has not taken bodily being at the movies very seriously—and, at best, it has generally not known how to respond to and describe how it is that movies 'move' and 'touch' us bodily. [...] we need to alter the binary and bifurcated structures of the film experience suggested by previous formulations and, instead, posit the film viewer's lived body as a carnal 'third term' that grounds and mediates experience and language, subjective vision and objective image—both differentiating and unifying them in reversible (or chiasmatic) processes of perception and expression.*[49]

Sobchack turns to phenomenology to find of a method capable of describing the existential structure of "cinematic vision," incorporating the body's radical contribution to the constitution of the cinematic experience. In *The Address of the Eye*[50] (1992), her first and most influential work, the author distinguishes between Husserl's transcendental phenomenology and Merleau-Ponty's phenomenology[51] of the body. According to her, the philosopher of *Phenomenology of Perception* transformed phenomenology into a semiotic exploration of "being," rejecting the idea of consciousness being transparent and reality being opaque. Instead, he argued that both thought and sensation can only occur within the existence of a

---

[49] Sobchack (2004, 59–60).

[50] Sobchack's book is a kind of a watershed in Anglo-Saxon cinematographic theory, although it arrived only timidly in Brazil—unlike the two other most influential works of the period, by Steven Shaviro and Laura Marks, of more Deleuzian heritage, whose influence on Brazilian academia is undeniably visible.

[51] Sobchack says of Husserl: "Ahistorical, acultural, and inherently static, the transcendental ego seemed a return to metaphysical idealism. That is, the goal of achieving a completely presuppositionless and all-encompassing description and interpretation of phenomena in the life-world ran counter not only to actual but also to possible experience with its countless ambiguities and variations of meaning and value" (2009, 438).

perceptive activity that is fundamentally understood as embodied. Sobchack will work within this theoretical framework influenced by Merleau-Pontian thinking.

> *My own discovery of Maurice Merleau-Ponty's existential phenomenology and my elaboration of its special focus on the radical semiosis of the lived-body as a practical method for describing the existential structure of cinematic vision might seem perverse. If so, however, I would argue that this perversity is profound. That is to say, my move to phenomenology emerges not from my desire to exercise transcendental phenomenology's capacity for describing 'essences' or demonstrating 'universal' structures, but rather from my desire to cry out my inherent qualification of the world of essences and universals, to allow for my existential particularity in a world I engage and share with others.*[52]

Sobchack criticizes and laments the fact that the embodied and existential nature of the cinematic experience is often overlooked. The author identifies three key points that reconcile realist, formalist, and contemporary theories (psychoanalytical, structuralist, gender, etc.): the act of vision as a priori data that constitutes cinematographic communication; the communication that requires a prior cinematographic "competence," an agreement without which there is no way to produce meanings; and the notion that film is an object to be seen, regardless of whether it was conceived as an object of expression (formalists), as an object of perception (realists), or as a rhetorical and reflective object (contemporary theories).

She then underlines three metaphors that predominate in film theory: the frame, the window, and the mirror. The frame is associated with formalism, while the window is associated with realism. They are almost opposite poles, with one emphasizing the apparatus, linguistic elements, and plasticity, while the other favoring notions such as mis-en-scène and depth of field. The frame reinforces the belief in the filmic object as an expression in itself. The window frames the film as perception in itself. Sobchack criticizes subjective psychologism in the former and objective empiricism in the latter. The third metaphor, the mirror, implies the joining of perception and expression and characterizes a significant portion of contemporary film theory. It reproduces the idea that the film reflects a context of which the spectator (and the director) is necessarily a part, and where the interpretation of any meaning is determined by ideological contingencies and an unseen, culturally established apparatus. The film is seen as mediation in itself.

[52.] Sobchack (1992, XV).

To these persistent metaphors—historical misconceptions, according to the author—Sobchack reinforces the vivid sense that vision in the cinematic experience is articulated at the same time by film and spectator. They both are engaged in two spatially distinct acts that converge on a common ground, although they never fully occupy it. The author does not deny the analyses that focus on sociocultural, political, or economic aspects, nor those that emphasize the formal and plastic side of the cinematographic image, nor those that explore gender or psychoanalytical perspectives. Instead, she looks for a way to situate the film and the spectator (and the director) in the same corporeal universe, sharing the same structure of vision. About her project, she says:

> the task of The Address of the Eye: A Phenomenology of Film Experience is to describe and account for the origin and locus of cinematic signification and significance in the experience of vision as an embodied and meaningful existential activity. My study here is less theoretical than it is empirical. Or, rather, if it is theoretical, it is radically—materially—so, grounding itself in an interrogation and description of the experiential phenomenon of sensing, enworlded bodies that can see and be seen. Given this task, both the philosophical reflection and eidetic method of existential phenomenology best provide me the basis and means to develop an existentially grounded and radical semiotics and hermeneutics capable of describing the origins of cinematic intelligibility and the signifying activity of embodied vision.[53]

Sobchack identifies an intersubjective communication in cinema as occurring between the film, the spectator, and the filmmaker. This communication is based on and activated by common structures of embodied experience, allowing for the perception of experience and the experience of perception. This circular and reiterative process accompanies her throughout her book. A film is the expression of an experience, and this expression is itself experienced in the act of watching a film. Consequently, this leads her to reformulate the equation as "an expression of experience for experience's sake." Cinema expresses life through life itself. The modes and structures of embodied existence are taken to be cinema's raw material. Sobchack, in her own way, resumes a widespread belief among authors of phenomenological inspiration. What interests her most is precisely the emphasis on the physical and concrete reversibility between

---

[53.] Ibid., XVII.

perception and expression, which constitutes both the film and our experience of it. She continues:

> *More than any other medium of human communication, the moving picture makes itself sensuously and sensibly manifest as the ex pression of experience by experience. A film is an act of seeing that makes itself seen, an act of hearing that makes itself heard, an act of physical and reflective movement that makes itself reflexively felt and understood.*[54]

For the author, in a radical transformation of photography, film made visible for the first time the dynamic action of vision, recording its objects as it envisions the world, moving in space, through time and reflection, and always engaging in the creation of meanings. She believes that cinema makes the phenomenological concept of "intentionality" explicit and tangible as a materially embodied and actively directed structure through which meanings are formed in an endlessly ongoing sensual and reflective process.

What is glimpsed, therefore, is the possibility of a film being considered as more than just a visible object. It demonstrates a perceptive and expressive competence on par with that of the director and the spectator. It is both the subject of vision and the object of vision. "We are certainly not suggesting that the film is a human subject,"[55] underlines the author. A film reveals the reversible structure of vision, making it visible through a perceptive and expressive performance that is equivalent in structure and function to the performances of the filmmaker and the spectator.

If Merleau-Ponty said that cinema was able to "make manifest the union of mind and body, mind and world, and the expression of one in the other,"[56] Sobchack not only concurs but also adds that this union is manifested within film itself and also between the film and its spectator. The cinematographic experience involves at least two subjects-who-see (film and spectator) in a dynamic and relational structure. Sobchack explores the fundamentally embodied, intentional, and significant imbrication of two perceptive and expressive subjects engaged in a dialogical and dialectical, intrasubjective, and intersubjective relationship.

In short, cinema is an extension of the spectator's embodied existence. The phenomenological model postulates mutual permeability and reciprocal creation

---

[54] Ibid., 3.

[55] Ibid., 10.

[56] Merleau-Ponty (1964b, 58).

between oneself and the other. Thus, the act of watching a film becomes a prime example of the intertwining between myself and the world. Instead of simply watching a film through a frame, window, or mirror, I share and shape the kinetic space dialectically and dialogically. Sobchack, building on Merleau-Ponty, emphasizes the spatial relationship between the image and the spectator. It is actually a bit curious. In *Matter and Memory*, Henri Bergson states that questions concerning the subject and the object, their differentiation and their unity should be considered in terms of time, not space. Deleuze approaches cinema from this perspective. It is not easy to definitively state—as Sobchack does—that Merleau-Ponty's "The Film and the New Psychology" prioritizes the spatial aspect of this equation. The author of *The Address of the Eye*, in contrast, is much more specific on the issue:

> *It is not time, but space—the significant space lived as and through the objective body-subject, the historical space of situation—that grounds the response to those questions and the question of cinematic signification in this present study. In this focus on embodiment and situation, existential, semiotic phenomenology is not out of step with the contemporary quest for an account of cinematic signification that grounds meaning as value-laden, com mitted, and socially active. Its aim is to locate the structure and meanings of phenomena in the contingency and openness of human existence.*[57]

It is no coincidence that Sobchack's work is subject to criticism, particularly from authors inspired by Deleuze. In general, Deleuze's criticisms of Merleau-Ponty and, more precisely, of phenomenology are reproduced, which, as we have seen, according to the philosopher of *The Movement-Image*, would be a pre-cinematographic current. In a book released in the early 2000s and highly acclaimed in the English-speaking world of film studies, Barbara Kennedy argues, for example, that Sobchack's ideas are "dangerous." They are dangerous because they grant a certain privilege to notions such as "subjectivity." Kennedy explains:

> *Sobchack's work is predominantly a phenomenological explanation of the cinematic experience and whilst it provides a stepping stone in my argument, it does not go far enough because it is based on a theory of 'natural perception' (that is the body and mind being separate entities) rather than a molecular coagulation of perception and the materiality of the brain/body/mind imbrication. Sobchack*

[57.] Sobchack (1992, 31–32).

does, however, break down the traditional oppositions between subject and object, mind and body, the visual and the visible object, arguing that the film has always been both a dialectical and a dialogical engagement of viewing subjects. But this still maintains a concern with subjectivity, with 'viewing subjects'. It still is locked into identitarian thinking and concern with psychic constructions of subjectivity as a fundamental element of the filmic experience.[58]

This excerpt reveals the author's lack of familiarity not only with phenomenology and its various ramifications but also with the tradition of cinematographic theory influenced by this source. There is also a somewhat intellectual arrogance, when the author states that Sobchack's work "still maintains a concern with subjectivity"—as if this was something to be overcome. Kennedy consistently display an absolutely inexplicable aversion to any analysis that delves into the theme of subjectivity in her book, as if this were a starting point not relevant to cinema or the experience of watching a film.

Sobchack, however, has her own problems. Similar to "The Film and the New Psychology," she goes very timidly to specific movies—a great exception is the inspired discussion of *The Lady in the Lake* (1947), by Robert Montgomery. While containing numerous interesting discussions and suggestions for further exploration, Sobchack may have overgeneralized her considerations of the cinematic experience and failed to propose a more specific phenomenological investigation of film form and the various aesthetic experiences associated with it. She is more interested in the receiving subject than in the filmic material. Daniel Yacavone,[59] for example, argues that Sobchack and much of the more recent phenomenologically inspired theory tend to marginalize the formal and aesthetic dimensions of cinema.

Furthermore, the terms used by Sobchack (subject, object, perception, meaning) may contribute to certain misunderstandings and oversimplifications. It is filled with newly coined words, hyphenated terms, wordplay, balanced phrases, and parallel structures, making it challenging to read. The purpose of this complexity, as she states, is "to force a certain form of attentiveness to what we say but hardly hear."[60] In any case, if the idea is to think about the dialogical and dialectical

---

[58.] Kennedy (2000, 57).

[59.] Yacavone: "Sobchack's overriding focus on what are presented as fundamental visual, spatial, and affective features of all live-action films, as tied to perceptual conditions of the film medium and its technology, stands in sharp contrast to Merleau-Ponty's emphasis on variable artistic form, style, and expression in cinema, together with temporality and rhythm" (2016, 160).

[60.] Sobchack (1992, XVIII).

relationship of mutual constitution between film and spectator, starting from the concept of "flesh" as the stuff of the world, then wouldn't we be in a realm where notions such as subject and object (for more than reversible) still would have a chance, or, rather, still would be instituted?

In this sense, what strikes me as most curious is the fact that, with the use of the term "flesh," of extreme importance to Sobchack, Merleau-Ponty inscribed temporality at the center of his reflection on being. "Flesh" is an expression that resists the abstraction that the word "time" easily induces. It is always worth remembering that, for Merleau-Ponty, the human being is a "l'être au monde" and not a "être dans le monde." One of his biggest challenges in *The Visible and the Invisible* is precisely to find a vocabulary that avoids spatial metaphors, which often result in two-dimensional conceptions of being. It is difficult to escape from almost automatic associations, such as the prefixes "in" and "ex," which subtly prompt us to think in terms of container and content, to envision meaning within and materiality outside the mind, or the mind situated within the body space, or the body within the world.

Merleau-Ponty himself acknowledges that he has fallen into this trap many times and agrees that in his first two works, he failed to completely detach himself from the perspective of transcendental philosophy, which conceives the primacy of consciousness over its object. Even at the level of language, the difficulty persisted. As the work notes progress, the phenomenologist becomes increasingly severe in relation to the *Phenomenology of Perception* in particular. The annotation "resume Ph.P." becomes more and more frequent. At one point, he says: "the problems posed in Ph.P. are insoluble because I start there from the 'consciousness'-'object' distinction."[61]

Another two banknotes from the late 1950s[62] envision an alternative path for the constitution of a new ontology: "our corporeality: not placing it at the center, as I did in *Phenomenology of Perception*,"[63] and, further, "starting from the results of *Phenomenology of Perception* and showing that it is necessary to transform them into ontology: 1/ moving from the affirmation of the 'perceived' to that of the brute Being; 2/ moving from the idea of the body as subject to that of the undivided being."[64] Merleau-Ponty expresses in these brief considerations the desire to reject the central role attributed to embodied subjectivity and to

---

[61] Merleau-Ponty (1968, 200).

[62] Published in Portuguese as an appendix in a book by Marcus Sacrini Ferraz (2009).

[63] Merleau-Ponty and Ferraz (2009, 307).

[64] Ibid., 308.

move forward in his project of describing a field of being that precedes the split between subject and object.

It is the very statute of the body that changes as Merleau-Ponty advances in a redescription of the sensible. In *Phenomenology of Perception*, the proper or phenomenal body is seen as irreducible to mundane objects. In other words, the body, as a site of perceptive productivity through which all things and events can appear as such, is not a thing and cannot be confused with one. This perspective underwent a complete change in the 1950s, when Merleau-Ponty emphasized that perceptive capacity is inherently linked to a sensitive foundation within the body. Seeing necessarily implies the potential for both seeing and being seen. The body, visible and mobile, exists among things, as one of them, attached to the fabric of the world. However, precisely because it sees and moves, the body maintains things around it, as a kind of annex or extension. "The world is made of the same stuff as the body,"[65] says the philosopher. This is its riddle:

> *The enigma is that my body simultaneously sees and is seen. That which looks at all things can also look at itself and recognize, in what it sees, the 'other side' of its power of looking. It sees itself seeing; it touches itself touching; it is visible and sensitive for itself. It is not a self through transparence, like thought, which only thinks its object by assimilating it, by constituting it, by transforming it into thought. It is a self through confusion, narcissism, through inherence of the one who sees in that which he sees, and through inherence of sensing in the sensed—a self, therefore, that is caught up in things, that has a front and a back, a past and a future.*[66]

That is, the relationship between the one who feels and what is felt is never given in a single sense. Now, if the distinction between subject and object is confused in my body, it is also confused in the thing, "which is the pole of my body's operations, the terminus its exploration ends up in, and which is thus woven into the same intentional fabric as my body."[67] Additionally, I do not perceive myself while I perceive. This non-coincidence is insurmountable. Totality is always present as an absence. The sentient cannot coincide with itself in pure interiority. It is only found and accessed through the depth of the world to which

---

[65] Merleau-Ponty (1964c, 163).

[66] Ibid., 162, 163.

[67] Ibid., 167.

it is open. The philosopher finds in this description a challenge to the prevailing idea of things and the world.

This is what leads the phenomenologist to say that it is no longer possible to think according to the cleavage between subject and object. Merleau-Ponty explores the concept of "flesh" (of an ontological nature) as a means of describing in the same movement the apparently paradoxical being of my body as a "two-faced" being, "a thing among things and otherwise what sees them and touches them."[68] It is well known how important the notion of "flesh" is to the late Merleau-Ponty. However, as Mauro Carbone (2015) reminds us, it is often overlooked that "flesh" is another name for the "element," which he also calls "Visibility." This term appears to have been chosen to avoid references to a specific subject or object, and to encompass both activity and passivity.

In *The Visible and the Invisible*, Merleau-Ponty argues that the element of "Visibility" does not pertain "neither to the body as a fact nor to the world as a fact," and thus, because of it, "the seer and the visible reciprocate one another and we no longer know which sees and which is seen."[69] This element of visibility, as Carbone reinforces, appears as both a challenge to the categories on which the Western philosophical tradition is based and an announcement of the opening of an ontological perspective. In fact, the being of visibility is defined as follows: "a being by porosity, pregnancy, or generality, and he before whom the horizon opens is caught up, included within it."[70] For Carbone, Merleau-Ponty pursues the existence of a connection between the visible and itself that runs through us and shapes us as seers. This thesis also shows how he conceives "our corporeity from the standpoint of the experience of the flesh of the world—namely, the experience of 'Visibility'—just as he had conceived the latter from the standpoint of the first."[71]

The vision is embodied and occurs in the midst of the world. It cannot be described as the unfolding of a wholly objective world in the presence of an ubiquitous consciousness. "This amounts to saying that vision advents as the actual presence of a visible world,"[72] says Barbaras. The world is never before me. It surrounds and overwhelms me. The world is immersed in me, invades me, and fills me. Although I am "in" it, there is no way to draw a line between the

---

[68.] Merleau-Ponty (1968, 137).

[69.] Ibid., 139.

[70.] Ibid., 149.

[71.] Carbone (2015, 2).

[72.] Barbaras (2014, 156).

world and myself, between what belongs to it and what I would consider mine. We are made of the same fabric. In other words, seeing something is not just seeing it in itself but seeing with or through it. The vision emerges as a moment of the thing, a moment that cannot be separated from it.

The flesh, therefore, simultaneously indicates the reversible nature of the body (visible and seer, phenomenal body and objective body, inside and outside) and of the world (surface and depth, visible and invisible, fact and "carnal essence," phenomenon and "being of latency," donation and retraction, light and darkness), as well as the fundamental unity between body and world. It is the "indivision of this sensible Being that I am and all the rest which feels itself in me."[73] This indivision, however, is also the fission that gives birth to the sensible mass of the body in the sensible mass of the world.

If *Phenomenology of Perception* emphasized the active role of the body, *The Visible and the Invisible* explores its background community with things. It is, indeed, true that the body cannot be reduced to a sensible thing among other things, as it serves as the general measure by which all things are perceived. However, it is only because there is a "being that in itself is imminent sensibility (flesh of the world) that corporeal flesh can exercise its active role."[74] The flesh, the stuff of the world, is what is visible by itself, sayable by itself, thinkable by itself, being, curiously, a porous plenum, a presence that contains an absence that never ceases to aspire to be. That is to say, the flesh always refers to an emptiness without which it cannot become. It is the meeting point of the visible and the invisible, the sayable and the unspeakable, the thinkable and the unthinkable, whose distinction, interchange, and reversibility constitute the stuff of the world. In this way, the reversibility, which in the *Phenomenology of Perception* characterized the relationship between subject and object, their intertwining and potential inversion, is described in *The Visible and the Invisible* as that which defines the flesh.

> *Where are we to put the limit between the body and the world, since the world is flesh? Where in the body are we to put the seer, since evidently there is in the body only 'shadows stuffed with organs,' that is, more of the visible? The world seen is not 'in' my body, and my body is not 'in' the visible world ultimately: as flesh applied to a flesh, the world neither surrounds it nor is surrounded by it. A participation in and kinship with the visible, the vision neither envelops it*

[73.] Merleau-Ponty (1968, 255).

[74.] Ferraz (2009, 271).

nor is enveloped by it definitively. The superficial pellicle of the visible is only
for my vision and for my body. But the depth beneath this surface contains my
body and hence contains my vision. My body as a visible thing is contained
within the full spectacle. But my seeing body subtends this visible body, and all
the visibles with it.[75]

Experience, then, is not simply an intentional exercise of powers separate from
the structures of the world. It can no longer be definitively located within one
of the polarities that define it (activity/passivity, agency/sentience, self/other,
interiority/exteriority) but rather in the interweaving of these aspects. What is
perceived is a reinterpretation of the sensory experience. Merleau-Ponty emphasizes
the sensitive nature of the body, leading to a revision of the excessively active
role of the perceptive subject. Now, perceptive activity arises from the sensible
characteristics of the Being itself. It is nourished by the inherent sensibility of
the world. This sensitive community believes that placing the body and things
in the same fabric ensures the accuracy and veracity of perception.

In this sense, it is interesting to observe the gradual shift from using the term
"perception" to favoring the notion of "perceptive faith" in *The Visible and the
Invisible*. The concept of "perception" in *Phenomenology of Perception* appears
to presuppose certain theoretical assumptions that should not be accepted as
self-evident. After all, perception shapes a system of subjective abilities capable of revealing every ordinary event or thing. The perceptive subject contains
within itself the potential for every conceivable existence. This is what leads
Merleau-Ponty to make problematic assertions such as "the thing presents itself
to the person who perceives it as a thing in itself, and thus poses the problem of
a genuine in-itself-for-us,"[76] or "the world remains 'subjective' since its texture
and articulations are traced out by the subject's movement of transcendence."[77]

When discussing how he intends to develop his approach in his last and
unfinished book, Merleau-Ponty argues that it is essential to abandon terms
such as "acts of consciousness," "states of consciousness," and "perception":
"We exclude the term perception to the whole extent that it already implies a
cutting up of what is lived into discontinuous acts, or a reference to 'things'
whose status is not specified, or simply an opposition between the visible and

---

[75.] Merleau-Ponty (1968, 138).

[76.] Merleau-Ponty (2002, 375).

[77.] Ibid., 500.

the invisible."[78] The rejection of these terms is based on the idea that perception implies a fragmentation of experience into separate acts, a spatial and material correlate, and appears to exclude a domain of the invisible, that is, in perceptive activity, the subject would only refer to the regime of what is present, without even acknowledging the existence of dimensions that are absent from sensitive donation. The use of the term "perceptive faith" could solve these problems.

If, then, we adhere to the originary donation of the world, what "perceptive faith" reveals, according to Merleau-Ponty, is that direct and effective access to the sensible world is not based on absolute certainty. It is a matter of faith, an openness to the world before certainty, "which does not exclude a possible occultation."[79] Perception, perceptive activity, pre-reflective consciousness, and pre-predicative consciousness are synonymous notions used in similar contexts. They were already indicated in *Phenomenology of Perception* as an original contact with the world that presents things as they are. The distinction between these terms and Merleau-Ponty's concept of "perceptive faith" in *The Visible and the Invisible* lies precisely in the potential for "occultation."

In *The Visible and the Invisible*, Merleau-Ponty acknowledges the possibility of the existence of Being beyond what is positively donated as sensitive data. It is exactly this possibility that the theme of the concealment of being seems to confirm: perceptive faith not only recognizes what presents itself in an original way but also what is absent in an original way. This is something that I can only identify as something that, by right, escapes my subjective powers. By describing perceptual experience in terms of perceptual faith, the rigid correlation between existence and manifestation to subjective abilities is disrupted, and it is not excluded that existence surpasses appearance.

The sensitive Being also encompasses non-perception and concealment. There are negative dimensions that could be embedded in positive data. It is necessary to consider certain inherent absences that manifest as absence, in order to describe the sensitive dimension as ontological. Merleau-Ponty explores this idea through the concept of the "invisible," a term that encapsulates that which goes beyond what is visible. The invisible is an "interior armature" of the sensible, which the sensible at the same time "manifests and conceals,"[80] and whose presence counts in the sensible as that of a cavity or an absence. Marilena Chauí (1999) explains that the invisible, for the French philosopher, is that by which or through which

---

[78.] Merleau-Ponty (1968, 158).

[79.] Ibid., 28.

[80.] Ibid., 149.

things become visible. It is not a third dimension but rather the fundamental condition of visibility. The invisible influences the composition of the visible, ensuring separation and differentiation.

In *The Visible and the Invisible*, the original phenomenon is no longer designated as perception, but as experience. "It is to experience therefore that the ultimate ontological power belongs."[81] Following this line of reasoning, it is no longer a matter of explaining the experience, but of deciphering it in its essence. Experience distinguishes the seer from the visible, the act of touching from the touched, the speaker from the spoken, and the thinker from the thought, just as it differentiates between seeing and touching, speaking and thinking. Abolishing these distinctions would mean returning to subjectivity as a representation of consciousness. Merleau-Ponty alludes to nuclear physics, which explains the origin of the universe through the conversion of mass into energy. This process produces new particles of the same species as those that created them. That is to say, the being itself is divided from within without separating itself from itself. It is important to understand that this differentiation, inherent to the experience is not created by it but rather manifests itself within it. This is because the world, as flesh, embodies a simultaneity of different dimensions. It divides terms without separating them, and unites them without identifying them.

> Philosophy is not a rupture with the world, nor a coinciding with it, but it is not the alternation of rupture and coincidence either. This double relation, which the philosophy of Being and Nothingness expresses so well, remains perhaps incomprehensible there because it is still a consciousness—a being that is wholly appearing—that is charged with bearing it. It has seemed to us that the task was to describe strictly our relation to the world not as an openness of nothingness upon being, but simply as openness: it is through openness that we will be able to understand being and nothingness, not through being and nothingness that we will be able to understand openness.[82]

The discovery of an operative and original meaning prior to any signification is ipso facto the discovery of a world before each presentation. The universal is no longer found in the realm of sense, but on the side of the world; it is what nourishes any expression, even though it is always absent from what unveils it. The world is what still needs to be articulated within the expression of it and,

---

[81] Ibid., 110.

[82] Ibid., 99.

therefore, it is still separate from what says it. To consider meaning based on expression is to consider the world based on Being. Thus, Merleau-Ponty observes that the world truly exists as it is, "more than all painting, than all speech, than every 'attitude,' and which, apprehended by philosophy in its universality, appears as containing everything that will ever be said, and yet leaving us to create it."[83]

In this book I will not defend either a fundamental break between Merleau-Ponty's early and latter works (as Marilena Chauí believes) or a return with different eyes to the same terms and perspectives (as is the case of Marcus Sacrini Ferraz). What interests me is that in this plunge into the sensitive, in this movement toward a new ontology, Merleau-Ponty outlined a rapprochement with cinema. In some of his last work notes, it is possible to identify the philosopher's desire for a philosophical approach to cinema, no longer to illustrate a pre-elaborated thought. Viewing cinema as a celebration of the vibrant embodiment of my specular carnality, a particular way to express the Being, an aesthetic that underlies a "dialectic of the visible and the invisible."

In "Eye and Mind," while rereading the relationship between the sensible and the intelligible, Merleau-Ponty employs the concept of "voyance." It indicates "clairvoyance," the "gift of double vision." At this point, a notable literary influence takes on a theoretically central position: "The Letter of the Seer," by Arthur Rimbaud (2002). Merleau-Ponty arrives at this reference through a statement by Max Ernst, who compares the painter's task precisely to that which Rimbaud's manifesto assigns to the poet: "Just as the role of the poet since [Rimbaud's] famous *Lettre du voyant* consists in writing under the dictation of what is being thought, of what articulates itself in him, the role of the painter is to grasp and project what is seen in him."[84] Or what, following Merleau-Ponty, we might also describe it as "passivity upon an activity,"[85] which is the reflexivity of Being itself. "The Letter of the Seer" serves as a symbol of this contemporary ontological concept, as it asserts the independence of language to declare the debauchery of poetry. Merleau-Ponty considers this "fundamental milestone"[86] as a transformation in the relationship between the visibility of Being and the writer's discourse.

Merleau-Ponty observes a contemporary need to rediscover in language the "transcendence of the same kind that occurs in vision" that he identifies

---

[83] Ibid., 170.

[84] Max Ernst and Merleau-Ponty (1964, 167).

[85] Merleau-Ponty (1968, 42, 43).

[86] Merleau-Ponty (1996, 187).

in Rimbaud's poetics. The transcendence in "The Letter of the Seer" does not involve a "second sight" directed at the intelligible but rather a vision that sees the invisible within the visible. This allows us to discover the invisible within the very fabric of music or literary discourse, as well as within the veil of the visible. Rimbaud's clairvoyance embodies the simultaneous nature of poetry, reflecting the frequent attempt to convey simultaneity to expression, which Merleau-Ponty views as one of the characteristic traits of contemporary ontology. Clairvoyance simultaneously defines the role of art and access to the Being. Therefore, it designates the simultaneous emergence of an aesthetic and an ontology.

This is precisely what Merleau-Ponty says about painting in "Eye and Mind":

> *For I do not look at it as I do at a thing; I do not fix it in its place. My gaze wanders in it as in the halos of Being. It is more accurate to say that I see according to it, or with it, than that I see it.*[87]

The analysis of the act of vision shows us that an artist's work consists, above all, in an ontological recovery of the world. Painting, for example, tries, through the spectacle of the visible that a painting celebrates, to express, in a certain way, all aspects of the Being.

In notes referring to "Cartesian Ontology and the Ontology of Today," a course that Merleau-Ponty was preparing to teach at the Collège de France in 1961, shortly before his unexpected death, the phenomenologist seeks to ascribe a philosophical formulation to contemporary ontology:

> *it is not the history of philosophy in the usual sense: what was thought is: what was thought in the frame and horizon of what is thought—evoked to make understanding what is thought—Objective: contemporary ontology—Starting from this to then go to meet Descartes and the Cartesians, then back to what philosophy can be today.*[88]

Merleau-Ponty opposes what he calls "Cartesian Ontology," which he particularly identifies in the literature of Marcel Proust[89] and in the painting of Paul

---

[87] Merleau-Ponty (1964c, 164).

[88] Merleau-Ponty (1996, 390–91.

[89] This observation is noteworthy for those who claim that the last phase of Merleau-Ponty's thought concerns only painting. It is true: Merleau-Ponty's discussion of artistic mastery actually focuses on painting, following the path already traced in "Eye and Mind." However, Merleau-Ponty also investigates the literary domain, especially the works by Proust, Valéry, and a few others.

Cézanne, as well as in other arts such as cinema. At one point, the annotation "(painting-cinema)" is followed two lines further down by "André Bazin: ontology of cinema," and then "In the arts Cinema ontology of cinema—the question of movement in cinema."[90] What is very clearly perceived is the philosopher's desire to incorporate cinema into the reflections he had been developing on literature and painting, capable, each in their own way, of establishing the relationship between the visible and the invisible.

It is then of no surprise, as Carbone points out, that most of Merleau-Ponty's later reflections on cinema address directly the issue of movement. This is what is at stake in the summary of another course, "Le monde sensible et le Monde de l'expression," in which the "use of movement" coincides not only with a particular question but also with the very nature of what Merleau-Ponty calls "cinematic art."[91] He continues:

> Cinema, invented as a means of photographing objects in motion or as a repre-
> sentation of movement, discovered with it much more than changing places, that
> is, a new way of symbolizing thoughts, a movement of representation.[92]

It is quite interesting: Merleau-Ponty employs the concept of "representation." It seems absolutely legitimate to argue that the "discovery" the philosopher refers to in the quote above will lead him to abandon the idea of representation, in order to explore, in all its implications, that of the "vision of," resolutely refusing to reduce it to an "operation of thought that would set up before the mind a picture or a representation of the world."[93] Therefore, his real interest lies in investigating the non-mimetic dimension of cinematographic realism—an observation of manifestly ontological scope.

It is precisely this question that emerges from one of Merleau-Ponty's few more direct references to movies. Still in "Le monde sensible et le monde de l'expression,"[94] the phenomenologist extensively discusses the well-known scene of a riot in a college dormitory, shot in slow motion by Jean Vigo in *Zero for Conduct* (*Zéro de conduite*, 1933). When analyzing this passage, Carbone leads me down a curious path by underlining the references to Maurice Jaubert,

---

[90.] Merleau-Ponty (1996, 391).

[91.] Merleau-Ponty (2011, 102).

[92.] Merleau-Ponty (1968b, 19–20).

[93.] Merleau-Ponty (1964c, 162).

[94.] Merleau-Ponty (2011, 113).

the French composer who composed the soundtrack for Vigo's film. In this scene, Jaubert offers a unique melodic inversion in the soundtrack, blending the faithful reproduction of movement with a feeling of estrangement. Indeed, says Carbone, "Merleau-Ponty's notes precisely refer to the effect produced at once by the reversal of the original music and the use of slow motion."[95] What interests Merleau-Ponty — and Carbone identifies so well — is precisely this essentially cinematographic combination between the impression of reality and the effect of derealization. At another point, he says:

> *The sound of a wind instrument bears in its quality the mark of the breath that engenders it and of the organic rhythm of this breath, as evidenced by the impression of strangeness that is obtained by emitting normally recorded sounds in reverse. Far from being a simple 'displacement', movement is inscribed in the texture of figures or qualities, it is like a revealer of their being.*[96]

Thus, according to Merleau-Ponty, cinema helps us identify the direction to be followed in order to avoid the fundamental dualisms of the Western tradition. Cinema imposes on me a definition of movement not as movement in Being but rather as movement of Being itself, which, in turn, reveals itself as being always in motion. This is precisely what the course highlights when it states: "Therefore, here the movement = revelation of the Being, the result of its internal config-uration and clearly different from the change of place."[97] Although he does not delve deeply into his comments on cinema, the phenomenologist's notes and final essays seem to suggest, or at least infer, the guidelines through which the last phase of Merleau-Ponty's thought could have developed an ontological consideration of cinema, emphasizing, above all, its non-mimetic character, as a presentation of an unpresentable.

This consideration raises the question of vision as the reversibility of the flesh, "this precession of what is upon what one sees and makes seen, of what one sees and makes seen upon what is,"[98] as "at a crossroads, all the aspects of Being."[99] The analysis of vision in action shows us that the artist's work consists, above all, in an ontological resumption of the world. Painting, for example, as

---

[95.] Carbone (2015, 53).

[96.] Merleau-Ponty (1968b, 15).

[97.] Ibid., 102.

[98.] Merleau-Ponty (1964c, 188).

[99.] Ibid.

I have already stressed in this chapter, attempts to express, in a certain way, all aspects of the Being. By studying the experience of the painter, Merleau-Ponty dwells on the moments in which seeing, hearing, or speaking cross the layer of the instituted and lay bare the origin of a visible, sonorous, and speaking world. Cézanne, for example, as Merleau-Ponty insists, stated his desire to transform impressionism into "something solid like the art of museums." For Merleau-Ponty, this mission is paradoxical. The painter aims to capture reality and rejects the conventional means of achieving it: "pursuing reality without giving up the sensuous surface, with no other guide than the immediate impression of nature."[100] Cézanne believed that it was unnecessary to make a choice between the two, separating the permanent things that appear to our gaze and the fleeting way in which they appear. He "wanted to depict matter as it takes on form, the birth of order through spontaneous organization."[101]

In this way, the debate over the objective or subjective representation of the world, which greatly impeded a new approach to thinking about images and the imaginary, is thoroughly reconsidered, restoring to vision its fundamental power to convey more than just itself. For Merleau-Ponty, vision involves the metamorphosis of things themselves into vision, visibility, and clairvoyance. To be or not to be seen are the attributes of things, of their becoming present. It is the idea of film not as a pure representation. When filming a landscape, the filmmaker does not simply copy or reproduce it. It is impossible to separate the subject from the object when considering what is seen; both are constituted in this relationship of equivalence. At the same time that the landscape inspires the filmmaker and is captured on film, his work is composed by seeking in the landscape what the image lacks in order to achieve its full expression. There is no cause-and-effect relationship. I cannot regard cinema simply as a creation based solely on the artist's intention.

I refer back to Merleau-Ponty's mention of Bazin. He could not be more thought-provoking. There is, in fact, a harmony between the critic and the phenomenologist that appears to have become more pronounced during the 1950s. Bazin and Merleau-Ponty view cinema as a compelling new language for expressing the Being, capable of reflecting on our promiscuity with the world and things. Both became aware of this ontological gamble inherent in the game of imagination: the emergence of the image wrapped in a coming and going, from things to form, from fact to meaning, and vice versa.

[100.] Merleau-Ponty (1964b, 12).

[101.] Ibid., 13.

In "The Ontology of the Photographic Image," Bazin wrote that the "logical distinction between what is imaginary and what is real tends to disappear. Every image is to be seen as an object and every object as an image."[102] In "Eye and Mind," when reflecting on the novelties of modern painting, Merleau-Ponty states that the image will no longer be considered as "a tracing, a copy, a second thing,"[103] more or less faithful to its model, and in any case produced by an independent vision of our sensible relationship with the world. For both, the imaginary cannot be conceived as a substitute for a faculty or a substitute for reality. The imaginary is not the opposite of the real, but emerges "precisely together with vision itself—from the sensible kinship between the world and us."[104]

In *The Prose of the World* (1973), Merleau-Ponty asserts that in a painting by Cézanne, the objects bleed, their substance spreads under my eyes, and it directly challenges my gaze and tests the pact of coexistence I made with the world through my whole body. When investigating the painter's experience, Merleau-Ponty focuses on the moments when perception, hearing, or speaking transcend established norms and reveal the origins of a visible, audible, and communicative world. For him, in modern painting, flesh is at stake—"both the flesh of things, and the flesh constituting each living creature's way of inhabiting the world."[105] The philosopher is referring to the work of Paul Klee, but I can extend it to cinema. Thus, the image can be characterized as a chiasm. It is a thing of the world—it is entirely in the world, but the world is entirely in it. It makes the world appear, and the world appears in it. Barbaras speaks of an "openness-opened":

> It is opened up, it is arranged, and it appears as a thing only if it is an opening, that is, on the condition that it leaves room for the world itself. It is opened up, then, only if it is itself the openness in which it appears. It is unified only in the measure that it is unifying; its unity overflows the limit that it nonetheless circumscribes; its unity is made generality, world.[106]

What emerges from this Merleau-Pontian rapprochement with cinema is the understanding that the seventh art is perhaps the one that, in the most

---

[102.] Bazin (2005, 15, 16).

[103.] Merleau-Ponty (1964c, 164).

[104.] Carbone (2015, 57).

[105.] Ibid., 21.

[106.] Barbaras (2014, 189–90).

paradoxical way, manages to express the simultaneity of all things. The potential of cinematographic techniques lies in their ability to promote an openness to things without a concept: the intensity of a face highlighted in a close-up, the long shot that conveys the possibility of whatever it is, the hesitant murmur of movements, gazes, colors, scenarios, all interconnected, interdependent, differentiated yet simultaneous. When it comes to painting, in a quote that comes to my rescue, Merleau-Ponty comments:

> *Art is not imitation, nor is it something manufactured according to the wishes of instinct or good taste. It is a process of expressing. Just as the function of words is to name—that is, to grasp the nature of what appears to us in a confused way and to place it before us as a recognizable object—so it is up to the painter, said Gasquet, to 'objectify,' 'project,' and 'arrest.' Words do not look like the things they designate; and a picture is not a trompe-l'oeil [...] The painter recaptures and converts into visible objects what would, without him, remain walled up in the separate life of each consciousness: the vibration of appearances which is the cradle of things. Only one emotion is possible for this painter—the feeling of strangeness—and only one lyricism—that of the continual rebirth of existence.*[107]

Like the filmmaker, the painter brings back to light what germinates in it, and that is why the painter's vision is a continuous birth. With inveterate rigor, a director like Hou Hsiao-Hsien compels us to relinquish the idea that we possess the world, challenging the things that gain visibility and show themselves as existing. This interrogation takes place within the image, through it, and is prolonged in us, the spectators, as a celebration of the mysterious and feverish genesis of things in our body, which supposes, in Merleau-Ponty, an ontological unity rather than a fracture between seeing and thinking. Hsiao-Hsien's shots in *Goodbye South, Goodbye* captivate our gaze with their raw edges, claiming an absolute presence by virtue of a sense of configuration whose idea is not given to us by a "theoretical sense." It is a strange world that sees itself as constituted, renewed, not yet tamed by any culture, and it asks us to create culture anew. That is why his films give the impression of nature in its original, its imminent presence.

Hsiao-Hsien's cinema expresses a unique relationship with the world, bridging the gap between image and discourse, contemplation and composition, and reality, meaning and figuration. Hsiao-Hisen transforms the cinematographic experience into a creative journey, prompting us to think not only about what

---

[107] Merleau-Ponty (1964b, 17, 18).

has already been thought but also what lies hidden behind those thoughts. A film like *Goodbye South, Goodbye* brings to Being what without it would deprive us of experiencing. It gropes around an intention to express something for which I do not have a model, since it is the film itself, in action, that opens the access route to the contact through which it is possible to experience. If "Being is what requires creation of us for us to experience it,"[108] the filmmaker's work is precisely to capture the instituting as creation.

This type of maxim can be seen in the works of other phenomenologically inspired authors. For them, cinema is a spontaneously phenomenological art that enables us to see rather than explain, creating a unique relationship with reality and encompassing concepts such as "mystery," "ambiguity," "revelation," and "feeling." The terms come from the movies (especially the neorealists, at least for Bazin and Ayfre). They emerge from a direct and immediate confrontation, and they show a constructive reliance on their examples. Throughout this process, the cinematographic image is even seen as an asymptote of reality, moving ever closer to it, forever dependent on it, to the point where Roger Munier feels paralyzed and impotent. Filmmakers must, therefore, fulfill this moral obligation, remaining faithful to the ontological dimension of cinema—whether through a rigid program, as is the case with Mourlet, or through an elaboration that is always situated and contextual, beyond styles, aesthetics, and theories, as suggested by Jean Mitry.

These authors often assume a certain transparency in the use of certain language procedures, insisting on the differences between film and the world. At the same time, however, even when this may not be obvious, the most important aspect is the understanding that a film primarily presents an ontological formulation. Cinema offers a different way of thinking about the world without entirely controlling or domesticating it. This insight, which helps me navigate through many of the dilemmas in which these authors find themselves entangled, will serve as my guiding principle from now on.

Ayfre, Bazin, Mourlet, Munier, and Mitry, each in their own way, complement much of what we observed in Merleau-Ponty, while also paving the way for new avenues of exploration. I will now highlight each one of them, and later we will look for another important ally in Gilles Deleuze. We will review the disagreements between the French philosopher and phenomenology, and identify in them a cinematographic project with countless similarities. The exploration of this overlooked tradition and the unexpected connection between Deleuze and

---

[108.] Merleau-Ponty (1968, 197).

Merleau-Ponty points to the cinematographic potential of an ontological nature that contemporary cinema explores.

1.2 Amédée Ayfre

The Art of Revelation and the Exercise of Freedom

Amédée Ayfre, who is practically unknown in the Anglo-Saxon world, was an abbot, a close friend of André Bazin, and a student of Maurice Merleau-Ponty. His work, interrupted by his premature death in a car accident in 1964, reveals a film theory project at the intersection of phenomenology, Sartrean existentialism, and Catholicism — a cocktail in perfect harmony with the French post-war environment. As the master of *Phenomenology of Perception*, Ayfre sees cinema as a spontaneously phenomenological art. His biggest concern is the subtle presence of things and the world that cinema, by its very nature, is inclined to unveil to us. This revelation is associated with the concept of "mystery," a term that Ayfre believes has religious meaning. This, however, can only be possible in an approach that is both respectful of reality and ethical toward the spectator.

Priest, philosopher, critic, and enthusiast of Christian cinema, Ayfre enrolled at the Sorbonne under the guidance of Étienne Souriau to study filmology with a research project entitled "Aesthetic Problems of Religious Cinema." The idea, at least initially, was to apply the phenomenological method in vogue in filmology studies to cinematographic works of a more religious nature. His primary intention was to help Christians reflect on cinema, "one of the most important phenomena of our time."[109] Contrary to one of the fears often expressed by the Catholic Church,[110] Ayfre believed that the "magic" of the images was not harmful. The illusion they create does not prevent us from accessing reality and, ultimately, from "being in the world" through cinema. Ayfre sees the seventh art as a gesture of faith, as a means of expressing the presence of the divine mystery in the most tangible form of human actions.

Italian neorealism awakened the abbot to cinema. If Merleau-Ponty had no familiarity with neorealism, the Italian movement served as a foundation not only for Ayfre but also for Bazin. The cinematographic production that emerged in Italy immediately after the end of World War II gained recognition through Roberto

---

[109] Ayfre (1964, 1).

[110] Both Pope Pius XI and Pope Pius XII issued guidelines regarding cinema, always underlining its qualities and dangers.

Rossellini's *Rome, Open City* public acclamation. It actually received a bunch of denominations: humanist cinema, naturalism, neopopulism, neoexpressionism, and neorealism. The latter, the consecrated term, indicates continuity, a way of inserting oneself into a tradition, as Mariarosaria Fabris (2007) warns us. The addition of the prefix "neo" signals a movement, a dialogue with classical realism, French poetic realism, Soviet socialist realism, as well as with the realistic experiences of the Italian cinema of the fascist period. I am referring to a production characterized by strict control and censorship, as well as of propaganda, works that have a realistic nature. For this cinema, man is understood as a worker who is a part of the state. Man exists only in relation to the state.

The early works by Luchino Visconti, Roberto Rossellini, and Vittorio De Sica not only challenged the banality that had been the dominant mode of Italian cinema for a long time but also reacted against the socio-economic conditions prevailing in Italy during that period. Italian neorealism is the expression of a philosophy[111] yearning for another relationship between man and reality.[112] Everyday, ordinary Italy, which had been absent from the cinema for twenty years, made a comeback on the big screen. The films unfolded through minor dramas of the daily life of the common Italian people, who were oppressed by sociopolitical circumstances beyond their control. Italian neorealism was the first post-war movement to liberate from the artificial constraints of Hollywood studios. With limited resources, in a country completely destroyed by war, filmmakers took cinema to the streets, using small crews, minimal equipment, local citizens, and a handful of professional actors.

Rome, Open City was the epitome of these ideas and ideals. The production conditions of the feature (filmed almost entirely on location, with only two professional actors, film purchased on the black market by Rossellini himself, and the team's headquarters, which operated in a deactivated riding ring under a brothel next to the newsroom of an American army newspaper)[113] contributed greatly to the many myths surrounding neorealism. The film also told the

---

[111] It is worth remembering that cinematographic neorealism coincided with the resurgence of realist literature in Italy, especially the works of Italo Calvino, Alberto Moravia, and Cesare Pavese.

[112] Pier Paolo Pasolini comments:

Neorealism is the product of a democratic cultural reaction to the stagnation of the spirit in the fascist period: from the literary point of view, it consisted in replacing decadent, hypothetical classicism, which instituted from above and implied a clear 'stylistic distinction' turned towards a *sublimis* style (in which, if there was realism, it was precious or anecdotal realism), by a taste for paratactic reality, which, as in a documentary, operated at the level of the reality represented through a process and mimesis, from which the discovery of interior monologue, lived speech and a stylistic mixture was born, with the predominance of a *humilius* (or dialectal) style. (Pasolini and Fabris 2007, 8–9)

[113] For more on the troubled filmmaking process of *Rome, Open City*, see Tag Gallagher (1998).

story of a group of resistance fighters who lived under German occupation at the end of World War II. In other words, not only were the filming conditions special, but the plot itself diverged from the conventional battle of good and bad guys that Hollywood had perfected. Instead, it embraced the uncertainty of the characters' motivations and the cause-and-effect connections. What made *Rome, Open City* the neorealist model was its daring combination of styles and tones, ranging from documentary to melodrama. It completely defied the rules of a then hegemonic narrative cinema and aimed to present an anti-spectacular portrayal of man facing a reality which a priori means nothing. More than a style, for Rossellini, neorealism was a moral stance. In this work, the translation of man was not achieved through psychological motivations and extensive dialogues but rather through his physical movements, gestures, and interactions with surrounding objects.

These ideas of a cinema of behavior, of the street, of an improvised mise-en-scène, of a non-ideological representation of everyday life, would be increasingly adopted as the 1950s progressed. They would serve as a rich base for phenomenologically inspired approaches. The very friendship between Bazin and Ayfre is curiously rooted in their mutual admiration for *Germany, Year Zero* (*Germania, anno zero*, 1948). Enthused by the criticism that Bazin had published in the fourteenth edition of *Esprit* magazine regarding on Rossellini's third feature, Ayfre sent him a long letter at the end of 1949. Bazin replied, surprised by the convergence of their respective approaches. Both saw the Italian movement as a new form of realism that relied on a constant dialogue with physical reality. Ayfre drew heavily on Bazin's criticisms of movies like *Bicycle Thieves*, while identifying in this cinema an appeal to the spectator's conscience, forced to leave his recognizing in this type of cinema a call to the spectator's conscience. The spectator is compelled to move beyond passivity and engage in a phenomenological description that can uncover the "mystery" of the world. Bazin, in turn, would adopt from the abbot the notion of a record of reality in its entirety. Although there were some divergences between them (which, however, never established a more direct confrontation), whether with regard to the machinic dimension of the seventh art or the religious character of the cinematographic experience or the emphasis given to the language of cinema, both celebrated an encounter with phenomenology and focused their attention on the nature of the relationships between reality, a film, and the spectator.

Ayfre was invited to write for *Cahiers du Cinema*, and "Neo-réalisme et phénoménologie," a dense article, probably his main essay on cinema, was published in November 1952. Interestingly, the abbot begins the text by arguing precisely about the validity of the term neorealism:

> *'Realism' is one of those words which should never be used without a determining correlative. Does 'neo-,' as applied to post-war Italian realist cinema, fit the bill? Judged in terms of the more or less universal usage it has acquired, the answer would have to be yes. But if, on the contrary, we sift through the innumerable critiques to which it has been subjected, even by artists themselves, and if we note that all those who use it do so with some reservation in the form of brackets or circumlocutions (in short, with a bad conscience), the temptation is to look for something to replace it.*[114]

Ayfre then traces an analysis in perspective and asks himself if neorealism merely redraws worlds already mapped in detail or if it actually offers something new. He ponders if the accent should be on the "neo" or on the "realism." Realism has been a fundamental aspect of cinema since the Lumière brothers, who, by placing a camera in a certain place, filming something for a certain time, and recording the world in black and white on a flat surface, established an inevitable abyss between representation and reality. This realism that is born with the cinema would develop, according to the author, through two trajectories that he names as "documentary" and "verism." Its objective is to understand whether the Italian movement would be another transformation of the latter or if it would have found an alternative to the dialectical impasse of the documentary.

In describing what he calls a documentary, Ayfre cites Dziga Vertov. The Russian would have realized that the pinnacle of realism in cinema would be the documentary. Hence, there is a need to step out of the studio, without any actors or scripts. The ideal for this cinema would be that of a camera that continuously records every street corner. Ayfre, however, asks: What would emerge from this ideal documentary situation? Would it be a film or a collection of moving photographs? Faced with this questioning, Vertov placed his bets on constructing a specific rhythm that would be imposed on the images through montage. However, for the abbot, Vertov's gamble consumed him to such an extent that he gradually lost interest in the individual elements at his disposal. "Thus," says Ayfre, "from the starting point of the rawest kind of realism we are thrown back into abstract art."[115]

The verista movement would be the one that rejects the naivety of an objective and direct contact with the real in favor of a digression around the notion

---

[114.] Ayfre (1985, 182).

[115.] Ibid., 183.

of "truth." What characterizes this cinema, according to Ayfre, is the belief that an event needs to be deliberately reconstituted in order to become credible. He quotes Maurice Cloche and Jean Grémillon as examples. Both French filmmakers, aware that the "real content" of their films must be trimmed, underlined, and explained, would always be striving to stylize the event recorded by the camera.

Neorealism creates a sort of short circuit between these realistic paths traced by the abbot. The author dwells at length on the final sequence of *Germany, Year Zero*. The boy, Edmund, wanders aimlessly through the devastated streets of Berlin and finally finds what appears to be his only escape route. Edmund commits suicide by jumping off a building. At no time does the boy appear to act. Ayfre says it is impossible to determine whether I am experiencing a good or bad performance, just as the spectator is not emotionally invested. This will be one of the hallmarks of Rossellini's cinema, a poetics of solitude that is entirely shaped by the exterior landscape. The boy walks as if he exists independently of my gaze. For Ayfre, not even emotions such as regret, remorse, or despair can explain what I am witnessing. What is at stake in this sequence is the confrontation with the question of "human attitudes as existential attitudes."[116]

Ayfre underlines that the documentary element of *Germany, Year Zero* is not based on a facade of passive objectivity in the cinematographic record. The "neutrality" of his representation is never cold or impersonal. Although it is not possible for us to judge the events narrated, we are always emotionally affected. Rossellini does not advertise but polemicizes. What most decisively differentiates Rossellini's film from the other two "realisms" described by Ayfre is the fact that "the objective, subjective, social, etc., are never analysed as such; they are taken as a factual whole in all its inchoate fullness, a bloc in time as well as volume."[117] The abbot refers to another Italian film, *Bicycle Thieves*, by De Sica:

> Here we have a man in search of his bike who is not just a man who loves his son, a worker desperately engaged in trying to steal another bike, a man who, finally, represents the distress of the proletariat reduced to stealing the tools of its trade. He is all that and a host of other things besides, indefinable, unanalysable, precisely because primarily he is, and not in isolation, but surrounded by a bloc of reality which carries traces of the world—friends, church, German seminarians, Rita Hayworth on a poster. And this is in no sense merely decor, it 'exists' almost on the same level as he does.[118]

[116.] Ibid., 184.

[117.] Ibid.

[118.] Ibid., 185–86.

It is not very difficult to identify the phenomenological roots of Ayfre's insights. He even referred to the Italian movement as "phenomenological realism." The author seeks in Merleau-Ponty[119] and Andre Lalande[120] two definitions for the phenomenological current that help him to approach what he sees as the most important aspect of Rossellini's film: the representation of the boy's experience. This representation is not seen as psychological or introspective, nor as a passive experimentation with stimuli from the environment, but rather as an "openness to the world." Therefore, a "total sense of existence" would emerge from the image, not in the form of a thesis that the film would like to demonstrate or even illustrate and which, in this way, would indicate a precondition for its conception. On the contrary, meaning is an integral part of a concrete attitude, hence its ambiguity.

Let us take another look at Edmund's suicide at the end of *Germany, Year Zero*. How can we explain it? Perhaps due to the economic disorder of a decadent society, where even the love of God cannot find a way. Perhaps the absurdity of polarization as a whole, in a sad and bloody world filled with superfluous people. "Rossellini," however, as Ayfre explains, "makes no decisions. He puts the question. In the face of an existential attitude, he proposes the mystery of existence."[121]

The notion of "mystery" will be extremely important for Ayfre. The ambiguity of the image for him inevitably results in the portrayal of mystery. It is not only a space for the exercise of freedom but also a real for the manifestation of mystery. "Ambiguity is the mode of existence of the Mystery which is the safeguard of freedom."[122] According to the French author, the main works of the Italian movement operate in an intersection with the sacred. Rossellini and De Sica, filmmakers mentioned by Ayfre, want to talk about things as they are, as they appear in my experience, they place issues such as character and narrative in parentheses, favoring a total apprehension, in which events and mystery are co-present.

This phenomenological realism, like the method that inspires it, would also be the result of an action of putting between parentheses, a kind of "encapsulation." Between parentheses is a fragment of reality that gives the spectator the sensation of not being in front of a spectacle, not even a realistic one. The filmmaker, however, is the one who knows the cost of the effort needed to achieve the

---

[119] "Essays in a direct description of experience as it is, without regard to its psychological genesis or the causal explanations which the scientist, historian or sociologist may provide" (Merleau-Ponty and Ayfre 1985, 185).

[120] "Descriptive study of a set of phenomena as they manifest themselves in time or space, as opposed to the fixed, abstract laws governing such phenomena, the transcendental realities of which they are a manifestation, or normative criticism of their legitimacy" (Lalande and Ayfre 1985, 185).

[121] Ayfre (1985, 184).

[122] Ibid., 190.

impression of reality and convey the feeling that he, the author, never set foot inside the parentheses. Ayfre proposes a notion of style that is similar to the one his friend Bazin defended. A style that negates itself and, simultaneously, brings forth the ambiguity and mystery of the world. The abbot outlines an ascesis of direction, script, and actors: "Art is therefore established within the very act by which it seeks to destroy itself."[123]

It is not by chance that Ayfre refers to the scripts by Zavattini and De Sica as examples of an asceticism to be pursued. Zavattini, something of an Italian film theoretician, was known for saying that the neorealist camera was "hungry for reality." For him, cinema should focus on what reality already has at its most spectacular: the ordinary man in his everyday actions, at any time, on any day. Each slice of reality would be able to reveal the real in its entirety. It is, therefore, necessary to trust the reality in front of each scene, to preserve it, to underline it, to immerse oneself in it, and to allow oneself to be fully traversed by the elements that constitute each filmed situation. That is, instead of fabricating stories, the Zavattinian project begins with mundane facts and emphasizes that the true importance of minor occurrences can be grasped through observation. He says:

> the real duration of man's pain and his daily presence, not as a metaphysical man, but as the man we meet on the corner, and for whom this real duration must correspond to a real effort of our solidarity.[124]

Hence, his big dream: a film shot in a single take, where the camera follows a man walking without any special occurrence. Now, as we saw at the beginning of this chapter on Ayfre's ideas, the abbot believes that the great novelty of Italian films was precisely the overcoming of the belief in the objectivity of the camera, capable of recording reality directly. "Phenomenological realism" aims to replace construction with description. Ayfre believes that "truth is not made, but found."[125] For him, I am no longer "in the domain of making, but in that of being."[126] In other words, the beauty of Italian films arises for Ayfre less from their formal aspects than from the rich texture of life within them.

The presence of the world in the image emanates from the possibility of it being captured as a whole, in its entirety, for the spectator. The spectator, in turn,

---

[123] Ibid., 186.

[124] Zavattini and Xavier (2005, 72).

[125] Ayfre (1964, 227).

[126] Ibid., 228.

experiences the world in its own original ambiguity, which reveals the mystery of existence. Contrary to what we will see in Michel Mourlet and Roger Munier, the meaning of this "revelation" is essential for the abbot, who goes deeper than Bazin in a theological dimension of the cinematographic experience. The "total meaning of existence" is revealed in the form of a fundamental ambiguity, which "is the human mode of existence of the mystery." Ayfre expressed his phenomenological argument in theological terms:

> The sacred for Christians is none other than God as he is, both accessible and inaccessible to men. Perhaps he has revealed himself to them, but even in that revelation he eludes them. In other words, to express the sacred, we will have to insert it in the universe of human experiences, even without humanizing it, so that it remains transcendent to these same experiences. [127]

Ayfre's thesis is intriguing. He argues that, for a Christian, the supreme divine revelation takes place in the person of Christ, who represents the human face of God. The church's liturgy evokes God in his invisibility, using "a style of reality, in indirect induction, with very sober gestures and extremely pure and simple elements."[128] The invisible, therefore, is much more suggested than represented. It is in this sense that Ayfre criticizes those who seem more concerned with the divinity itself when expressing sacred interests and attempts to assign a predetermined meaning to events that the very "finger of God" has kept open in ambiguity. In fact, the theme of ambiguity, always associated with the expression of mystery, highlighting the "finger of God," is much narrower than in Bazin's essays—although we cannot, in any way, reduce the work of the abbot to the spiritual field. Ayfre is interested in the form and scope of the revelation of reality provided by cinema. Cinema brings us closer to the mystery of God. For him, films exist as the ever-changing face of the divine:

> Great masterpieces of art, at all times, have always intended to evoke a sacred reality which, by definition, is rightly located beyond human reach. Cinema, although it was born very late, in a world largely dominated by a secular lifestyle, has produced numerous films with the same objective.[129]

[127.] Ayfre (1960, 106).

[128.] Ibid., 107.

[129.] Ibid., 105.

It is not surprising that Ayfre demonstrates an enormous appreciation for the cinematographic work of Robert Bresson—an oeuvre very different, it must be said, from Italian neorealism. The abbot describes films such as *Diary of a Country Priest* (*Journal d'un Curé de Campagne*, 1950), *A Man Escaped* (*Un condamné à mort s'est échappé*, 1956), and *Pickpocket* (1959), as "a long and progressive cleaning of the universe of appearances."[130] In fact, the French filmmaker does films that are simultaneously expansive and concentrated, precise as few others in mapping and recording gestures and actions, but also equally attentive to the imaginative resonance of his images and sounds. This tension between what is seen and heard and what is felt, what is understood and what is indefinable, is at the heart of his cinema. Bresson works by precisely coordinating all the elements of cinema—camera distance, sound, subject, narrative, movement, color, and human action—so that it works with perfect rhythmic clarity.

Diary of a Country Priest, for example, accurately depicts the daily life of its protagonist. Bresson immerses us in a state of heightened or transcendent perception. I am particularly fond of the way in which he works with sound. In Bresson, sound is almost always denaturalized, detached from its context and isolated. Many times, sound is even privileged over image, precisely because of its greater imaginative potential. When I see and hear something in Bresson, I really see and hear it. Its purpose is precisely to make the profound mysteries concealed within the spaces between objects, actions, and emotions.

The priest of Ambricourt strives to be a bridge between the parish and the local community. The film tells, above all, a story of confinement, of an announced failure, to be more specific. This is a man unable to make an impression on the world, someone who tries his best but finds himself weighed down by the weight of the world and the order of things. The film is marked at the same time by the emphasis on the physicality of the cinematographic record of the character's day-to-day life, as well as by a nameless void that persists, oppresses, and over-whelms the images. For Ayfre, it is "through the interplay of this presence and this absence, orchestrated with discretion as well as fullness by all the stylistic resources of a film, the sacred cannot but be manifested."[131]

Ayfre is always in search of what can make the presence of others effective for the spectator, in a realm beyond what the objectivity of the machine seems to guarantee us. This is one of the aspects that make his essays unique: It is not solely the automatism of the machine that brings forth reality in its ambiguity

---

[130.] Ibid., 110.

[131.] Ibid.

but rather the presence of a conscience that defines what "is situated in front of the real and interrogates it, describes it and finally reveals it. A living conscience, and not a cold conscience that refuses to exercise itself under the pretext of being more objective."[132] The cinematographic camera, a soulless machine as Ayfre likes to say, is incapable of capturing human presence. Cinema reveals the world through an engagement between this "conscience" and the spectator, who has access to images in the exercise of his freedom.

The story of this engagement, however, is not completed with the end of the film. Ayfre even had a curious metaphor to illustrate the phenomenological connection between film and spectator. In the relationship between a psychoanalyst and a patient, the former uses reason and logic to address the dreams and oneiric images of the latter. Through their dialogue, understanding and healing[133] can be achieved. According to Ayfre, a spectator is both patient and doctor, learning new meanings as the film's narrative progresses. Stimulated by the power and mystery of the cinematic experience, movie audiences are presented with a remarkable opportunity: to perceive humanity in a transcendent new perspective, as sacred companions on the path to eternity.

According to Ayfre, a spectator, who is enriched by the images and the cinematographic experience, must return to reality in a different way. For the author, there will always be a moment when you have to leave the movie theater. In "Cinéma et présence du prochain," an essay presented at a congress in Toulouse in 1956, Ayfre emphasizes that the cinematographic image, as long as it is not separated from the entire dynamic process that goes from "reality to idea and from idea to reality," can play a vital role in revealing the presence of another. When I watch a film like *Umberto D.*, I do not feel paralyzed by the banality or tenderness of the images. Nor is it useful to turn the feature into a thesis on old age or something similar. The spectator must bring the images to life as much as possible,

> *It is only on the street that this gentleman whom I passed without seeing will be able to assert himself, if I so wish, through the mediation of a film by Vittorio de Sica, Umberto D, as my neighbor. I will then have retraced the circuit and rediscovered for myself, thanks to the mediation of his images, the reality from which another departed.*[134]

Ayfre has written several articles attempting to unravel the universe of the cinematographic experience. His method consisted of identifying how a filmmaker

---

[132.] Ayfre (1964, 229).

[133.] Andrew (1976, 252).

[134.] Ayfre (1957, 630).

reveals not the "essence" but the "existence," and how he helps the spectator to apprehend the reality of human existence. As Dudley Andrew (1976) aptly determined, the abbot defends a cinema of dialogue with the world, where the spectator can actively play a role while looking for the depth of the spirit behind the shadows on the screen. A good film should turn the spectator in a witness of concrete human actions recorded as wholes and revealing a humanity in which the profound mysteries of the universe are intertwined.

Although the abbot believed that few directors could achieve such profound insights into the presumption of God, he felt that an approach to the transcendent need not be limited to Christianity. What interests me most about Ayfre is the potential to honor the inherent ambiguity of reality and its subsequent revelation to the spectator through the exercise of his own freedom, without being limited to formal elements or specific procedures. As in Bazin, and even in Mourlet, cinema is, above all, the art of revelation. Filming is filming the world. Cinema is an ontological machine. Once this potentiality is established, Ayfre finds himself, however, forced to broaden the range of stylistic alternatives in order to attain the revelatory experience.

This conviction opens up the possibility of praising different genres of films. Ayfre speaks at one point about "a translucent art, an instrumental kind of beauty which is plenitude and transparence at the same time."[135] He refers to the plastic beauty of Vermeer's paintings and compares them to Visconti's fishermen: "in this case it is impossible to avoid seeing in the formal shaping a kind of onto-logical humility which is to the deliberate neutralism of *Bicycle Thieves* what mysticism is to asceticism."[136] The abbot expands on the somewhat cruder realism of *Un homme marche dans la ville* (1950), by Marcello Pagliero, recognizing a method and a different concern with the concreteness of reality, and, therefore, a complement to previous analyses about the Italian feature films.

> *Since, without any obvious distortion, he [Pagliero] ends up impressing on the audience such a clearly directed vision of the world and of man, it seems that Heidegger was right to oppose Husserl in asserting that a description of existence always and necessarily confirms the idea one has of it, since that idea is already an element, mode and factor of existence itself. It was therefore possibly a little premature to congratulate, as we just did, Rossellini, De Sica and Zavattini, for their reserve and the freedom of interpretation they allowed the audience.*[137]

[135.] Ayfre (1985, 187).

[136.] Ibid.

[137.] Ibid., 189).

Ayfre shows, perhaps more clearly than Bazin, that Italian neorealism was the movement that, up until that moment, knew best how to use cinema to depict the accidents of life and the mystery that underlies our existence. However, the aesthetic superiority that he initially sees in these films is something that the abbot finally leaves open.[138] For the author, it is more important to identify the dense texture of life that a film is capable of incorporating and revealing than recognizing and defining a certain "way of making" cinema. Andrew summarizes: "What interested Ayfre was the manner in which a given series of images could transcend its author, its audience, and the normal rules of cinema, becoming adequate to itself, fulfilling rules of its own creation."[139]

In other words, the concept of cinematographic experience is privileged. For Ayfre, most studies on this experience seek to penetrate it from the outside. The abbot, like Merleau-Ponty and Bazin, cautions me against attributing all-encompassing power to reason. He asserts cinematic experience as something that takes us out of the labyrinths of logic. Art is a formal gesture that organizes our body and imagination in response to our most immediate and concrete experiences. Art, according to Ayfre, is ethereal; it exists only as an experience. This point must be my point of departure and of constant return.

This is what makes Ayfre able, like few others, of defining what was most decisive in Rossellini's films: a different way of filming man and the world we live in, and an alternative way of telling (or refusing to tell) a story. It is this impulse, this posture, this objective of starting cinema from "year zero," evidenced in his films by the search for new language tools and procedures, by the ruins and broken bonds between individuals, families, and social institutions, that leads Jacques Rivette to state in "Letter on Rossellini," published in *Cahiers du Cinéma* in 1955, that it is impossible not to see *Voyage to Italy* (*Viaggio in Italia*, 1954) "without receiving direct evidence of the fact that the film opens a breach, and that all cinema, on pain of death, must pass through it."[140]

Ayfre, therefore, focused on cinema's ability to reveal transcendence within immanence: the expansion of human consciousness and of the world, constantly reminding me of the limitations of my own perception. Cinema is of interest (always and above all else) for this ontological intention of making me glimpse the possibility of a different connection between the image and the world, a

---

[138.] In this sense, it is quite curious the praises Ayfre (1960) makes in relation to several Japanese and Indian films, such as *The Harp of Burma* (*Biruma no Tategoto*, 1956), by Kon Ichikawa, and *Song of the Road* (*Pather Panchali*, 1955), by Satyajit Ray.

[139.] Andrew (1976, 252).

[140.] Rivette (1985, 192).

link that is not based on the mechanical element of the apparatus. Although it depends on conceptions of scene, dramaturgy, and language, this connection can also be found in something more abstract and impalpable, in expressions such as sensoriality, sensation, and intensity.

The privilege given to the concept of cinematographic experience, where one must formally analyze a specific film, searching for the elements and strategies that, between the visible and the invisible, the concrete and the ethereal, manage to express the mystery, the ambiguity of the world, is a bet that proves to be very profitable for the subsequent clash with the films of Tsai Ming-Liang, Pedro Costa, Claire Denis, and Apichatpong Weerasethakul. A cinema that radicalizes the movement to break down all boundaries (between concept and feeling, between the "real" and its spectral extensions, between mise-en-scène and the exercise of the gaze, between documentary and fiction, between the shot and the flow, between those who "believe in the image" and those who "believe in reality") that characterizes modern cinema in all its ramifications.

1.3 André Bazin

Cinema and the Apprehension of Reality

French critic, André Bazin wrote for several magazines (*L'Esprit*, *L'Ecran Français*, *La Révue du Cinéma*, *Radio-Cinéma-Télevision*) and newspapers (*France-Observateur* and *L'Observateur*). In 1951, he co-founded, alongside Jacques Doniol-Valcroze and Joseph-Marie Lo Duca, the most influential publication in the history of the seventh art, *Cahiers du Cinéma*. Bazin was the most brilliant representative of the new French post-war criticism. He did not share the pessimism of the older generation, who were still mourning the loss of silent cinema, and defended Hollywood cinema like few others. Imbued at the same time with the Catholic idealism of his time and the existentialism[141] of Sartre, Bazin envisioned great pedagogical potential in cinema and proposed a new history for it.

[141.] According to Dudley Andrew's (2010) detailed reports, Sartre's *The Imaginary* (2010) was decisive in Bazin's formation, specially regarding its association between art and ontology. Bazin read and reread the book, underlining various passages, writing them down compulsively. He also had ties to Maurice Merleau-Ponty and Gabriel Marcel. According to Andrew, it was Bazin who invited Merleau-Ponty to give his lecture on cinema at the Institut des Hautes Études Cinématographiques (IDHEC) on March 13, 1945. In 1956, the two engaged in a public discussion at the École Normale Supérieure on Jean Renoir's *Diary of a Chambermaid*, 1946. Bazin also talked with Marcel (closer to Amédée Ayfre) about cinema on a radio broadcast in 1948.

Bazin has not left us with any systematic books on film theory, although this by no means indicates a lack of system in his thinking.[142] As a critic, he always began with the appreciation of a film, its values, contradictions, and challenges, and, through a process of reflection, arrived at a theory. A method that makes reading Bazin exciting but also makes synthesizing his ideas a somewhat slippery endeavor, an easy target for a series of oversimplifications that persist this day. The fact is that Bazin was perhaps the first to challenge the formative tradition. He was undoubtedly the most important voice to defend an understanding of the seventh art based on a belief in the potential of mechanically recorded images and not in the power seized by artistic control over such images. Bazin sees the trajectory of the seventh art not as a development toward the absolutely plastic or non-narrative but as a progression toward an increasingly realistic style.

Alongside Amédée Ayfre and Albert Laffay, Bazin sealed the marriage between the phenomenology of his time and the neorealism of the early 1950s. Essays by him gained popularity through the films of Rossellini and De Sica, and helped to connect them with their intended audience. In the preface to Bazin's book on Orson Welles, André Labarthe emphasizes that the main insight of the French critic's work on cinema was the recognition of a novel connection between film and spectator, brought about by the emergence of what would later be called modern cinema. What made this cinema something new? What made it possible to have a different relationship with the spectator? What changes in the world and in the seventh art paved the way and/or demanded a different relationship between film and spectator? These would be the fundamental questions for Bazin.

Serge Daney (1993) once referred to a kind of editorial line of the *Cahiers du Cinéma*, something that would be equivalent to the genealogy of an "idea of cinema," embodied in the films of Rossellini, Jean Renoir, and the authors of the New Cinemas around the world. Daney described a type of axiom that, in his opinion, connects us to Bazin: "that cinema has a relationship with reality, and that the real is not what is represented."[143] Indeed, as Andrew (2010) points out, Daney borrowed this axiom from Eric Rohmer, who wrote a eulogy for Bazin in the January 1959 issue of the *Cahiers*, suggesting that in the critic's compiled works,

---

[142] For Dudley Andrew (1976), this illustrates one aspect of Bazin's personality, the sociability of his knowledge. Andrew makes a curious comparison between the German theorist Siegfried Kracauer, who spent years alone in a library to write his main work, *Theory of Film* (1960), and the French critic, who always maintained direct contact not only with other essayists and filmmakers but also with a wide range of artists and intellectuals.

[143] Daney (1993, 301).

each article, but also his entire work, has the rigor of a true mathematical proof. All of Bazin's work is centered on one idea, the affirmation of cinematographic objectivity, in the same way that geometry is centered on the properties of the line.[144]

Bazin, portrayed by Rohmer, unhesitatingly developed a realistic system. Just like "Euclid's straight line," the mechanically generated photographic image would serve as the initial foundation of this system. It is in his essays on Italian neorealism that these themes were originally treated and developed. Indeed, Bazin's thinking demonstrates a constructive reliance on several examples. The analysis of the narrative and aesthetic elements of a series of works by certain directors will provide the necessary substrate for the critic to outline the main characteristics of this new cinema and its key distinctions in relation to conventional or classic "realism." A neorealist film does not arise from a collision and cohesion of elements but from the ontological presence of things in themselves, filtered through the sensibility of a filmmaker. A "conventional" feature film creates situations, characters, and facts, while a neorealist film subordinates itself to them.

In general, the most significant differences between realism and neorealism can be identified in two main aspects of cinematographic language: dramaturgy and montage. Bazin sees greater freedom in the work of Rossellini, Visconti, and De Sica in relation to the rules of dramatic necessity inherited from the theater, as well as a break with the mechanisms of the spectacle. This rejection of the classic and seductive rules for the development of action and drama, evidenced, for example, in the recurrent use of non-professional actors and real locations, reveals a differentiated dramaturgy that aims to give voice to events and facts: "in this new perspective, the important sequence can just as well be the long scene that 'serves no purpose' by traditional screenplay standards."[145]

In an inspiring metaphor, the Frenchman compares traditional realism to bricks specifically manufactured to build bridges, while neorealism more closely resembles stones found in a river. A person can use these stones to cross the river, but they may not necessarily be intended for this purpose. That is, the "reality of the stone" will not change depending on its use:

If the service which they have rendered is the same as that of the bridge, it is because I have brought my share of ingenuity to bear on their chance arrangement; I have added the motion which, though it alters neither their nature nor their

[144.] Rohmer (1959, 32).

[145.] Bazin (2005b, 90).

appearance, gives them a provisional meaning and utility. In the same way, the
neorealist film has a meaning, but it is a posteriori, to the extent that it permits
our awareness to move from one fact to another, from one fragment of reality to
the next, whereas in the classical artistic composition the meaning is established
a priori: the house is already there in the brick.[146]

Driven by his enthusiasm for Italian films, Bazin proposes an approach to the novel. Cinema's references to music and painting, which predominated during the 1920s and 1930s, then undergo a complete reversal. The ideal filmmaker was someone who sought out his powers on the literary side. It is Bazin's celebrated conclusion: "The filmmaker is no longer the competitor of the painter and the playwright, he is, at last, the equal of the novelist."[147] For the French critic,[148] film appears to arrive at adulthood. It is not dependent on the visual, as it was the case in the silent era. It is not dependent on the theater, which was often the case in the early years of sound. Neorealism, in a broader sense, went beyond simple evocation through montage and the description of action through decoupage, and embraced its "romantic virtualities."

Bazin indicates an essential affinity between cinematographic narration and certain fundamental aspects of a more "objective" novelistic style, typical of American writers of the twentieth century, like John Dos Passos and Ernest Hemingway. It is in this sense that Bazin describes *Paisà* (1946) as the first feature film whose structure resembles that of a short story. *Paisà* seems to respect the duration of reality, breaking down a continuous representation of events. A film would present itself as a succession of fragments of reality, and their meaning are determined by the order and duration in which they are presented. Along these lines of reasoning, Bazin will elaborate his main criticism of montage, favoring alternative rhetorical devices, offering a fresh perspective on history, and emphasizing the unique characteristics of the cinematographic apparatus.

Bazin underscores the distinction between finding and creating a world, between using the pre-existing materials of reality and organizing them into a prefabricated vision, between striving to uncover the inherent order of things, separated from the spectator, and recognizing the order created by the spectator in his act of seeing. Cinema rediscovered another specificity in Italian neorealism, which had been

---

[146.] Ibid., 99.

[147.] Bazin (2005, 40).

[148.] Bazin does not mention it, but he does return, in this sense, to an earlier idea put forward by Alexandre Astruc in 1944: "A film is not an album of stylized images, nor is it a filmed theater play. It's a story told with pictures, just as a novel is a story told with words. It is necessary to count, and this is the primordial problem" (1992, 260).

abandoned by the montage theories of the early twentieth century: its intrinsic realism. Italian neorealism had the ability to represent reality without human intervention, preserving it in a multitude of senses. In his famous essays, such as "Ontology of the Photographic Image" and "The Evolution of the Language of Cinema," Bazin traces the history of verisimilitude and realism in the visual arts. He identifies photography and cinema as the arrival of a differentiated stage, where there is a possibility of a better adaptation between the image and the object. He says:

> In achieving the aims of baroque art, photography has freed the plastic arts from their obsession with likeness. Painting was forced, as it turned out, to offer us illusion and this illusion was reckoned sufficient unto art. Photography and the cinema on the other hand are discoveries that satisfy, once and for all and in its very essence, our obsession with realism. No matter how skillful the painter, his work was always in fee to an inescapable subjectivity. The fact that a human hand intervened cast a shadow of doubt over the image. Again, the essential factor in the transition from the baroque to photography is not the perfecting of a physical process (photography will long remain the inferior of painting in the reproduction of color); rather does it lie in a psychological fact, to wit, in completely satisfying our appetite for illusion by a mechanical reproduction in the making of which man plays no part.[149]

I realize that the statement about cinema realism is not based solely on a physical notion of reality but also on a psychological sense. "Photography affects us like a phenomenon in nature, like a flower or a snowflake."[150] But Bazin never said that photography was a phenomenon of nature, only that it affects us in this way. For him, realism has to do not only with the accuracy of the reproduction but also with the spectator's belief in the origin of the reproduction. In painting, this origin involves the talent and mind of an artist when they confront an object. That is why Bazin believes that the painting's greatest contradiction, or its main "defect," is its lack of objectivity. No matter how successful a painter or painting is in reproducing an object, the work will always lack credibility. "All the arts arc; based on the presence of man, only photography derives an advantage from his absence," said Bazin.[151]

[149.] Bazin (2005, 12).

[150.] Ibid., 13.

[151.] Ibid.

A photograph is an image that shares something of the reality it represents. It receives a "reality transfer" from the thing it portrays, says Bazin. A painting is an image created by hand and carries in it something of the hand. A photographic image is made of light. It employs a physics of light rather than the painting's spiritual or transcendent light. The light that the camera captures from reality is a material that belongs to the object being depicted. Bazin is the one who taught us that light leaves a trail like any other body, leaving a mark that the camera captures in an image. A photographic image is a light mark, a trace left by a real body. Something of the thing itself is captured in its photographic representation.

For Bazin, cinema is an asymptote of reality, moving closer and closer to it, forever dependent on it. Ismail Xavier (2005) alerts that for the French critic, cinema does not exactly provide us with an image of the real. It is actually capable of constituting a world "in the image of the real," which gives an idea of how slippery Bazin can be. He goes even further: Not only is the reproduction of a world in the image of reality a possibility of cinema, but it is inherent to its nature. Bazin tries, for example, to prove that the advent of sound, as well as the entire technological evolution of the industry (color, the different screen formats, and three-dimensional photography), would bring cinema closer to its underlying spirit. The seventh art has a moral obligation to remain faithful to its ontological dimension, to capture the passing of reality and reveal what is essential in it.

According to Bazin, cinema initially followed the path of transforming empirical reality into abstraction, imitating painting and the visual arts. The value of the first films was limited to their ability to create an illusion. The crude appeal of cinema to reality was actually vehemently condemned by the early theorists of the seventh art. Montage was not only the main focus of thinkers such as Hugo Münsterberg and Rudolf Arnheim, but it was also regarded as the primary creative film force for directors like Sergei Eisenstein and D. W. Griffith. Montage is a technique used by filmmaker to convey meanings to images. So, as Bazin believes, by rejecting the potential offered by the automatic mechanism for perceiving reality, cinema ultimately acquired the contradictions of painting.

Bazin takes a stand against not only the montage symbolism of the Russian constructivists but also against the manipulation carried out by classic Hollywood decoupage. By breaking with these uses of montage, the French critic proposes an evolution (also technological) toward realism. He divides cinema from this perspective into two opposing tendencies: those of the directors who believe in the image and those who believe in reality. The first are those that add, through plastic resources (the scenery, the interpretation of the actors, the light, the framing) and montage, elements external to the represented event.

The second privilege reality in its own transparency and duration. Bazin identifies a link between directors who, for their realism, were subjugated by the aesthetic evolution of silent cinema (Erich von Stroheim, Friedrich Wilhem Murnau, Carl Theodor Dreyer, and Robert Flaherty), and a new realist tendency that he sees in William Wyler's films and Orson Welles, and most notably, in neorealism.

The main difference that Bazin identifies in the advent of what we will call modern cinema is the reintroduction of ambiguity in the structure of the image. For him, reality itself would be ambiguous, and it is up to cinema to bring forth this ambiguity. Bazin starts from the perspective that our natural experience corresponds to a continuous and gapless perception of reality. The film, in turn, given its ontological nature, must respect this integrity by projecting on screen an experience equivalent to the sensory experience we face in reality. In this manner, cinematographic elements must be used to replicate a certain natural logic. It is from this perspective that Bazin develops his famous critique of classical montage.

The montage that manipulates reality or transforms it in order to produce a particular message is condemned not only for political reasons but also because it violates one of the truly original aspects of cinema: the mechanical recording of reality without human intervention. In "In Defense of Rossellini," one of his most famous essays, and part of a dialogue with the essayist Guido Aristarco, an ardent critic of neorealism, Bazin, first of all, affirms the Italian movement in opposition not only to traditional dramas but also to realism in both literature and cinema. Second, he points out that neorealism would distinguish itself in an integral, global description of reality. This notion of a record of reality in its entirety comes from Ayfre, which Bazin quotes glowingly. He claims:

> *Neorealism by definition rejects analysis, whether political, moral, psychological, logical, or social, of the characters and their actions. It looks on reality as a whole, not incomprehensible, certainly, but inseparably one. This is why neorealism, although not necessarily antispectacular (though spectacle is to all intents and purposes alien to it) is at least basically antitheatrical in the degree that stage acting presupposes on the part of the actor a psychological analysis of the emotions to which a character is subject and a set of expressive physical signs that symbolize a whole range of moral categories.*[152]

Montage opposes the continuity of space "as well as its duration." This is because when analyzing and organizing reality, montage assumes and/or imposes a unit

---

[152.] Bazin (2005b, 97).

of meaning onto the event. Bazin offers a different interpretation of Kuleshov's experiment. Instead of preserving the enigmatic quality of the actor's face, the montage would diminish its inherent ambiguity by assigning a singular meaning to each connection. Pascal Bonitzer, in a position similar to that of Bazin, maintains that "the Kulechov effect is the lowest common denominator between the spectator's blissful passivity and the director's creative laziness. It is cinema's principle of inertia."[153] Bazin still associates the experience of the Russian filmmaker with classic decoupage and its *raccords* and shot and reverse shot techniques. Hollywood cinema asserted itself at the expense of an invisible manipulation of the spectator.

Against the assumed abstraction of Russian constructivists and the camouflaged discontinuity of Hollywood cinema, Bazin defends respect for the unity of space and the concrete duration of the event. He even proposes a rule: "When the essence of a scene demands the simultaneous presence of two or more factors in the action, montage is ruled out."[154] An example: *The Red Balloon* (*Le Ballon Rouge*, 1956), by Albert Lamorisse, where the boy and the balloon are always filmed together in the same shot, emphasizing their co-presence within a continuous record. Through this record, the balloon and the boy shared the same regime of light and duration, the same ontological plane. It does not matter if the movement of the balloon depends on some effect or gimmick. The key is to respect its raw presence, which is physically apprehended in contiguity with the equally concrete presence of the boy, without the intervention of editing.

> *Lamorisse's red balloon actually does go through the movements in front of the camera that we see on the screen. Of course there is a trick in it, but it is not one that belongs to cinema as such. Illusion is created here, as in conjuring, out of reality itself. It is something concrete, and does not derive from the potential extensions created by montage.*[155]

He insists:

> *Montage which we are constantly being told is the essence of cinema is, in this situation, the literary and anticinematic process par excellence. Essential cinema,*

[153.] Bonitzer (1999, 87).

[154.] Bazin (2005, 50).

[155.] Ibid., 45.

> *seen for once in its pure state, on the contrary, is to be found in straightforward*
> *photographic respect for the unity of space.*[156]

It is based on this conviction that cinema must photographically respect the unity of space-time in an event and the inherent ambiguity of reality that Bazin advocates for two other narrative procedures: the long take and the depth of field. When analyzing the films of Jean Renoir, William Wyler, and Orson Welles, Bazin points out a more systematic use of both techniques. He already saw in the works of these filmmakers an attempt to replace the frequent cuts of classic cinema with a continuous flow of the image. The spectator is invited to actively participate, as the meaning of an image begins to depend on their will.

I feel close to Ayfre once more. The reason for this is that they both rely on spectatorial reception. As we saw at the beginning of this exposition on Bazin's thought, his essays are based on the intuition that a new relationship between film and spectator was envisioned in contemporary cinema at that time. A cinema that rescued us from the passivity we maintained with classical cinema, where an author manipulated cinematographic techniques to create at his own will an image that the spectator could not "read" in any other way than the one prede-termined. For Bazin, the ontological relationship between the image and reality asserts itself in the process of presenting itself (without pre-determinations) to the spectator. The realistic cinema defended by Bazin is rooted not only in the mechanical process of the cinematographic camera but also in the act of percep-tion and the subjective experience of watching a film.

It is all of these elements (the abandonment of interventionism and discourse through montage, the use of the long take and the depth of field, the preservation of the spatial and temporal unity of the recorded event, and the invitation for the spectator's active participation) that make Bazin see neorealism as a more accurate representation of life as we live it. This is his most important criterion. It is in these terms that he analyzes one of his favorite films, *Umberto D.* The temporal structure of this feature is portrayed as closely as possible to the actual passage of time. Instead of using two or three shots to convey the maid's awakening, De Sica and Zavattini divided this event into smaller events, such as crossing the corridor and the flood of ants, all shown in their continuous real time.

What is evident in essays like this one is that for Bazin, more than a style that can be applied or an effect to be induced in the spectator, neorealism is an attitude, a posture, an impulse, a goal. In other words, the most important thing for Bazin

---

[156.] Ibid., 46.

is the establishing of a cinema that is solely based on immanence. It is in this sense that he approaches phenomenology, which also supports this same idea of a world presented just as I perceive it: without any predetermined meaning, open to all the meanings that we want to attribute to it. Bazin himself refers to a "phenomenological integrity" of the facts in certain Italian films, underlining an operation of "between parentheses," in which reality is not corrected in terms of psychology and the demands of the drama, nor in the name of an ideology. He even proposes a definition for what he calls phenomenology:

> *The originality of Italian neorealism as compared with the chief schools of realism that preceded it and with the Soviet cinema, lies in never making reality the servant of some a priori point of view. Even the Dziga-Vertov theory of the 'Kino-eye' only employed the crude reality of everyday events so as to give it a place on the dialectic spectrum of montage. From another point of view, theater (even realist theater) used reality in the service of dramatic and spectacular structure. Whether in the service of the interests of an ideological thesis, of a moral idea, or of a dramatic action, realism subordinates what it borrows from reality to its transcendent needs. Neorealism knows only immanence. It is from appearance only, the simple appearance of beings and of the world, that it knows how to deduce the ideas that it unearths. It is a phenomenology.*[157]

Bazin's phenomenology asserts itself as a respect for the given appearance, as a faith in the phenomenon as something that reveals itself. This conviction somewhat distances him from Maurice Merleau-Ponty. Despite some common expressions and the attraction to the theme of ambiguity, there is a considerable difference between the phenomenologies of Bazin and Merleau-Ponty. They seem to agree that cinema is capable of showing us the world as it is, but this statement harbors different beliefs. For the philosopher, cinema presents us with a symbolic and sensorially realistic representation of the world, and is not defined as a place where things are present. The ambiguity for Merleau-Ponty concerns the denial of any Absolute and the recognition of the essential incompleteness of perception, given the condition of man as a being deeply connected to the world.

Bazin believes that cinema shows us the world as it is, allowing us to speculate what it has to do with Being. Xavier already warned that Bazin does not examine the element that constitutes the fundamental starting point within what can be more commonly called phenomenology. Rather than addressing the examination

---

[157.] Ibid., 64, 65.

of perception as an activity and investigating the conditions and implications present in this activity, he "assumes its nature reasonably known (within the model of contemplation) and concentrates his efforts on the expulsion of any activity extraneous to it."[158] Bazinian phenomenology implies a contemplation that reveals the presence of a transcendent that is insinuated in reality. For the Catholic critic, the world and things really do have a meaning, even if, as Jacques Aumont reminds us, "it should remain God's secret, hidden from our sensibilities."[159]

Bazin's perspectives, when viewed in an absolute manner, especially in relation to montage and the evolutionary concept of cinema toward realism, can lead to the reductions that usually surround the interpretation of his ideas. The possibility of a form of representation that excludes man and his subjectivity would allow reality to speak for itself. Photography, as a way of capturing moments, preserves them, immortalizes them, and brings them back into the world for us to notice and appreciate. The concept of "ontology" comes at least initially from this reasoning. Bazin, however, was well aware that the camera is not the only machine that makes the film. The projector, the magic lantern, animates the light trail with its own light, brings the imprint of life to new life on the screen. The images on the screen carry something of the world itself, something tangible yet altered transmuted into a different realm. Hence, both its peculiar proximity to reality and its equally singular tendency to suspend reality: the material ghost, as Gilberto Perez describes it so well.

It should be noted that Bazin referred to the ultimate goal of achieving a full and comprehensive representation of reality as a myth, and he had several reasons for doing so. As an ideal, and I believe Bazin would not object to the term, I should aim for it knowing that I will never fully get there. According to him, it was this ideal that motivated the development of cinematographic technology, and not the other way around. The seventh art was not created by two entrepreneurs. Thomas Edison and the Lumière brothers would be part of a group of now forgotten dreamers, "the fanatics, the madmen, the disinterested pioneers"[160]—all obsessed with the power of moving images.

In this sense, I should especially refer to the essay "The Myth of Total Cinema," when Bazin discovers in the origins of cinema a theory of its essence, highlighting the relationship between realism, illusion, and deceit. The critic placed this essay right after "The Ontology of the Photographic Image." Together, these

---

[158.] Xavier (2005, 90).

[159.] Aumont (2006, 120).

[160.] Bazin (2005, 22).

two essays form the basis of a theoretical argument that prioritizes realism in cinema. However, it is striking that "The Myth of Total Cinema" does not rely on the indexicality of the photographic image, evidenced by the constant references to painted animations and/or drawn from the *Pantomimes Lumineuses* by Charles-Émile Reynaud.

In the essay, Bazin attributes to film the power to reveal something about the world to the spectator that they cannot know through imagination nor can through perception. For Bazin, photography captures and allows us to envision a reality that eludes both perception and imagination, uniting mechanical objectivity with affective subjectivity. For him, the unique potential of the photographic medium is to stage an encounter between the camera and the spectator. In this encounter, the image of an object emerges both in its rational concreteness and in its irrational essence. Bazin continues: "Every image is to be seen as an object and every object as an image. Hence photography ranks high in the order of surrealist creativity because it produces an image that is a reality of nature, namely, an hallucination that is also a fact."[161]

What exists in Bazin is a dialectical relationship between realism, imagination, and illusionism. When writing about of *White Mane* (*Crin blanc: Le cheval sauvage*, 1953), another film by Lamorisse, he says: "its documentary reality, but if it is to become a truth of the imagination, it must die and be born again of reality itself."[162] From this quote, depending on the meaning given to each use of the word "reality" (which Bazin hardly makes explicit), cinema can be understood as an agent of transformation that both intervenes in a process of change and renewal through a kind of self-annulment, and constitutes an act of appropriation involving the destruction of what one wishes to preserve. This passage demonstrates that Bazin is not at all naive. For in his essays, reality and illusion, truth and belief, are often seen as interdependent rather than opposing categories. The demand for realistic cinema, free from ideological and psychological manipulations, does not fundamentally contradict the creation of fictional worlds. Quite the contrary, Bazin insists that "realism in art can only be achieved in one way-through artifice…a fundamental contradiction which is at once unacceptable and necessary."[163]

At another point, when discussing with the non-professional actors of neorealist cinema, Bazin states, "It is an understatement to say that these temporary actors

---

[161.] Ibid., 15, 16.

[162.] Ibid., 47.

[163.] Bazin (2005b, 26).

are good or even perfect. In these films the very concept of actor, performance, character has no longer any meaning."[164] This is a strange statement. It has nothing to do with the cinematographic ideal Bazin saw in these films. For him, *Bicycle Thieves* is one of the first examples of pure cinema. "No more actors, no more story, no more sets, which is to say that in the perfect aesthetic illusion of reality there is no more cinema."[165] This quote suggests that artifice and style have the power to manifest as life, as if the world were akin to an accessory to cinematic action. What Bazin identifies is actually a kind of "coincidence" between cinema and reality. "Cinema is over" means, instead, that there is nothing in *Bicycle Thieves* that was understood as cinema until then: the spectacle, the star system, and the chained plot. At the same time, if cinema can disappear, it is because it no longer needs actors, a story, or direction to offer us an experience of the world.

This passage shows that Bazin is perfectly capable of defining an "ontology" of cinema without limiting it to indexicality. Bazin's appreciation for Lamorisse's movies stems from his dialectical understanding of the interplay between realism, imagination, and illusionism. For him, the artifices at play in these works do not diminish their realism. On the contrary, its magical effects are successful precisely because the staging and montage imprint a unique "spatial density" on the flow of images:

> *If the film is to fulfill itself aesthetically we need to believe in the reality of what is happening while knowing it to be tricked [...] So the screen reflects the ebb and flow of our imagination which feeds on a reality for which it plans to substitute. That is to say, the tale is born of an experience that the imagination transcends.*[166]

The complete elimination of montage was never in question in Bazin's essays. He wanted the logic of montage to be integrated with the principles of long takes and the depth of field. Nor was he an advocate of non-narrative cinema. A film with dozens of long takes of birds landing in a square would not be cinema for Bazin. I can, following the lead of Luiz Rezende Filho, take another example: *Sleep* (1963), by Andy Warhol. It's just over five hours of uncut footage of a sleeping man. Could this be a kind of hyper-Bazinism? Was Andy Warhol a radical neorealist? "Would he have led cinema to its own erasure, to the total

---

164. Ibid., 56.

165. Ibid., 60.

166. Bazin (2005, 48).

disappearance of its elements (actors, plot, *misé-en-scène*)?"[167] asks Rezende Filho. Oddly enough, no. If, on the one hand, a film like *Sleep* fulfilled a neorealist dream, on the other hand, it presented a series of challenges. By pushing to the extreme the desire for an ambiguity that would emerge from the real, minimizing his own intervention as a director, Warhol, in fact, created it something without any meaning.

Warhol was not after a perfect expression of reality or the world as we see it. Quite the opposite. His experiments sought to install a different relationship between film and spectator, who, without the usual references (actors, plot, mise-en-scène), was led to relate to it in a different way. That was the theme of his cinema. The intrinsic meaning of the film was of little or no importance. If we observe the different trends that modern cinema would trace from the Nouvelle Vague (which Bazin, the deceased, did not witness), we will realize that the seventh art did not exactly take the path of an increasingly realistic representation and did not abandon the idea of film as a means of discursive enunciation, although the notion of ambiguity and the invitation to a more active participation by the spectator remained on the agenda. A filmmaker like Jean-Luc Godard would make ambiguity and the multiplicity of meanings central to his films, more a product of a discursive formulation than exactly a natural feature of the image or the cinematographic apparatus. That is, the ambiguity does not come from the theme, the image or one or another cinematographic language procedure, but from an intention or discourse that does not establish a single meaning for what it shows.

Let us consider a feature by Hou Hsiao-Hsien like *Goodbye South, Goodbye*. The film explores the underworld of petty crime in suburban Taipei. We follow the entrepreneurial misadventures of Kao and his misfit partner Flatty. Kao devises a plan to get some easy money. Everything goes downhill when the temperamental Flatty annoys the wrong people. The curious thing is that, strictly speaking, there is not exactly an action in this supposed gangster film. Hsiao-Hsien empties the characters, the plot, and the narrative of their classical, psychological, and narrative anchor points, and, as usual, offers us descriptions of a series of situations, of rituals: the motorcycle race, the conversations in the restaurant, the fights, the train rides, etc. Nothing is done to dramatize or even to "mean" or "tell" anything.

Goodbye South, Goodbye begins with a long sequence-shot of a train leaving and ends in another long, still shot of a car stuck in the middle of nowhere. The

---

[167.] Son (2023).

long take dilutes the characters and the situations in which they are involved. Depth of field takes the story to the background, privileging in front of the screen things that apparently have little to do with the film. The cinematic frame extends its roots far beyond its limits. The camera decentralizes everything it shows, and, in a kind of vicious circle, it is constantly moving away from and getting closer to the characters. If we add the amount of non-actors what we will have is an absurd reality effect.

Would it be an exaggeration to think of a hyper-Bazinian cinema, of the minimal intervention of the long take, of the "open window" to the everyday world? Would this cinema then be a type of degree zero of enunciation? On the contrary. Despite the fact that this cinema provides us the most concrete sensation of being-there, for everything that appears there is the initial intention of the director. He is concerned, down to the smallest detail, with distributing lines, shapes of people and objects within and of the frame. Narrative seems to be in check, and, in the end, is reinforced. A sense is created.

Bazinian ontology is more a theory about inscription and time storage than about mimesis or representation. The "spatial density," although exemplified by Bazin through techniques such as the long take and depth of field, is not confined to these stylistic choices. Furthermore, these techniques are not inherently more "natural" or "ontologically grounded." Bazin has always maintained a more nuanced aesthetic view, arguing that realism is a result of artifice and that it is achieved through faith. His thought is unique because he does not separate the anthropological perspective of the social historian from the aesthetic value judgment of the critic. Besides, reflection on the ontology of the image has never denied its epistemological dimension. Just remember the final sentence of "Ontology of the Photographic Image": "On the other hand, of course, cinema is also a language."[168]

Cinema is certainly primarily defined as a mechanical record, and while this may be a common way of identifying Bazin, what is often misunderstood is the fact that the cinematic record is not just a product of its mechanics. Because during any filming, something else is happening, something is filming and being filmed. Robert Bresson, in one of his most beautiful maxims, says that cinema is "a mechanism that gives rise to the unknown."[169] Something that Bazin—who had initially defined cinema as a mechanical record, beyond the other arts—discovered precisely with films by certain directors. The cinematographic record is, in fact,

---

[168.] Bazin (2005, 16).

[169.] Bresson (1977, 32).

not just a product of its mechanics. I am not exactly in the realm of reproducing the same but rather in that of the appearance of a "new," an "unknown," not necessarily unknowable or divine but rather something not yet known.

That's exactly what Bazin seems to do. He makes it clear that belief in the existence of what I see in the image is an inescapable conviction that persists despite rational reflection. He, thus, proposes a psychological and aesthetic thesis concerning its power to carry perceptual conviction: a pre-reflexive belief in the veracity of what I perceive through the image. This is the real magic of cinema: not its ability to reproduce nature but something more elusive, the possibility of creating something that escapes, that makes the rough terrain of the everyday and the dizzying heights of transcendence and the supernatural emerge from the same soil, which is not of the order of either the subject or the object. Or, as Lisabeth During and Lisa Trahair put it, "in an attempt to bring divinity back down to earth, the cinema makes the secular and the profane the sole theatre of grace."[170]

Daney was right. Bazin went beyond Rohmer's Euclidean view. For Daney, Bazin is closer to a calculation where negative and imaginary values also come into play. Objectivity is a matter of approximation. Bazin, as Daney and someone like Andrew underline, is in part a theorist of absence, whose mission was to show that before signifying or resembling, cinema embalms the real. Bazin never claimed that the photographic portraits represented his subjects. They are "grey or sepia shadows, phantomlike and almost undecipherable…presence of lives halted at a set moment in their duration, freed from their destiny."[171] Andrew is right: Bazin's theory is founded not only on photography but on the spectral. "Cinema confronts us with something resistant, to be sure, but not necessarily with the solid body of the world. Through cinema, the world 'appears'; that is, it takes on the qualities and status of an 'apparition.'"[172]

An ontological approach to cinema is based on an endless interrogation, a dialectic without synthesis. Bazin, through crooked lines, teaches me that the aesthetic possibilities of cinema are not given. It is the films that map and explore these possibilities, and the discovery of a new possibility implies the encounter with a new cinema. The seventh art is something through which or through which something specific is done or said in specific ways. It provides, one might say, particular ways of reaching someone, of making sense (whatever definition you may have for the term). It is no coincidence that the only book that Bazin published

---

[170.] During and Trahair (2012, 5).

[171.] Bazin (2005, 14).

[172.] Andrew (2010, 9).

during his lifetime was called *What Is Cinema?* No one has had the courage to ask and answer this question as many times as Bazin. This question is actually a kind of compass for him. A question that will never go unanswered and will be asked time and time again. Because Bazin is ultimately of the understanding that cinema is always ahead of us.

Bazin is important to me precisely because he turns theory into an endless question, a never ending wonder. It is, on the one hand, the demand for a cinema that reveals the mysterious ambiguity of things, and, on the other hand, the understanding that in order to achieve this objective it is necessary to create. A creation that imposes itself not only on films but also on spectators. It is this fleeting moment of creation, emergence and construction of meaning, the continued birth of the world and its elements, so keen to Hsiao-Hsien's cinema that interests me. His shots, as exercises of the gaze, as ways of experiencing a certain distance and time, are like "half-open doors to the time and space of the shot, a door whose doorframe is music, a sound, a voice, that which takes us by the hand and guides us there where the image leaves us at a distance."[173] The challenge in the cinema of the Taiwanese filmmaker is one that Bazin had already circumscribed in a certain way: that of living an experience, a form of sharing the perspective on the experiences of the characters that exist in the world created in the film. Hsiao-Hsien immerses me in a unique experience of disorientation within the core of the most familiar experiences. It is a meticulous, serious undertaking, always to be taken up again and again.

1.4 Michel Mourlet

Human Dramas Sculpted in the Sensitive Matter of the World

To speak of Michel Mourlet is to speak of mise-en-scène. The term, imported from the theater in early cinema,[174] is one of the richest and most complex in the history of film criticism and theory. It gained unprecedented prominence in post-war France amid the explosion of film clubs and the launch of various specialized magazines. Originally coined to describe a theatrical practice,

---

[173] Baecque (2011, 34).

[174] The expression "early cinema" or "cinema of attractions" generally covers more or less the first two decades following the first public showing of the film *The Arrival of the Train at La Ciotat* (*L'Arrivée d'un train en gare de La Ciotat*, 1895), by the Lumière brothers. From the point of view of history and film theory, there is now a certain consensus on the characteristics of this early cinema: it works as a kind of stage of a variety theater. It is not interested in telling stories. It shows something "exciting."

"*mise-en-scène* acquires a phenomenological dimension in cinema: showcases human dramas by sculpting them in the highly sensitive material of the world,"[175] says Luiz Carlos Oliveira Jr.[176] It encompasses, in a single gesture, the art of placing bodies in relation to space and affirming our existence in the world, as well as our fascination with moving images. It serves as a means of understanding, an exploration of the phenomenon of perception, and an examination of the nature of thought.

"Everything is in the *mise-en-scène*,"[177] says Mourlet, in line with the discussions that captivated the ranks of André Bazin's *Cahiers du Cinéma*. The term became popular among of French critics in the 1950s. True aesthetic manifestos were dedicated to it. This is the moment when Jacques Rivette, Éric Rohmer, Claude Chabrol, François Truffaut, and Jean-Luc Godard, the so-called Young Turks,[178] made mise-en-scène the central criterion for assessing the greatness of a work and adopted it as a way to demonstrate the pinnacle of the classic style in Hollywood. They elevated names like Howard Hawks, John Ford, and Alfred Hitchcock, while also highlighting the emergence of a new cinema on the horizon.

Although it had an undeniable relationship, at least initially, with the Nouvelle Vague nucleus of *Cahiers du Cinéma*, Mourlet was part of another group formed by other cinephiles and critics who frequented the Le Mac Mahon cinema[179] in Paris. The theater, still in operation, was inaugurated in 1938 and did not have, at least initially, a specialized program. It would often be occupied by the military: first, by the Nazi occupation troops during World War II, then by American officers after the conflict—the latter were very present in the neighborhood as part of NATO activities. It was at this moment that Émile Villion, the owner of the place, decided to capitalize on the various benefits offered by commercial

---

[175.] Oliveira Jr. (2013, 2).

[176.] The work of Luiz Carlos Oliveira Jr. is certainly the one that most rigorously and passionately investigates the writings of Mourlet and his colleagues, tracing the history of the term mise-en-scène from classical cinema to the flow aesthetics. This chapter is largely indebted to his work.

[177.] Mourlet (2022, 494).

[178.] Faced with angry criticism of the famous and equally aggressive essay by François Truffaut, "Une certaine tendance du cinéma français," published in January 1954, Bazin was forced to take a stand. In February 1955, he adopted the expression "Hitchcocko-Hawksian," created by Jacques Doniol-Valcroze and disseminated as a kind of mockery by Georges Sadoul in one of his most important texts, and wrote a letter to the latter, in which he admitted the impertinence and insolence of the young critics of *Cahiers* and claims not to agree with much of what they say, although he defends the erudition, talent, and passion of his disciples, calling them "young Turks." To learn more about this story, see Baecque (2003).

[179.] Mac-Mahon is a polysemous proper noun. He is referring to General Patrice de Mac Mahon, commander of the successful siege of Sébastopol in the midst of the Crimean War, in 1855, as well as to one of the main avenues of the French capital, where the cinema, incidentally, is located.

agreements[180] between the United States and France. He chose to shift his focus to Hollywood films, much to the chagrin of veteran and communist critics who were still mourning the end of silent cinema. However, his decision brought great joy to a new generation of moviegoers.

From 1951 to 1952, a group of young people—most of them studied at the Carnot school, located a few kilometers away—began to gather around one of them, Pierre Rissient. This first group would be formed by Rissient, Georges Richard, and Michel Fabre: they form the founding trio. The second wave includes Marc Bernard, Alain Archambault, Jacques Gouzerh (the future Jacques Serguine) and Mourlet, also known as the "Boileau Mac Mahon."[181] The group was completed in the following years with the addition of Pierre Guinle, Simon Mizrahi, Jacques Lourcelles, and the Viennese Alfred Eibel. They founded a magazine, *Présence du Cinéma*, and went on to systematize a certain ideal of beauty contained in the exercise of mise-en-scène—they would also defend other names in the pantheon of great filmmakers: Fritz Lang, Raoul Walsh, Otto Preminger, and Joseph Losey. The latter was almost a novelty brought by the Mac-Mahonists, as they would be called. They were initially close to the *Cahiers du Cinéma* and were responsible, in 1960, for publishing a special issue dedicated precisely to Losey. At the end of one of the texts in this edition, Serguine tries to explain what "Mac-Mahonism" would be:

> *The 'Mac Mahon' is not the geometric center of world cinema, but of an idea of cinema. It does not involve anything, except perhaps friendship. Friendship may be nothing more than a shared demand. From which what follows is that 'Mac Mahon' is by no means a school narrowed into a funnel, but rather a starting point, that funnel turned upside down [...].So is being 'Mac Mahonian' a new snobbery? There are always labels for those who seek beauty, that other name of truth [...] It doesn't seem important to me to ask: how can one be 'Mac Mahonian'? What matters is to reflect: how can one be Raoul Walsh? And Fritz Lang, and Joseph Losey? I still do not know. I know they are, and nothing else. The beautiful is the evidence of the beautiful, that is the paradox.[182]*

[180.] The Blum-Byrnes agreements were a series of Franco-American trade treaties signed on May 28, 1946, by U.S. Secretary of State James F. Byrnes and French government representatives Léon Blum and Jean Monnet. The agreements aimed to eradicate France's debt to the United States and obtain new credits in exchange for opening French markets to American products, especially cinematographic productions.

[181.] The nickname refers to Nicolas Boileau-Despréaux, French critic and poet of the seventeenth century. His works, especially the satires, first published in 1666, mark a moment of renewal in French art criticism.

[182.] Serguine (1960, 44).

These notions of beauty, evidence, and the world, which are prominent in this passage by Serguine, as well as in the essays of his fellow cinephiles and critics, bring us back to ancient Greece. The Greeks had a word to "designate the universe as ordered, the world understood as order of the world: cosmos," says Marc Cerisuelo in the preface to Mourlet's last book, *L'écran éblouissant* (2014). Everything is in its place. Planets rotate without collapsing into nothingness. The seasons return with remarkable regularity. Young people do not have a lot of gray hair. We will all die. By a kind of semantic blessing, the word also means jewel, adornment, or ornament. Not only is the world in order, but its beauty is evident to the eye. This is the thesis and philosophy of life of those who are called "Mac-Mahonists."

In August 1959, the *Cahiers du Cinéma*[183] published the essay-manifesto of the Mac-Mahonism signed by Mourlet, "On a Misunderstood Art." Oliveira Jr. underlines the fact that the magazine edited the text in italics, as if to mark a certain foreignness of those ideas, and with an introductory paragraph most likely written by Rohmer, that warns of the extreme nature of its content.[184] For Jacques Aumont, "On a Misunderstood Art" is "one of the most direct artistic manifestos ever written about cinema."[185] In it, Mourlet revisits the concept of mise-en-scène that had been explored at the *Cahiers du Cinéma* itself but takes a more essentialist approach. Cinema would be dedicated to portraying the "truth of the world," providing a unique realistic experience.

According to Mourlet, cinema has been misjudged as an art. It was necessary to define and differentiate it better in relation to the other arts, as Bazin attempted to do, albeit in a different manner. This is the theme of the first segments of "On a Misunderstood Art":

> *Art had always been a mise-en-scène of the world—that is to say, the chance given to a contingent and unfinished reality to be accomplished with certainty according to human desires. But this world could only be grasped by a middle term; immediate possession being impossible, it had to be recreated in an*

[183.] The relationship between *Cahiers du Cinéma* and the Mac-Mahonists was short-lived, as was to be expected. After issue 111 of September 1960, dedicated to Losey and entirely edited by Mourlet's group, the Mac-Mahonists disappeared from the magazine. Mourlet (and Rohmer, then editor in chief) were immediately condemned for the issue by most of the more regular editors, such as Luc Moullet, Louis Marcorelles, and Fereydoun Hoveyda. In October 1959, Moullet jokingly calls Mourlet "the bitter Michel" and asks for his departure from the magazine. To know a little more about this story, see Baecque (1991).

[184.] The paragraph states: "Although the *Cahiers'* line of conduct is less rigorous than is sometimes thought, this text only clearly deviates from it in a few points. However, being respectful of any extreme opinion, we submit it to the reader, without further comment" (Mourlet 2022, 23).

[185.] Aumont (2006, 78).

*indirect way, transposed, presented by way of allusions and conventions [...]
In these conditions, the value of the artwork was measured in absolute terms,
without regard to its technique, the renewal of which was not so much a matter
of progress as the simple exploration of a new domain. In other words, with art
creating its own material, it was not susceptible to improvement, and the most
primitive works equaled by definition the most refined. Then, at the end of the
nineteenth century, came a significant event that shook up this state of affairs
[...] A glass eye and a silver-bromide memory gave the artist the possibility
of recreating the world from what it is and hence of providing beauty with the
sharpest weapons of truth.*[186]

Cinema would reverse the path taken by other arts, which moved from the abstract
to the concrete, by affirming a representation without an ontological connection
to the world. Unlike a painter, who recreates the world by "exchanging its form
for its truth,"[187] the filmmaker recreates the world "from what it is."[188] Film is
the first of the arts to have before it not an idea of the world but rather the world
itself. In this sense, Mourlet establishes an essence for cinema by highlighting its
ability to immediately apprehend reality. No wonder, as we shall see, the critic
will have an extraordinarily selective list of "true" filmmakers. Because for him,
more than the existence of films, movements, and directors, what is paramount
is this ideal essence of cinema.

This essentialist perspective opens the door to an evolutionary theory. Cinema
would rely on technique in a mechanical and technological sense and would
be structurally linked to a progression toward a more accurate portrayal of the
sensitive world. In fact, Mourlet embraces Bazin's myth of total cinema. That
is, for both, the seventh art is making effective and continuous progress toward
an ideal state of perfectly reproducing of all phenomena in their sensorial dimensions. An ideal of cinema: to capture "the spectator, immersing him in the
most directly sensory and emotional ways possible, without the interposition of
a 'language' of images."[189] Mourlet derives some aesthetic consequences from
these ideas, and anything that does not align with the concept of total cinema is
subsequently rejected.

[186.] Mourlet (2022, 489–90).

[187.] Ibid., 489.

[188.] Ibid., 490.

[189.] Aumont (2006, 82).

The history of the seventh art would be that of a kind of "purification," where it gradually aligns itself with the ideals of immediacy and transparency advocated by Mourlet. For the French critic, true cinema was not born from the superimpositions of the impressionists, nor from discontinuous montage, or from a displaced expressionism, and it certainly did not come from a supposed new realism from Italy. "Cinema begins with the talkie,"[190] says Mourlet, who is indebted to the post-war cinephile movement. Their project aimed at recognizing the value of talking films, while also acknowledging the nostalgia for silent images. This unwavering defense of the talkies is certainly a radical consequence of Bazin's thesis. Bazin's realism certainly consists not only of a defense of the long take and the depth of field but also of an intensive recovery of fifteen years of neglected discourse to reflect on cinema. Bazin is the first to challenge the formative tradition, laying the groundwork — along with Roger Leenhardt, Alexandre Astruc, Albert Laffay, Amédée Ayfre, and a few others — for what was to come next. In a note to "On a Misunderstood Art," Mourlet himself admits his debt to the *Cahiers* (Rivette, Rohmer, and Philippe Demonsablon[191] in particular) for clearly designating the notions of author and mise-en-scène as the alpha and omega of contemporary reflection on cinema.

However, for a Mac-Mahonist like Mourlet, it is simply inconceivable to love Preminger as much as Alfred Hitchcock or Orson Welles. True cinema emerges spontaneously under the guidance of an Aristotelian logic of action, propelled by the power of the gestures on the stage. Mac-Mahonism is a form of classicism insofar as, for its defenders, art must remain hidden: Anything that disrupts the allure created by the "spontaneous logic of vision" must be avoided. Although there is no explicit citation to the Hegelian system of the arts, Oliveira Jr. underlines the influence of the German philosopher and identifies the three stages of Hegel's aesthetics adapted to the historical and theoretical field of cinema.[192] The symbolic art of the Egyptians can be compared to silent cinema, while the classical art of the Greeks can be associated with a certain classicism, particularly in Hollywood, represented by few filmmakers. The romantic art, in turn, can be seen as a precursor to the auteur cinema,

---

[190.] Mourlet (2022, 491).

[191.] "The note in question reads: Let us recognize our debt to the 'Hitchcocko-Hawksian' critics, who, especially with Éric Rohmer, Jacques Rivette and Philippe Demonsablon, were the first to prepare the ground, even if they seem to hesitate in drawing the consequences of their actions. premises" (Mourlet 1922, 34).

[192.] Aumont states that this Hegelian model had become popular in France through André Malraux: Each art should know the same history, with primitivism, classical apogee, and, later, decline. These ideas were widespread in the critical mindset of the 1950s.

characterized by an exaggerated expression, as Orson Welles exemplified in Mourlet's opinion:

> *An art whose singularity is that it is founded on technique, in the mechanical sense of the term, is consequently capable of progress — a notion that is incompatible with the traditional concept of art. Its first principle, the recording eye, indicates its vocation to place people before the world, and hence its ideal accomplishment is to be endowed with senses as subtle as human senses.5 The less refined these senses, the greater the feeling of incompletion and malaise given by the work. We must dare to say that cinema begins with the talkie. What we are accustomed to calling the masterpieces of silent film are just preliminary steps; they need to be recontextualized in their inchoate, approximate perspective, regardless of the talent of the filmmakers. This talent is not in question, but rather the means employed to serve it.*[193]

Neorealist cinema would focus solely on one of the dimensions of cinema, namely the documentary genre. It would refrain from organizing the phenomenal world, and relinquish what Mourlet refers to as "féerie." This would be Alfred Hitchcock's dominant dimension, equally criticized by the critic for imposing his directorial vision on every last detail, suffocating reality with symbolism. Mourlet also harbors a genuine dislike for Sergei Eisenstein's intellectual montage technique, which involve a harsh intervention that overlaps the camera's gaze and undermines the captivating experience that cinema should create for the spectator. Mourlet once again echoes a Bazinian theme, that of the forbidden montage, although he does so with a more radical approach. Montage is not only prohibited when the essence of an event depends on the simultaneous presence of two or more elements of the action but also in most cases. For Mourlet, this is not only an ontological question but also a pragmatic one. Montage must always respect the duration, rhythm, and nature of an event and never disrupt the spectator's fascination.

Mourlet and his companions favored Hollywood cinema. Every spectator who visited the Mac-Mahon in those days was immediately greeted by four stunning black and white photographs: Fritz Lang, Otto Preminger, Raoul Walsh, and Joseph Losey. Authors, no doubt. Directors, obviously. Perhaps somewhat "minor," in a Deleuzian sense. This theme of the minor is at the center of Gilles Deleuze's philosophy, explicitly since his work on *Kafka* (1986). The philosopher

---

[193] Ibid.

distinguishes between the majority and the minority based on quality rather than quantity. Majority implies a consistency or pattern. It's about being White, male, heterosexual, and urban. Minority implies deviation and fissure, both in political contexts. The minor is a type of potentiality that offers escape routes to the model. It is this creative use of cinema that breaks away from the dominant system, the current regime, and the hegemonic discourses and notions of art. That is the Kafka's process as described by Deleuze and Félix Guattari. It deterritorializes the dominant language and creates its own. That's what interests not only the Mac-Mahonists but also seems to concern a theoretical and critical attitude that propels the film forward.

And what would differentiate these specific filmmakers? A sense of self-evidence and transparency; an ability to captivate the spectator, engrossed in an experience of fascination/exaltation; a reverence for the world, space, locations, probability, and characters; a naturally Aristotelian understanding of fiction in which the power of action always triumphs over the artifices. The filmmakers whom Mourlet admires are those who capture the unfiltered essence of the world through what he refers to as "method." They do not reject the phenomenality of the eye and the intuition of the moment and seek to combine them with a certain subjective freedom. The mechanical process that enable cinema to capture the appearances of the world must be controlled by a "heartfelt intuition and precision such that the slightest lapse disrupts the fever curve—this will only come as a surprise to those who are satisfied with little."[194] This is what he sees, for example, in Otto Preminger's movies. A cinema that identifies the central element of the scene in each shot and suggests a meaning without imposing it or reveling its features. Indeed, there is a clarity in Preminger—a transparency that, as Aumont claims, makes Hitchcock seem excessive, Ford sentimental, and Hawks more primitive and less varied. It is not by chance that Mourlet employs terms such as "beauty" and "sublime" to describe watching a film by Preminger, Losey, or Lang. A cinema that opens itself to a form of liturgy or contemplation of a "rediscovered cosmic order."[195] For the critic, the ultimate goal of cinema, achieved only in rare moments by these filmmakers, "consists in stripping viewers of all conscious distance to precipitate them into a hypnotic state sustained by an incantation of gestures, gazes, minute movements of the face and the body, vocal inflections."[196]

[194.] Mourlet (2022, 493).

[195.] Ibid.

[196.] Ibid., 492.

"Everything is in the *mise-en-scène*," says Mourlet. Mise-en-scène is precisely in the "bodily presence of actors in a setting."[197] It designates "the placing of actors and objects, their movements within the frame must express everything."[198] It is in this sense that the critic expands on the prominence of the actor's body on stage, as it serves as the raw material of his concept of mise-en-scène. The actor's body should occupy the center of the shot and fully immersed in a world whose concrete presence is ensured by the camera—when used without trickery. Mourlet speaks of an "art of the epidermis," of a "carnal universe," of the "reconciliation of man with his flesh," which can be revealed through the direction of gestures and intonations.

> To see what I mean, just take Hitchcock's recent Vertigo or a shot from The Wrong Man as examples of what not to do. The camera swirling around Henry Fonda's face to express anxiety or the succession of changing colors showing James Stewart in the throes of a vertiginous nightmare proceed from the same impotence before the actor; they compensate for an incapacity to reveal the actor's passionate potentialities—from the inside—with a contortion of all that is not the actor, of all that is outside, just as mediocre writers will belabor style and brutalize words in an attempt to make the reader feel what they do not feel.[199]

In this passage, Mourlet curiously echoes a passage from "The Cinema and the New Pychology," by Maurice Merleau-Ponty. In it, the philosopher gave an example of a hypothetical scene involving a character experiencing vertigo, and criticized the filmmaker who relied on camera movements to convey it. Both Merleau-Ponty and Mourlet emphasize the notion of behavior and the ideal that cinema is able to better convey sensations such as vertigo through the gestures, scenery, gaze, and movements of the characters. The good filmmaker, therefore, should not make pirouettes with the camera to express vertigo but rather "tacitly to decipher the world or men."[200]

Mourlet's vocabulary ("flesh," "world," "body," "sensitive") is essentially phenomenological, which demonstrates his alignment with the other authors discussed in this chapter. The mise-en-scène conceived around these terms acquires a phenomenological dimension by showing human dramas through

---

[197.] Ibid., 496.

[198.] Ibid., 494.

[199.] Ibid., 491.

[200.] Merleau-Ponty (1964b, 58).

the delicate world's sensitive matter. For Mourlet, it is the mise-en-scène that ensures the direct presence of the world in a film. This does not mean that the filmmaker should remain silent behind a purely sensory perception. Cinema is not a passive reflection of reality. The mise-en-scène is precisely an exercise in organizing the unorganized. A combination of observing the delicate world and possessing the intelligence to reshape it, to find harmony with it.

Mourlet never explicitly engages in dialogue with phenomenology, unlike Bazin and Ayfre. However, "On a Misunderstood Art" shares with the others the privilege of the cinematographic experience and, most importantly, the premise that cinema eliminates the separation between the interior and exterior, allowing the sensible and the intelligible to align. For Mourlet, cinema is also a spontaneously phenomenological art, as it brings to life the experience of our inherence to the world, to things, and to others. It serves as an interrogation about the sensible appearances that constitutes the world. Like the artist, the spectator also finds himself in a relationship of immediacy with the world through cinema—although "the majority of viewers have not yet learned to see, and thus they sift images through a mental filter unsuited to the realities of the screen."[201] Watching a film is not the same as reading or even understanding it; it is being consumed by something that may not have any sense or whose meaning is not given to me.

It is, however, curious, the movement that the mise-en-scène affirms and reveals, according to Mourlet. The filmmaker is the one who dedicates himself, first and foremost, to a realm of data assimilated in full evidence. He needs, in a typically phenomenological operation, to enclose within parentheses, to circumscribe a sphere of pure evidence, in which true cinema must be established. After all, unlike other arts that use metaphors to represent the world, cinema is made in an immediate and transparent relationship with it. Mourlet then conveys the initial thesis that the existence of the world is equated with its phenomenal appearance—something that he sometimes appears to regard as self-evident. However, cinema, for the critic, is based on the need to reform the world and reconcile with it.

The mise-en-scène provides access to the presence of things, to the feeling of the being of things. This "presence of being" corresponds to a balance between a phenomenological gaze and an awareness of the representational act, between the "mise" and the "scène." This communion would be capable of conveying an essence and an absolute. Mourlet, in a second moment, then describes being as something that cannot be reduced to mere phenomenal appearance. In fact,

---

[201.] Mourlet (2022, 498).

he bases his defense of certain filmmakers on their ability to make people see beyond what initially appears, and to transcend. That's what he sees in the latest Fritz Lang films. Aumont acknowledges in Mourlet a belief that we cannot attain a rational understanding of reality or existence but only of an intuition or feeling. I would not go that far.

> *As cinema is a gaze that is substituted for ours to give us a world in accord with our desires, it will focus on faces and bodies, radiant or bruised but always beautiful, from the glory or the heartbreak that testifies to one and the same original nobility, of a chosen race that we recognize with exhilaration to be ours, the ultimate advance of life toward god. This is unlike Rossellini's work wherein the groping of the creature toward the creator is a theme exterior to the mise-en-scène, but man becomes god in the mise-en-scène, by the revelation of its powers, an abyss abruptly opening on the surface of things and engulfing us. A hymn to the glory of the body, the cinema recognizes eroticism as its supreme motivation. I mean that cinema did not choose eroticism among other possible avenues but rather that, given its twofold condition as art and gaze on the body, it was destined to eroticism as the reconciliation of man with his flesh.*[202]

This passage[203] implies a series of complicated pre-assumptions, as well as dangerous, especially political, consequences. It is once again the idea of the Greek cosmos that emerges. Not only does the world exist, but there is an agreement that resonates in it. There is harmony between our desires and what we see on screen, and that is exceptional enough to become a defining aspect. It is the world that defines the work of the director (whose objective is to recreate the world, restore it to its appearances) and also that of the spectator (who, in front of a film, must only receive the world and look for nothing else). This world, restored by the mise-en-scène, is, however, the realm of wonderful characters, bodies radiant with beauty, of Beauty. Making cinema the art of mise-en-scène and then describing it as creating a world "in accordance with our desires" is, as Aumont states, "wanting to transcend fiction into myth. Taken to the extreme, this conception does not correspond to any existing film, it is a pure idea of 'staging.' "[204]

---

[202] Ibid., 496.

[203] The phrase "cinema is a gaze that is substituted for ours to give us a world in accord with our desires" stamps the beginning of Jean-Luc Godard's *Contempt* (*Le Mépris*, 1963), being, however, "erroneously" (there are those who believe in the premeditation of this error) attributed to Bazin.

[204] Aumont (2006, 85).

The cinema advocated by Mourlet existed only fleetingly. In fact, it is difficult to discern from his passionate manifesto a more concrete meaning of mise-en-scène (the direction of movement and intonation of a body on stage) and its most ideal notion (of the constitution of a world of radiant beauty, according to our dreams). Furthermore, there are few examples that Mourlet offers, suggests, and indicates, and all of them are debatable.

It is understandable that he was fascinated by Preminger's style. I am thinking, for example, of *The Human Factor* (1979), a film of concealed feelings, hidden from the camera—the images seem designed to express, in a distressing way, nothing more than their own inexpressiveness. Preminger achieves a drama of pure surfaces, devoid of emotional appeals, free of judgmental character identification, and purged of the seductive highs and lows of traditional storytelling. The film presents itself as a smooth, uninflected flow of events and images, as a careful exposition and collection of information, as a kind of theorem. And as it unfolds, the relentlessly mundane images take on a kind of beauty. This is, however, a functional beauty, insofar as it is only possible because it embodies the precision and clarity that have always been the basis of Preminger's mise-en-scène. *The Human Factor* refers to a very specific set of ingrained attitudes and stylistic preferences of a particular filmmaker. Preminger's transparent and clear discourse is exactly that: a discourse.

What, however, seems to be the most problematic in Mourlet's essay is the glimpse of mise-en-scène as a "hymn to the glory of bodies." For him, reconciling "man with his flesh" is to establish, through the mise-en-scène, a "kingdom of Beauty." Fascination with the beautiful and violent body, as well as disgust for the grotesque body, not only have formal correspondences in the pursuit of an aesthetic characterized by objective lines of action but also have ideological equivalents. The French's tone and terminology sometimes align with an aesthetic sensibility that resonates with Nazi-fascist ideals. I am not accusing him of being a fascist, but some of his ideas are quite slippery. When discussing, for example, the portrayal of war and violence as something inherent to the restorative activity of the mise-en-scène, Mourlet praises a type of hero, exemplified by actors like Charlton Heston and Jack Palance. "A brutal and noble, elegant and virile hero, who reconciles strength and beauty and represents the perfection of a lordly race, made to win and to foresee or know all happiness."[205] Mourlet himself recognizes: "the Mac-Mahonian *mise-en-scène* that exalts the fascinating beauty of a chosen race, ends up tending towards what some call 'fascism.'"[206]

[205.] Mourlet (2008, 61).

[206.] Ibid.

In "Fascinating Fascism," Susan Sontag, when dealing with the process of purifying Leni Riefenstahl's reputation from its Nazi rubble, explains the connection between the celebration of a classical beauty and reverence for the idea of a hero, and the ideology of Nazism. For the American essayist, unlike the official art of countries like the Soviet Union and China, which aims to expose and reinforce a utopian morality, fascist art exhibits a utopian aesthetic. She continues:

> *National Socialism—more broadly, fascism—also stands for an ideal or rather ideals that are persistent today under the other banners: the ideal of life as art, the cult of beauty, the fetishism of courage, the dissolution of alienation in ecstatic feelings of community; the repudiation of the intellect; the family of man (under the parenthood of leaders). These ideals are vivid and moving to many people, and it is dishonest as well as tautological to say that one is affected by Triumph of the Will and Olympia only because they were made by a filmmaker of genius. Riefenstahl's films are still effective because, among other reasons, their longings are still felt, because their content is a romantic ideal to which many continue to be attached.*[207]

Mourlet's work[208] undeniably exudes a totalizing aspect. The author aims to analyze individual films and filmographies using some universal laws (the balance between the documentary and the *feerie*, the pre-eminence of the actor and the presence of the world, and the aim to fascinate the spectator in a reconciliation with the world) and the establishment of a certain cinematographic nature (its capacity to reveal ontologically the truth that exists in a latent state in the phenomenal world). It is not a coincidence that at times, especially when Mourlet talks about precipitating the spectator into a state of hypnosis, he seems to refer to a cinema like the one I am studying in this book, by Hou Hsiao-Hsien and Apichatpong Weerasethakul, among others. However, we have to be very careful.

> *without significant events tensioning the narrative and dialectically justifying that moment of rest and relaxation; they are bodies given over to sensible duration, to the installation of an ambience; the film is an assemblage of pure temporal forms, Apichatpong's most 'literal'—and, by the way, its best.*[209]

---

[207] Sontag (1981, 96).

[208] In 2022, none of the Mac-Mahonists were openly involved in far-right movements. Apoliticalism remained the rule. It was only a few years later that Mourlet wrote in Maurice Bardèche's far-right magazine *La Defense de l'Occident*.

[209] Oliveira Jr. (2012, 12).

What is quite interesting in Mourlet is the cultivation and appreciation of a sense of control, a clear direction of the scenic elements, and, at the same time and in the same hierarchy, the rejection of excessive and suffocating intervention. The author seeks to be captivated by the hidden truths that exist in the phenomenal world. This revelatory experience cannot be achieved through total and absolute control or calculation. The opposite is also rejected. The mise-en-scène, in this sense, as Aumont rightly underlined, is a kind of "trap thrown at the real." A filmmaker must always be on the lookout for moments of grace and sublimity that, when organized around a drama, a narrative, exude the "feeling of being."

This apparent paradox is at the core of modern cinema. It is the notion of encounter, of accident, that is felt in the work of completely different filmmakers, such as Robert Bresson, Jean-Luc Godard, John Cassavetes, and Jacques Rivette. It is the idea that a film results from the circumstances of filming, some unforeseen and others provoked. Staging is reacting to the encounter between the actors, a setting and a dramatic situation. It would be a mistake to look for these perspectives in Mourlet, who sees many dangers in this management of the unexpected, the uncontrolled. However, what characterizes his conception of mise-en-scène is precisely, as we have seen, the organization of the unorganized. Here is an intention that will accompany me throughout the chapters that follow.

It is a cinema that simultaneously says yes and no to the world and to cinema. It is a meditative state that awaits the dispensation of something to us, characterized by an absence. It can be described as a "serenity," to use Heidegger's expression. The contemporary cinema that interests me has radicalized this paradox to the point that the terms of this equation can no longer be seen as opposites. Quite the contrary. It's like they're one and the same thing. Hsiao-Hsien empties the characters, the plot, and the story of their classical, psychological, and narrative points of reference, and bets on a record that does not seem to apprehend anything beyond the act of recording itself. Speaking of *A City of Sadness* (*Beiquing chengshi*, 1989), a true mark in the filmmaker's filmography, Antoine Baecque reinforces the theme of presence and the inability to find satisfactory answers in the midst of the overwhelming mystery of the world. I agree with him:

> However, some sense is created, as in the eyes of the deaf-mute that occupy a long shot in City of Sadness. Wen-Ching, in prison, watches the last moments of two death row inmates who are being picked up by guards for execution. The camera resumes his point of view, from a distance, through the half-open cell door. He observes the last gestures of the condemned, their slow dressing, their impotence, their fear. For a long time the end of the shot is postponed, like a last

sensation of life before the ineluctable death. Wen-Ching's eyes saw everything: the shot is an sorte of an evidence, infinitely elongated and yet very short; it is thanks to them that hope remains, but it is through them, nevertheless, that the act unfolds, the gestures are carried out, the minutes are thrashed. The apogee of the shot never comes: it suffices to last in order to exist.[210]

1.5 Roger Munier

The Paralysis of Reason and the Silence of Conscience

Roger Munier, as Adrian Martin (2011) stresses, is something of a lost moment in the international annals of film theory. Even in his country of origin, France, he is still rarely discussed or quoted—although a filmmaker as prominent as Raul Ruiz has acknowledged that Munier's essays "brought up a storm of declarations, counter-declarations, and reprimands, enough to fill dozens of volumes"[211] during his youth in the streets of Chile. A philosopher by training, a former student and one of the first translators of Martin Heidegger into French, Munier is also the author of a body of work that transcends various genres and disciplines. Poet, painter, and sculptor, he always sought to overcome the limited framework of a particular field (literature, philosophy, religion, etc.) in order to foster dialogue and, if possible, the harmonious blending of different languages, particularly the intimate fusion of poetry and theory. Throughout these pages, we will see how much of his work resonates with that of Stanley Cavell (1979) and Jean Mitry (1965, 2000)—even paving the way for other more recent theorists such as Gilles Deleuze (1989, 1997) and Nicole Brenez (1997).

A man of his time, Munier began to ponder in the early 1960s about the increasing influence of visual imagery. We live in the age of the verb and we are in the wake of a new culture. Our civilization is today under the sign of the image. For the author, in a world now dominated by illustrated magazines, film, and television, images replaced the written form, becoming prominent mediums of global expression due to their suggestive power. Although he praised photography, especially the work of Henri Cartier-Bresson, he was more cautious in his appreciation of cinema. In his opinion, film is an art that had not yet attained the status of a fully developed language. According to Munier, the presence of the visible world in cinema is an attraction, the source of an unprecedented form of social alienation.

[210.] Baecque (2011, 34).

[211.] Ruiz (1995, 32).

In 1963, in a dialogue with André Bazin, Siegfried Kracauer, and Jean Epstein, always based on Heidegger's hermeneutic ontology, Munier focused on what he referred to as the "objective image." For Munier, a photograph and a film are composed of images of another order, unique in the history of art, which go beyond what they help to narrate, and announce a pre-logical world that dominates and controls our imagination. *Contre l'image* ("against the image," in English) is the paradigmatic title of his pamphlet work—a summary of which was published earlier in English, in 1962 under the name "The Fascinating Image."

The first part of Munier's work reflects on the ontological connection between an image and its referent. As Bazin and Michel Mourlet did, the philosopher also strives to single out the mechanically generated image. It is once again the machinic basis that allows for understanding a more immediate apprehension of the reality, which defines, for the philosopher, the nature of the photographic or cinematographic image. Munier diagnoses an inversion: It is the world that takes the initiative in a photograph. It replaces the simple appearance of things with a kind of "discourse" of the world. Photography only speaks of the world by capturing it in images. This argument is initially presented through a comparison with the pictorial image. The pictorial image invites us to perceive the world in a transformed way, whereas the objective image imposes the world upon us, causing to immerse ourselves in it silently. He says:

> *By its very structure, the objective image tends to establish a new rapport between man and the world. One can hardly, if at all, speak of 'image' in connection with photography. Originally the word signified: imitation, copy. The image which imitates the world remains distinct from it. In a drawing, faithful though it might be, there is always a distance, an interval between the object represented and its plastic transcription. This distance disappears entirely in photography. There, the image coincides so much with the given data that it is somehow destroyed as an image. It is this very data, magically repeated, covering the surface of the paper or of the screen with its presence, its double, so to speak. The photographic image is no longer a copy.*[212]

Painting and drawing deny the world, not in terms of its colors and shapes, in its essence. The world that both envision is a transposed world, in which man has left his mark, interpreting it in plastic terms. Munier cites the painting *Orchard* by van Gogh, which, according to the philosopher, is not just a representation

---

[212.] Munier (1962, 85).

of an orchard but an image that invites us to see the world transfigured by the vision of the Dutch painter. For Munier, van Gogh's hand traces a transmutation: It appropriates the substance of the world to incorporate it into the realm of humanity, and subsequently molds the world to align with our vision and taste. The objective image, on the contrary, depends on the predicates of the world, its autonomy and difference, so that an image can be created from it. Where there was once an exercise of power, now there is nothing but submission.

This is what Munier investigates under the concept of "objective image": an image that creates an object in a proportion that deprives the human being. The latter would be just a moment in the dialectic process of making an objective image, as it solely relies on man in the act of capturing it. It does not belong to him; it excludes the man instead of summoning him. For the philosopher, it is as if we were not merely taking pictures of the world—rather, it is the world that is being photographed through us. What we are left with is a pure and serene feeling. For Munier, this is the true meaning of the word "fascinated": a total paralysis of reflective power. "Filled to the brim, but at the same time inert. Inert to the same degree that it is filled to the brim, without any reaction in the face of this enthralling world, uttered in itself and for itself, indifferently."[213] Photography and cinema would disrupt the centrality of man and render us powerless against the profound impact of the world. "It is the world," continues Munier, "in its pure state, in the pure projection of its essence, beyond all prehension."[214]

Munier investigates the fascination exerted by the cinematographic image on the early spectators of the beginning of the twentieth century. According to him, the impact caused was not restricted to a mere discomfort or the potential for a physical threat—it is known that, in 1895, some people actually ran out of the exhibition hall in fear that the train filmed by the Lumière brothers would advance on toward them. The fascination extended to every natural movement: the sight of smoke rising into the sky, waves crashing on a beach, and a tree swaying in the wind. For Munier, the leaf projected, and shaking in the wind holds more "reality" and feels more authentic than the leaf that was used as a reference for that image. What is fascinating, then, is not simply the spectacle of the replica but the paralyzing power it expresses:

> In the cinema, however, the smoke itself is rising, the leaf really trembles: it declares itself as a leaf trembling in the wind. It is a leaf like that which one encounters in

---

[213] Ibid., 88.

[214] Ibid., 87.

nature and at the same time it is much more, from the moment when, in addition to being that real leaf, it is also, indeed primarily, a represented reality. If it were only a real leaf, it would wait for my observation in order to achieve significance. Because it is represented, divided in two in the image, it is already signified, offered in itself as a leaf trembling in the wind. What fascinated the spectators who saw the Lumiere projections was, much more than the exact repetition of a natural rhythm, this self-expression of the moving image.[215]

I can try to explain or interpret the rising smoke or the trembling leaf, but in order to do so, I must insert myself into the image. Therefore, the immanent meaning of this movement will remain elusive to me. In cinema, it is this imma-nent meaning that is simultaneously revealed and hidden. "The trembling of the leaf is enunciated insofar as it is a trembling, in its nudity."[216] Munier's emphasis is on the potential or limitations of discourse to intervene in what transpires on the screen. A tree expresses itself only through its own means. A street speaks, but no one knows exactly what it says or how it says it.

Anyone who has had the chance to see the props, costumes, sets, or trappings of a beloved film (in a museum, for example) understands Munier's point. The reader who has gone through this experience is fully aware of the horrible disappointment that is at stake: Removed from the context of the film, these paraphernalia are not even a fraction of what they appeared to be on the screen. The lighting, movements, camera filters, and enlarged scale are missing. It lacks, in a word, cinematic quality. In fact, it is not simply a matter of extracting something from its audiovisual context and its original narrative or symbolic purpose. Martin elaborates:

A worse, far more depressing, anti-magical and de-auratic process is going on here, as the wonderful fetish object is returned to its banal reality. The threads of our imaginary investments, our unconscious projections, are being untied here and reduced to dust. Nothing, no possible refilming, will ever bring that fallen object back to life now.[217]

It is not by chance that Munier employs the term "photogenic," a concept that belongs to a real akin to magic. It was Louis Delluc who proposed the

---

[215.] Ibid., 91.

[216.] Ibid.

[217.] Martin (2011b).

term to designate the unique quality of the cinematographic image: "Few have understood the interest of photogenics. Besides, they don't even know what it is."[218] Photogenic indicates a mysterious relationship between photography in general and certain subjects that lend themselves to it. Jean Epstein made it the central focus of his films and thinking. What Epstein glimpses when it comes to photogenics is its character of aesthetic value, which is essential but indescribable, felt but not explained, and constitutive but not analyzable. At the same time, this mysterious substance is, in fact, the substance of cinema, which serves not only as a means of representing the world but also as a way of delving into it, uncovering a universe beyond human experience.

For Munier, as it had been for Epstein, the objective image is not merely an improvement on painting. It possesses certain qualities that occasionally present the objects it captures to us in an unexpected, enchanting, and fascinating manner. It is this "great mystery" of a kind of sensory and sensitive intensification of the world through its footage that Epstein came to call photogenics. It expresses the revealing power of the world registered by the objective image. It designates the mute discourse of things. For both Munier and Epstein, photogenic is the meaning that things inherently possess. "The objects or scenery of the world thus repeated are photogenic because they are self-significant in the objective image. Being photogenic expresses the cosmophonic character of the revealing image,"[219] says Munier.

Epstein, however, explains photogenics as a result of the dual nature of cinema: mechanical and human. Human intelligence operates indirectly, but functioning as a self-sustaining organ, like a robot-brain that is part human and part machine. Cinema is an autonomous intentionality machine that creates its own vision of reality, dismantling false dichotomies between continuity and discontinuity, quality and quantity — and proposing alternative concepts of spatiality, time, and causality. Sensibility and reason are no longer seen as antagonistic; rather, they merge into a unified lyrosophical aesthetic (1947). It is, therefore, capable of creating its own philosophy, its anti-philosophy, in the words of Epstein. It is the task he pursues in his various works, as if he were pursuing the philosopher's stone.[220]

[218.] Delluc (1985, 34).

[219.] Munier (1962, 90).

[220.] Epstein says:
Like the philosopher's stone, the cinematograph has the power to effect universal transformations. But this secret is extraordinarily simple: all this magic boils down to the ability to vary temporal dimension and orientation. The true glory, the most surprising and, perhaps, dangerous achievement of the Lumière brothers, is not to pave the way for the creation of a 'seventh art'—which, incidentally, seems to be abandoning its own path and contenting itself with being a substitute to the theater—but to have created sorcery— […] that frees our vision of the world from the enslavement of the only external, solar, terrestrial rhythm. (Epstein 1947, 163–64)

This dialectic between the sensible and the intelligible as something that explains the fascination that cinema is capable of generating is not present in Munier. His argument is much more based on the idea of the world's self-manifestation in cinema. The world would no longer need my mediation or interpretation as a filmmakers or spectator. The world of the objective image is not constituted "for us"; we are, on the contrary, placed at its mercy. Photography and cinema are akin to a magical repetition of the world, where magic serves as a means to subvert technology, ultimately challenging the dominance of mankind over the world. The objective image feeds a kind of "photogenic revenge on the world," which is said to be perpetuating itself in its "alogical" nudity, to use Munier's term. In a 1973 conference, the philosopher comments: "To the discourse about the world, which places man in front of the world to name it, (photography and cinema) oppose the simple appearance of things, a kind of discourse of the world."[221]

The idea that the world speaks to itself was introduced by phenomenology in its various forms, from Edmund Husserl and Maurice Merleau-Ponty to Paul Ricoeur and Heidegger. Munier remains within this theoretical framework, favoring the notion of experience. He is always interested in the seventh art as a new way of relating to the world. The cinematographic image would be the very place where entities are shown, to use the Heideggerian expression that is dear to him. For Munier, this exhibition is simultaneously manifestation and refusal of manifestation: "We must understand it in its sense and self-manifestation, in which what is manifested, conserving the initiative of unveiling, at the same time refuses and closes itself off."[222]

The presence of Heidegger is evident. On a radical critique of the philosophical tradition of Western metaphysics since Plato, Heidegger sought to propose a new direction that would also serve as a quest for something more authentic and fundamental: the revival of ontology. This revival would overcome the "forgetfulness of being," which persisted throughout the history of Western thought. For Heidegger, we are facing an essentialist tradition that confuses "Being" and "being," which leads to the division of being into substance and accident, and to the habit of classifying and objectifying the "Being." The question of "Being" had transformed into the question of what sorts of things exist. It is against this backdrop that the philosopher defends the recovery of ontology, focusing the theme of the meaning of the Being as an unveiling and manifestation. Philosophy has forgotten the Being of beings, however, every being is present

---

[221] Munier (1989, 14).

[222] Ibid., 45.

in Being. Entities are bimorphic. They are characterized by their ability to both show themselves and disappear, to appear and manifest, and also to dissimulate and wander. From this perspective, beings are always in a state of Being and non-Being. In Heidegger, phenomenology serves the purpose of allowing things to be seen in their own right. It deals with the concept of veiling and unveiling, in the context of the being-there.

In this return to a "fundamental ontology," Heidegger resists the neo-Cartesian emphasis on consciousness and maintains that the most common ways of relating to things are manifested in practical activities, such as hammering. In his famous analysis of the tool being, Heidegger points out that our primary way of interacting with things is through their absence. While our conscious efforts are always focused on some explicit purpose, they rely on a hidden infrastructure of objects. None of them are visible while functioning correctly—although they are all invoked. For Husserl, not only must I begin with what is present in consciousness, but I must also end there. Any notion of things in themselves that remain forever beyond the reach of intentionality is treated by the father of phenomenology as nonsensical. Heidegger, in contrast, argues that something surpasses its mere presence for us. The entities are biomorphic. This is the background of Munier's struggle with cinema:

> At the cinema, it is this opacity which is projected by itself, reaching us without our being able to exercise any real grasp upon it, without the possibility of any dialectical relationship between it and us. The screen gives us only an exteriority represented, and then sealed. I have said 'cosmophonic' and this must be understood in its meaning of self-manifestation, where what is manifested, protecting the initiative of its disclosure, at the same time keeps itself aloof and conceals itself. Orson Welles has correctly stressed the self-revealing character of the cinematographic image. 'The camera...,' he writes, 'is much more than a recording apparatus, it is a means whereby messages from another world come to us, a world not ours, leading us to the heart of the great secret'. But how can one subscribe to this last affirmation? The camera by itself would not know how to introduce us 'to the heart of the great secret'. In order that we should be led to that, it would still be necessary that we play a part in the expression. Now, this world ignores us, in the name of its self-definition. This 'great secret' remains closed to us. It is as a secrets that it expresses itself in the shadow of darkrooms.[223]

[223.] Munier (1962, 93).

In passages like this, I am always reminded of Cavell. For him, photographs provide us with transparent access to things. This photographic-transparent dimension can be broken down into at least three main questions that, in a certain way, define the capabilities of the seventh art: the fact that it absolves us from the burden of answering (we are not obliged to correct the errors that I observe on the canvas, because I cannot enter in it); the fact of overcoming subjectivity (the magical reproduction of the "invisible" world in the film, "explains our forms of unknownness and of our inability to know"[224]); and the fact that it saves us from solipsism (it gives us a vivid, necessary, experimentally rooted symbol of the possibility of the world existing independently of my mind).

Cavell argues that cinema promises us a direct connection with reality, a sort of nostalgic return to a more innocent time. In *The World Viewed* (1979) he asks himself, "What happens to reality when it is projected and screened?"[225] And while there are undoubtedly many points of contact, Cavell's rich and complex responses make any reconciliation with Munier a challenging one. The concept of "automatism," for example, may seem to be, at first, a promising approach. However, automatism means many things to Cavell. Automatism comprises an agreement with the same universals that govern each of the arts. This is what leads him to claim that cinema is a moving image of skepticism. Cavell is interested in exploring the potential for reconciling the experience of watching a film with the profound impact of being thrown into the world, thereby mirroring the circumstances of our own traumatic entry into the world. Munier partly follows this path.

Cavell, in turn, proposes a disjunctive argument. The photographic image is a reproduction of the visual representation or manifestation of the subject being photographed. In a way, it can be considered as the actual appearance of the thing itself. However, he maintains that photography cannot be the reproduction of the appearance of the object because, for the sake of ontological parsimony, we must be cautious in postulating that things have appearances that can be accurately represented. That is to say, if we accept apparitions into our ontological inventory of what exists, our metaphysics will swell into inordinate magnitude, since every object that exists will also be connected to an infinitely large number of appearances, that is, ways in which the object appears virtually at infinite angles and distances. However, if photographs do not re-present apparitions to spectators, it must be the very things that they represent.

---

224. Cavell (1979, 40–41).

225. Ibid., 16.

Following this path, I run into a problem that belongs to both Munier and Cavell. The latter asserts the transparency of photography in his argument that aims to demarcate the border between the photographic and pictorial image. One is transparent, while the other is not. I perceive the object itself through photography, and that is why cinema has the ability to present the world to us. However, could the same argument not be applied to painting? "Consider," speculate Noël Carroll and Jinhee Choi:

> paintings since the time of Plato, if not before, have been said to traffic in the appearances of things. If it is problematic to speak about appearances, for meta-physical reasons, when it comes to photography, it should be equally problematic to do so with respect to paintings. So if paintings do not represent the appear-ances of the objects that they are paintings of, what do they represent? The only alternative Cavell offers us is 'the objects them-selves.' But then paintings are transparent pictures too. This would appear to be a counterintuitive result for most people.8 But, in addition, it is an unhappy one for Cavell since he appears to need transparency to pertain uniquely to photography, not only to distinguish it from painting, but to pave the way for his 'world-viewed' hypothesis.[226]

Cavell was fully aware of these knots, and made an effort to clarify and re-solve them — Munier not so much.[227] Thinking that things speak their language of things in the image, and that cinema's role is to capture this indescribable essence, could be considered a concise definition of a specific cinematic mo-dernity. Defending, however, that it is only in accordance with their supposed essence (when things speak their language of things) that things can convey their signifying reality is a separate issue. To consider the cinematographic image as a "declaration of the real world," as "cosmophonic in its essence," is to claim the world "in itself" and to define this "in itself" as necessarily identical to the object. However, this perspective fails to acknowledge that the object is what it

---

[226.] Carrol and Choi (2006, 57).

[227.] For example: Munier's argument even holds true for the special effects. And on this point, the history of cinema since George Meliés contradicts the philosopher. It would not even be necessary to indicate the radical break that the electronically generated image glimpses on the horizon of this theoretical perspective. It is enough to highlight the increasingly intense narrative use of CGI and the consequent gasification, volatilization of the bodies on stage that no longer need the cut to take them from one space to another. What can we say about those abundant shots in *Spider-Man* (2002) in which the hero jumps from one building to another, and the film, instead of making the *raccord*, moving to the next shot, prefers to incorporate the malleability of the character's body moving inside of the same image? The more the hero moves, the less demands are placed on the body of the person who made that image possible during the filming stage.

is by virtue of my perception.[228] Marc Cerisuelo (2001) traces this problem back to the confusion of two "returns to things": Roberto Rossellini's and Husserl's. The famous *motto* of the Italian filmmaker—"Things are there. Why manipulate them?"—does not concern the things themselves but rather a Copernican form of cinematic revolution, the way of looking at things. In a similar vein, but in reverse, Husserl's willingness to return to things always privileges the structured consciousness of a subject.

Munier is absolutely right: when a camera is positioned in front of something, we have a spectacle, a *cliché*, a flattening, a transmutation of the world into an image. It would, however, be naive to think that we could avoid this confusion between the real and the mediated, the imaginary and the experienced, and human sensibility and machine intelligence.[229] By carefully examining the objects, we can observe the identification of the signifier and the signified is entirely relative. Furthermore, while analogous to what it unveils, it constantly adds something to the revealed content. In reality, objects are involved only by their presence; in cinema, objects are involved in a narrative reality that has a beginning, an end, and a purpose, regardless of what that may be. They cannot be different from the way they are presented; they cannot fail to take part in the action that is foreign to them but involves them. They are in the film and are a part of it.

It is, indeed, true that Munier even went so far as to argue that the silence of the image, referred to as "alogos" by the author, is not necessarily unavoidable. The image can speak to us and address us through a dialectical succession of equivalents, which the author, in turn, qualifies as "analogues." This speaking image, finally cured of its inhuman silence, is discussed in the last chapter of *Contre l'image*. The term "analogues" does not imply the negation of the repetitive and non-discursive structure of the image. The non-discursiveness of the image becomes fuel for another type of discourse. It is necessary to create a syntax of images. It is the link between the images that would unite them in a discourse that looks at me, which is no longer the self-mediation of the world. We would then be capable of a new alchemy of language, of expressing something that is both partially spoken and the essence of the thing itself. The filmed world has a magic that fascinates man, that plunges us into the incomprehension

---

[228.] Not to mention that the way the camera works and the subsequent projection of images also depend on an entire optical system designed by man so that its "reproduction" effectively emulates human vision. If this optical system happened to show a vision that revealed a "transcendental reality," we would reject it as incongruous and perhaps call it misleading.

[229.] Or, as Alfred North Whitehead, an author who begins to gain ground in this book, says: "If we desire a record of uninterpreted experience, we must ask a stone to record its autobiography" (Whitehead 1978, 15).

of a hypnotic sleep. Man, however, due to the very properties of cinema, could appropriate this magic.

Munier praises the qualities of "certain works" (those of Bresson, no doubt), that, by converting the image into logos, bring the image into "conformity with its essence," that is, as a declaration of the world itself, "because it is only when things speak their language of things in it that they can register their reality as a sign."[230] If, on the one hand, I agree with Munier regarding the conversion of the image into logos, on the other hand, I feel equally disappointed when the author limits the reality of an image to the idea that things must speak their own language of things. In addition to the metaphysical imprecision that emanates from this "aesthetic," it is still necessary to challenge the illusion that drives it: making images the "words" of the world. This analogy between image and word, which an author like Christian Metz diagnosed at the beginning of his career, has generated many misunderstandings over the years. Mitry leaned over it as well. If verbal meaning is composed of a combination of signs, meaning in cinema is the outcome of a connection between facts. In other words, "the significance of one in a linguistic sense is a circumstantial factor."[231]

Munier's two great references in terms of cinema are Andrei Tarkovsky and, most importantly, Robert Bresson, whom he was friends with and dedicated his book *Contre L'image* to. Tarkovsky and Bresson are filmmakers that who, at first glance, have few points in common. Both, however, believe in the "truth" of the cinematographic image in its relation to the world. I cannot perceive the world in its totality, but for these two filmmakers, the image can convey this totality. It is not possible to know the truth of the real directly because it has neither guarantee nor signifier. However, it is possible to perceive it, even if with difficulty and fleetingly, as if by flashes. Bresson adopted the term "cinematograph," defined as "a writing with imagens in movement and with sounds"[232] and in a opposition to the cinema, seen as a synonym of "filmed theater," an immediate and definitive expression "by a mimicry done with gestures and intonations of voice."[233] He embarks on a rigorous style, stripped of any kinds of excess, in an effort to capture the essence of the "real."

The greatness of his films comes from the ineffable that emanates from their images. Bresson flattens his images, as if working with an iron, as he used to say,

---

[230.] Munier (1989, 94).

[231.] Mitry (2000, 319).

[232.] Bresson (1977, 2).

[233.] Ibid., 5.

in an attempt to refine the quality of the shots. He saw in the automatism of life an opposition to theatrical exteriorization, betting on his "models," automaton beings whose mechanized exteriority would preserve a virgin or pure interiority. He refers to a " 'visible parlance' of bodies, objects, houses, roads, trees, fields"[234] that makes us undertake "a voyage of discovery on an unknown planet."[235] The filmmaker also emphasizes the immense potential of the mechanical aspect of the cinematographic apparatus when he states that "what no human eye is capable of catching, no pencil, brush, pen of pinning down, your camera catches without knowing what it is, and pins its down with a machine's scrupulous indifference."[236] All this aligns with Munier's ideas. When dealing with *Balthazar* (*Au hasard Balthazar*, 1966), the author says:

> *We see a close-up of the donkey Balthazar and everything is said in his gaze, which is no longer simply evoked, but it is present in and through the image. Bresson had probably already chosen the moment to capture this image, determined its framing, the potential of the environment, and proposed, isolating this look, to communicate to us a certain truth about the animal, its docility, the abyss of humility of its patience, calm…Certainly, the living image of that sweetly obstinate head, directing its clear and heavy gaze towards us, is precisely what the filmmaker sought to record. But at the end of the day, this image is a sign of itself in its immediate figuration. Bresson speaks of the soul in capturing the image, and, between what he wants to say and what is said, there is no intermediary.*[237]

Interestingly, in a short essay, "S'isoler des arts existants" (1971), Bresson mentions his friend Munier:

> *Roger Munier was right when he wrote his book Contre l'image. But if the cinematograph (like literature with the words in the dictionary) arrives, through the clash and sequence with other images and with sounds, to give us a face, a value, a new power to the image, and if the image, as a result, becomes something other than what it is, and if the films draw their expression only from this prodigy, then a magnificent and very powerful language is born, which does not take root in the world of literature, nor in the theater, nor, thank God, in*

---

[234] Ibid., 7.

[235] Ibid., 12.

[236] Ibid., 14.

[237] Munier (1967, 38–39).

painting: no more postcards! Movies take off. The directors are getting up and they won't fall anymore.[238]

This quote is intriguing because Bresson, perhaps unintentionally, creates a distance between himself and Munier. The filmmaker always emphasizes the fundamentally relational nature of cinematographic art. This search for a definition of what cinema is and the fulfillment of its essence necessarily involves affirming a plurality at its foundation. After all, I am constantly oscillating between stillness and motion, a single image and several images, images combined with sounds (and language), a multitude of frames and shots. This is precisely what Bresson suggests in *Notes on the Cinematographer*: "Cinematographic film, where expression is obtained by relations of images and of sounds, and not by a mimicry done with gestures and intonations of voice (whether actors' or non-actors'). One that does not analyze or explain. That recomposes."[239]

The originality of Bresson's conception is rooted in the desire for a certain indeterminacy of the profilmic, as well as in the necessary modulation of the film's components—which are what they are only in relation to others: "An image must be transformed by contact with other images, as is a color by contact with other colors."[240] Or, shortly after, radicalizing with great firmness a rejection of the very idea of image: "No absolute value to an image. Sound and image owe their value and their power only to the use you put them to."[241] Bresson expresses in these aphorisms the desire to eliminate any preconceived meaning from an image. He claims vehemently in capital letters: "IN THIS LANGUAGE OF IMAGES. ONE MUST LOSE COMPLETELY THE NOTION OF IMAGE. THE IMAGES MUST EXCLUDE THE IDEA OF IMAGE."[242]

In other words, a closer analysis of Bresson's cinema helps me to identify Munier's naivete. After all, the director's ability to surprise us with the familiar and reveal the mystery at hand, is a result of his dual status as both a formalist and a realist. The cinematographic image, as an artistic image, is born from the paradoxical conjunction of desire and reluctance, artistic intentionality and submission to being-there of the world. The Bressonian cinematograph seeks the manifestation of the real through a kind of writing. For Bresson it is all a question

---

[238] Bresson (1971, 153).

[239] Ibid., 5.

[240] Ibid.

[241] Ibid., 11.

[242] Ibid., 33.

of "writing," of personal expression that is neither immediate nor definitive, whose means and elements do not vanish. Bresson's mise-en-scène is as articulate and interventionist as any meticulously planned staging.

The visualization of space, the way he tells stories, the use of sound, his models, all these aspects are a direct result of the French director's unique temperament and vision. It is precisely this aspect that causes his work to elicit extreme reactions from all sides. To many moviegoers, his films seem disturbingly apathetic and emotionless. Kent Jones draws parallels between popular reactions to atonal music and abstract painting, as if his models' lack of emotional range could be compared to Mondrian's lack of representation or Webern's absence of melody. The sensation of a reality that only exists through the filter of personal perception is perhaps the central issue in Bresson's work. This is my experience when watching a film like *Mouchette* (1967): It feels like an intimate portrayal of my connection with the world, which is then recreated and transformed into a narrative. "The great lesson that Bresson's work teaches those who are paying attention," underlines Jones, "is that when you make a film, you resist all conventions and stick to the world as you and only you experience it."[243]

Munier, however, comes to the fore when I come across a filmmaker like Hou Hsiao-Hsien. The same paralysis of reason or silence of conscience is evident, for example, in the forefront of a film like *Millennium Mambo* (2001). The camera struggles to focus on the fluorescent bulbs that illuminate a pedestrian walkway. Together, the lights blend and resonate throughout the shot and appear to create an artificial corridor on the ceiling of the catwalk. The camera slowly pans as if navigating and begins to synchronize with an electronic and somewhat melancholic beat that gradually intensifies in the soundtrack. From the left corner of the frame, Shu Qi, the young and beautiful protagonist of the film, appears sweetly. In a voice-over, she says: "That was ten years ago. It was the year 2001, the whole world was welcoming the 21st century and celebrating the new millennium." The sequence continues for a few minutes. Shu Qi gracefully walks down the runway, wearing a smile, smoking a cigarette, with her hair flowing and in slow motion. Time seems suspended yet reintroduced by the narration.

Millennium Mambo invites me in, directly and effortlessly. It provides me with something to see, contemplate, witness, and feel. Hsiao-Hsien is always seeking to revive a specific sense of awe in cinema. The subtle camera movements in Hsiao-Hsien evoke a feeling of longing, discovery, and revelation. *Millennium Mambo* re-enchants me with images. It is what the critic Shigehiko Hasumi

---

[243.] Jones (1999, 23).

(2008) refers to as "the archaeological rapture": the act brings forth the same fascination as the early silent films, and this sensation is repeated in later cinema:

> *The speeding train passing through tunnels and screeching around the many curves of the tree-draped tracks cannot help but remind one of the exhilarating sense of motion in the film* Passage Through a Railway Tunnel at the Front of a Locomotive *(Passage d'un tunnel en chemin de fer pris de l'avant de la locomotive, 1898) taken by the Lumière brothers at the end of the nineteenth century. Pressed right up against the scenery taken by the camera from the driver's seat, the viewer can only be impressed with how one characteristic of film, hibernating since its earliest days, has been reawakened in this shot in Hou's film (*Dust in the Wind *[Lianlian fengchen], 1986).*[244]

Hsiao-Hsien claims my attention to movement, color, music, atmosphere, humor, the flesh of the actors, as well as what is hidden, invisible, daydreams, fantasies, and ghosts. It is as if the elements (movement, color, sensation, sound, etc.), which are typically shaped and combined to tell a story, create characters, and deliver speeches, have been set free to operate independently. It is as if cinema found in Hsiao-Hsien a direct access to the world through a kind of celebration of the mystery of the sensitive. His staging is a kind of writing about the ephemerality of the movements that shape the world, be it a train, a motorcycle, a walk, or the wind that sways the tree.

Munier's work reinforces something that is evident in all the authors who have accompanied me here: Cinema is capable of removing us from the realm of reason toward the universe of experience. It is this perspective that seems best suited to delve into contemporary cinema: discussing not necessarily meanings but shapes, contours, and rhythm. I can coldly isolate and analyze each component and procedure described in Hsiao-Hsien's film, but I can live in that rhythm and feel that vibration with even greater enthusiasm. However, suspending the cultural world and revealing what still remains unnamed cannot be seen as an immediate and unavoidable outcome of the mechanical recording apparatus. Hsiao-Hsien's cinema always offers a unique perspective on the world, an enigmatic object that is more than just an object. It is not really an object at all. It is not in front of me but rather sustains and connects us in a significant way. This look needs to be created, instituted, and expressed. Before it, we wake up to a communion of a sensitive order that disorients and silences us.

---

[244] Hasumi (2008, 184).

What can be gleaned from Munier's essays, which is immensely useful to me in the confrontation with this contemporary cinema, is the notion that a film already meticulously describes, before the spectator or critic delves into it, all kinds of things: the world, spaces, objects, bodies, behaviors, atmosphere, and rhythm. That is to say, a film not only records something prior to itself. It does not simply refer to something prior to it but rather delineates and animates, represents and narrates, figures and sets in motion, all at once. This perspective opens up the possibility that cinema is more than just a technological device; it is a way of thinking, one that is based on visual and temporal properties.

The image invokes the objects. An invocation that materializes and suddenly takes on a new and different meaning. The cinematographic image always compels me to contemplate the objects it portrays, while simultaneously requiring me to engage in critical thinking about them. It can be said that any object presented in moving images acquires a meaning (a collection of meanings) that it does not have in "reality." We can never fully explore all the aspects, senses and meanings of an object. The emphasis on the absence of reality is manifested in the image of the film, especially because film is not so much about the object itself, but rather an aspect of the object, namely an image.

The philosopher is correct when he stresses that the meaning of a cinematographic image is not determined by the objects represented in it. Sense is something that naturally emanates from objects and is intensified in their moving representation when we see them. Hsiao-Hsien seeks to capture nature in its nascent state, the raw energy and fulguration of the world before man. This is something that Munier believed to be the essential quality of the cinematographic image. I reiterate once again: The cinematographic image does not prohibit, exclude, or oppose human intervention. Instead, it expresses something that the cold logic of analysis conceals, overlooks, or is incapable of apprehending.

1.6 Jean Mitry

The Image as Frame and Window, at the Same Time

Jean Mitry[245] left his mark in the history of film theory. By resorting at the same time to both the formalist and phenomenologist traditions, and already pointing, albeit timidly, to the semiological turn that was brewing on the horizon,

---

[245]. His given name is Jean René Pierre Goetgheluck Le Rouge Tillard des Acres de Préfontaines. He borrowed the name "Mitry" from a small commune (Mitry-Mory) about 25 km from Meaux.

the two volumes of *The Aesthetics and Psychology of the Cinema*, the first one published in 1963 and the second in 1965, marked the beginning of a new era in film research. Christian Metz,[246] who was a student of Mitry in France, would say that his teacher's work can be seen as a synthesis of the ideas on film that came before him. An extremely ambitious work, based on a new, more scholarly approach to theorizing, which is skeptical of simplistic or far-reaching solutions, yet aims to present a comprehensive aesthetic of cinema.

The Aesthetics and Psychology of the Cinema is as much about cinema as it is about film theory. This work is made up of at least three major ambitions that Mitry seeks to realize comprehensively: a psychology of the film experience, an aesthetic-linguistic theory of film as a medium for symbolic expression, and a critical history of film theory. First, Mitry focuses on the structures of the cinematic experience. These structures would define the experience of sitting and watching a movie. He describes the mechanisms that enable me to perceive movement and depth, the fundamental psychological duality of the moving image as both real and unreal, the structuring aspects of framing, and the tangible qualities of sound. He contrasts the perceptual and psychological aspects of the cinematic experience with the experiential characteristics of other arts, establishing the basis for the claim that cinema possesses a unique potential and vocation. Cinema is an art form that engages all the senses simultaneously. Then, Mitry analyzes how different film styles and modes of cinematographic experience function, without succumbing to the temptation of suggesting an essential nature. Soon after, he explores the expressive and symbolic capabilities of cinema. How does a movie create meaning? How does it speak? What can it say? This is the second major question of his work and the core of his aesthetic and critical theory: an investigation of cinema as a language system that enables the expression of ideas through the narrative depiction of concrete reality. This research leads him into lengthy discussions about the nature of perception and cognition, the symbolic abilities of the arts, and the expressive capabilities of discursive language itself. He describes cinema's unique status as a means of expression that is simultaneously a reflection of reality, an art and a type of language. It truly takes your breath away.

What is still curious is the fact that Mitry is the oldest authors with whom I dialogued in this chapter. He was born in November 1907, a year before Maurice Merleau-Ponty. He lived and worked during the so-called golden era of silent cinema. In Paris, as a young man, he associated with the Prévert brothers, Artaud,

---

[246.] Metz (1972, 32).

Aragon, André Breton, Alberto Cavalcanti, Jean Epstein, and Louis Delluc. His first book on the seventh art, a critical study of the work of the Swiss actor Emil Jannings, was published in 1928. It was expected that, similar to his contemporaries Epstein, Abel Gance, and Rudolf Arnheim, Mitry would develop a theory centered on the superiority of silent films. What we will see, however, is a particularly modern theory that believes cinema cannot be understood and constructed based on an essence, nor can it be discussed ideologically. For Mitry, the seventh art is eminently a field of research.

Dudley Andrew explains this perspective of the French author based on three aspects of his career. The first of these concerns his historiographical inclination, which involves the desire and ability to analyze and categorize types of films and cinematographic genres. He founded the first film club in the French capital. He wrote and edited many of the first specialized film publications. He was one of the creators of the French Cinematheque, along with Georges Franju and Henri Langlois, and he always had the demeanor of an archivist. Unlike André Bazin, whose essays were the result of a certain sensitivity and intuitive brilliance, Mitry always relied on extensive bibliographical explanations. Besides the two seminal volumes of *The Aesthetics and Psychology of the Cinema*, he published a work on the history of cinema in five volumes, a book on the history of experimental cinema, a critique of semiology in film, monographs and studies on John Ford, Chaplin, Eisenstein, and René Clair, as well as a film dictionary and an enormous universal filmography spanning thirty-five volumes. The second aspect of his trajectory is the pedagogical. Mitry began teaching at IDHEC in 1945 and became one of the first professors of film at the University of Paris and later at the University of Montreal. The third concerns is regarding his cinematographic work. Mitry collaborated on a series of well-known productions, such as *Napoleon* (*Napoléon*, 1927), by Gance. He met Sergei Eisenstein,[247] worked briefly with Jean Renoir in *La nuit du Carrefour* (1932), edited Alexandre Astruc's award-winning short film, *Le rideau Cramoisi* (1953), and directed a few others, including *Pacific 231* (1949) and *Images pour Debussy* (1952). These are all experimental projects that embody much of what Mitry would theoretically support. "Only Eisenstein," says Andrew, "exceeds him in time and energy spent in editing rooms."[248]

[247.] In *Sergei Eisenstein* (1961), Mitry recounts the days in 1929, when, at the invitation of Léon Moussinac and his film club, Les Amis de Spartacus, he toured Paris with the Soviet filmmaker and theorist in 1929. Eisenstein spoke of cinema, formalism, signs, symbologies, and language. The encounter had a lasting impact on Mitry.

[248.] Andrew (1976, 186).

Mitry believed that Russian filmmakers, particularly Eisenstein, had developed an aesthetic theory with limited scope. They would have focused all their attention on just one aspect of cinema: montage. While montage is certainly one of the defining components of the seventh art, it is only an element of language and structure, and not a precondition for its existence. This would also be the problem of other theorists such as Béla Balázs and Arnheim, both committed to the attempt to define and codify the elements that generate visual expression. For Mitry, their work cannot be generalized since they do not start from the fundamental principles of this expression but rather from some notions that, although important, are not sufficient to encompass the entirety of cinema.

Similarly, Bazin's positions on the relationship between the cinematographic image and reality, as well as on the use of the long take in depth, are also rejected. The value of Bazin's analyses is recognized as invaluable. However, since they permeate all of the critic's essays, his points of view end up limiting his overall conception. He says:

> *Some younger theorists, doubtless alienated by this categorization but categorical in their own way, have tried to deny the fact of 'montage,' merely to replace it with a certain use of 'depth-of-field'-without realizing that the latter is nothing more than a particular manifestation of the former. A system of aesthetics can never confine, within one interpretation, notions which must include them all.*[249]

Unlike his predecessors, Mitry wants to establish truly universal principles, escaping previous limitations. According to him, these limitations have hindered a comprehensive understanding of the field of philosophy, linguistics, logic, and psychology. Mitry believes that each question must be dealt with individually. The idea is to bring together all the theoretical problems that have emerged in the first fifty years of film theory and outline the main positions taken in relation to these questions. It is not without reason that Andrew likens Mitry's work to a "treatise on the human body or on the life of insects."[250] The concise summary of the two volumes of *The Aesthetics and Psychology of the Cinema* highlights the significant focus on the occasional, albeit unsuccessful, attempt to encompass everything within his reach.

Mitry will point to a middle ground between Bazin's revelatory realism and formalist cinema. For the theoretician, the qualities of the cinematographic image

---

[249] Mitry (2000, 2).

[250] Andrew (1976, 188).

synthesize the realistic and formative fields. A cinematic theory must account
for both the language and the psychology of film. His hypothesis is that cinema
derives from life and immediate reality, and that it is necessary, therefore, to place
the seventh art in the context of this "objective reality." In this way, even before
embarking on the aesthetic question and the material aspects of the image (the flat
surface, the frame and its limits, the point of view, and the montage), the author
ventures into long explanations regarding notions such as language, structure
and perception. For him, these expressions help him define the cinematographic
image in relation to other arts—and also to map the role and possibilities of
the cinema, which, in his opinion, forms the foundation of any filmic aesthetic.

That is, although he emphasizes the formalizing dimension of the camera as
the foundation of image construction, Mitry attempts to establish a connection
with Bazin's ontology—without, however, as the critic of *Cahiers du Cinéma*
sometimes seems to do, trying to lay down a essentialist definition of the seventh art. For Mitry, images cannot be discussed outside of their relationship
with the objects they represent. It is insufficient to talk about an image without
discussing objects. In a typical Husserlian formulation, the author points out
that every image is an image of something. This places cinema in a different
category than verbal language. If, in a novel, an action can be conveyed through
an abstract idea, enabling us to contemplate the world "out there," in a film, it
is always essential to depict concretely whatever it is. The cinematic image is
already "out there." It incorporates many of the objects' actual visual qualities,
including their movement.

The author does not see the cinematographic image as a "sign" that reminds us
of the represented objects but as "analogues" of the objects, their doubles. This
inherently connection to reality also sets cinema apart from the pictorial image.
What Mitry sees in a painting is a fictional representation of reality. A painting
of a bouquet of flowers would no longer capture the true essence of the actual
bouquet of flowers that served as its reference. This indicates that, for the author,
the main objective of painting is the pictorial representation of the bouquet and
not really the bouquet seen by the painter, or, rather, the representation itself. For
Mitry, in painting, the represented object disappears behind its own representation. Transformed into a painted work, it no longer exists. This representation
remains as a new object. This new object is an imitation and carries a somewhat
fictional character. In the movies, things would be different:

> *Whereas the painter's bunch of flowers is the effect of various colors applied by*
> *him on a canvas following an intention, the bunch of flowers recorded by me on*

film is devoid of all intentionality. The image is identical in all respects to the object in the viewfinder. It is not the effect of an artist but (dare one say it) the effect of the object itself, reproducing itself on film by means of light reflected onto it and captured by the lens. The object is transferred onto film as a completely faithful copy [...] What I see, in fact, is no longer the bunch of flowers but, through and by it, the bunch of flowers itself. It is the real bunch of flowers my consciousness observes through my perception of an image immediately forgotten as an image by reason that it is perceived 'as an object of which it is the image.'[251]

The raw material of cinema, according to Mitry, is the image that provides us with an immediate perception of the world. The cinematographic image is in the world. It is always possible to inquire into the underlying meaning of what I see in a photograph. This question makes sense in the context of cinema because it is a medium that reflects reality and provides answers. The world of a painting, in turn, is not continuous with the world of its frame; being framed, the world establishes its boundaries. A painting is a world. A photograph is of the world. The camera cuts out an indefinitely larger portion of the world. The implied presence of the rest of the world and its explicit rejection are essential to the experience of a photograph, just as important as what it specifically presents. It is the arrangement of elements and relationships between them that define a space. Films create characters who, in turn, detach themselves from their creators and are effectively presented and brought to life through motion. Their existence is not just an idea or concept; it is always situated in the here and now. In this sense, initially, the cinematographic image coexists with the world it portrays. Unlike the world, it designates nothing; it simply presents itself as something analogous to it, distinct but made of the same visual characteristics. "Thus," says Mitry, "reality is no longer 'represented'—signified by a symbolic or graphic substitute."[252]

This short excerpt brings Mitry closer to Bazin's conception of cinema as the "asymptote of reality." However, if the latter insisted on a certain harmony in the alignment of the filmic analogue with the world, the former endeavored to identify the distinctions between the cinematographic image and the parallel world that exists beside it and that it so faithfully reflects. If initially Mitry emphasizes that the things represented in cinema have a "dimension" and "thickness," forever engaged with their surroundings, just like in reality, then, the author resorts to various fields of knowledge and insistently weaves several distinctions. These

---

[251] Mitry (2000, 47).

[252] Ibid., 15.

distinctions are not only between an object and its image but also, and perhaps above all, between an object and its image in sequence. For Mitry, the cinematographic image, even though it is analogous to what it shows us, always adds something to what is being shown, and it does so in motion, in time.

The image of a chair is perceived both as an image and as a physical object. "It is the chair presented as an image."[253] Any object depicted in moving images acquires a meaning that it may not possess in "reality." Mitry argues that an image belongs not really in between reality and fiction but rather in between essence and existence. The image invokes an essence through a concrete existence, while also conveying a presence through an absence. Reality in cinema is both present and absent. It is present because it is effectively represented, but it is absent precisely because it is only represented. In this way, the image of a chair confirms the absence of the actual object, even though the spectator perceives the chair through its image. He comments:

> We must emphasize that we mean 'essence' here in its phenomenological sense, i.e., as pure potentiality and not in the Kantian or Platonic sense. It is imperative to stress this point so that errors of interpretation may be avoided. Moreover, it is this way of regarding the 'essence' as an 'in-itself' or as a transcendental 'a priori' which gives Bazin (and a few others) the idea of the camera discovering the world 'beyond the world,' the world of essences, pure spirits, beyond the human eye, a camera, as it were, 'discovering the divine,' whereas it is our minds which find, through the images of objects (and because the image 'makes the object unreal'), the essence it conceives 'beyond the objects themselves.' In the cinema, the immanent finds expression in a certain transcendence but not in the 'transcendental. '[254]

This is the tone of the criticism that Mitry makes not only of Bazin but also of other authors who take equally phenomenological approaches, albeit with more spiritualist accents, such as Amédée Ayfre, or more "cosmological," such as Roger Munier. Bazin and Ayfre understand the presence of the world in the image as an opportunity to reveal a mystery that transcends the very shapes and movements that I see on a frame. Mitry rejects this perspective and sees with irony the affiliation of both authors to phenomenological thought. For him, his countrymen take an operation of consciousness for a metaphysical reality. The

---

[253]. Ibid., 45.

[254]. Ibid.

primacy of existence over essence would have in Bazin or Ayfre no other mission than that of "preserving an essence of which existence would be no more than a pale reflection."[255] Munier, in turn, believes that the cinematographic image would be something like a "preface of the world." A world, until now debased as an object, that seems to regain its status through the image. This notion of the image as an impenetrable declaration of the world, as an objective phenomenon separated from human perception, is also dismissed as naive and simplistic. He says:

> To consider the film image as a 'statement of the real world,' by virtue of its objectivity considered as absolute, to say that it is 'cosmophonic in its essence,' is to posit the world as 'in-itself' and to posit this 'in-itself' as necessarily identical (and yet 'purer') with the object as we know it, without realizing that the object is the way it is only by virtue of our perception. [...] This might almost be conceivable were the vision of the camera to transcend human vision. However, not only is this vision 'directed' but it is dependent on an optical system designed by man so that its 'reproduction' is effectively the same as human vision. If by chance this optical system showed a vision revealing a 'transcendental reality,' we would reject it as incongruous and call it 'bad.'[256]

Mitry's criticism of Bazin, Ayfre, and even Munier is more effectively developed in the discussion of the compositional dimension that structures the cinematographic image. For the author of *The Aesthetics and Psychology of the Cinema*, the image has a life of its own. It has some particularities with which reality must combine in order to create an analogical impression. Film offers us imagens that are based on the visual forms and qualities of the world, but it can only bring us the image of a world constituted in representation. The presence of the real in the image is cut out by framing; it is intrinsically associated with the cinematographic frame. This notion of frame, seen as a window by Bazin and a frame by the formalist tradition, is revised by Mitry.

For him, the cinematographic image is both a frame and a window. It establishes a series of visual tensions, orders the elements present in the image, the way they are presented, and, at the same time, never fails to point to the world it represents. The mise-en-scène essentially consists of structuring a space that is confined within a frame. The image is necessarily organized according to this frame, which defines the living and active geometry it contains. Captured

---

[255.] Mitry (1965, 13).

[256.] Mitry (2000, 45).

by the camera's lens, things are recorded with a formalist intention that imbues them with meaning. The representation is, therefore, a form, an organic whole, different from reality, which, however, serves as a reference. Returning to the example of the bouquet of flowers, he explains that when I see a bouquet on the screen, I see the real object through the image offered to me. This object is given to my consciousness as an immanent reality, as something free of intentionality, but, at the same time, as a structured reality, with a distinct form. The bouquet transcends itself: "It becomes in some way self-transcendent, the existential manifestation of an idea. Seen as a reality and assimilated as the organic element of a structure, the object seems thereby to be in some way both subject and object, immanent and transcendent."[257]

Mitry's project aims to bridge the gap between realism and idealism. Both currents insist on distinguishing between subject and object as a starting point—realism giving precedence to the object and idealism to the subject. Although they come close, phenomenologists like Husserl, Sartre, and even Merleau-Ponty would not have been able to overcome this old and persistent dualism. What needs to be shown, therefore, is that neither the object nor the subject precedes experience; that is, neither one comes before the other in our relations with the world. Mitry invokes quantum mechanics to demonstrate that, even though there exists something in an undifferentiated state, such as power or energy, independent of my perception, it is not considered an object in itself. "The object," he says, "does not pre-exist the perceptive act, it completes it."[258] What is perceived, despite belonging to a reality or totality that is external to us and from which it is drawn, does not exist prior to perception as an object. It only becomes an object through the mediation and framing of sensation and consciousness, although consciousness neither creates nor invents or precedes it. "To perceive," continues Mitry, "is to build a world; to be aware of it is to give yourself this world as an object."[259] Similarly, the subject only comes into existence or becomes self-aware when I become aware, through perception, of what I am not, namely the object of perception. Mitry uses the principles of quantum physics to illustrate that objects that emerge in perception cannot be, as objects, identical with the physical world, that is, with that undifferentiated something that exists independently of us. Likewise, quantum physics conceives time and space not as a priori but as emergent properties of the world (quanta)

---

257. Ibid., 48.

258. Mitry (1965, 186).

259. Ibid., 191.

expressed by fields and successions (that is, by relations)—just like in Mitry's view, objectivity and subjectivity are expressions of the perceptual act from where they emerge.

The mission to bridge the gap between idealism and realism represents an unprecedented endeavor in the history of cinema, aiming to merge the formalist and realist traditions within a single theory. In other words, the image for Mitry cannot be conceived as essentially objective, but neither is it possible to detach it from the world. It no longer enjoys revelatory powers, although it retains with it the presence of things and seeks to depict a facet of the world. According to the author, this is one of the secrets of the cinematographic image. It is a reflection of a constant antagonism between the unity of the thing and its countless potentialities. In no other art it is possible to feel this "division between reality and appearance, between the concrete and abstract, between the immanent and transcendent—all complementing and justifying each other in a formal unity, the image."[260]

What is also perceived in this process is the author's desire to emphasize the presence of a subjectivity in the creation of cinematographic representation. I am always perceiving a particular version/view of the world. Mitry points out that it is not my attention that brings this or that image to my view, but rather someone who insistently directs me to look at specific aspects of the world. If, initially, reality cannot be ignored, in a second moment, at the narrative level, it becomes necessary to consider man, someone who submits the analogues of nature to his "own insatiable need to signify." A new world is created by the filmmaker with the collaboration of the world "out there." In film, for Mitry, the authors are those directors who were compelled to write their own scripts, transforming their filmographies into an obsessive exercise on a certain personal vision of the world and things.

When assembling a sequence of images, a filmmaker always guides us to search for motivation. Why choose these shots or takes over others? How do you explain these cuts, this order, and this rhythm? The spectator, on his own, will try to give these images some human sense and significance. And, most of the time, the images are motivated by a narrative in which each one finds its proper place, contributing to the understanding of the story at hand. The filmmaker cannot escape reality, but he can and must assert his own interpretation. That is, reality, at first, cannot be avoided; in second, however, it is the man who cannot be stopped—the man and his shots, his desires, his prejudices, his senses and

---

[260] Mitry (2000, 49).

meanings. For Mitry, a new world is created in collaboration with the world. No other art does this.

Only cinema, says Mitry, can speak to us through the virtual perception of concrete reality, evoking emotions, reasoning, and deeply suggestive symbolic meanings. Cinema, initially expressed through perception and emotion, opens a door, enable us to experience and understand the world in a different manner. "Film absolves us of the need to imagine what it shows us, but it requires us to imagine with what it shows us through the associations which it determines."[261] I am informed of something. I am influenced by something. Simultaneously. The cinematic experience offers, according to Mitry, something between contemplation and interaction, or, rather, a form of active contemplation.

The example Mitry used was a scene from Eisenstein's *Battleship Potemkin* (*Bronenosets Potyomkin*, 1925). During the insurrection on board the ship, right at the beginning of the film, the tsarist doctor finds himself in an extreme situation. After showing the doctor being brutally thrown overboard, Eisenstein inserts a single shot of his pince-nez hanging from a rope. Mitry distinguishes three levels of meaning in this scene. First, the pince-nez presents itself as a type of "glasses." I immediately recognize that this is a pince-nez, and the filmmaker is intentionally presenting it in a specific position and frame. Second, I contextualize the image within the film. I understand the human significance (that the detestable doctor was killed) of it. Third, due to the sequence's arrangement and the combination of the pince-nez image with those images that came before, as well as because of the composition, rhythm, and other resonances, the object in question becomes a symbol of the fragility of the doctor's social class and his downfall.

In other words, cinema is founded on the "production of new meanings," and in pursuing this goal, no stylistic procedure is more or less valid. Depth of field and long takes cannot be understood as the "zero degree" of cinematographic stylistics, as Bazin sometimes seemed to defend. For Mitry, on the contrary, these procedures are compositional. The author will define montage more broadly than any of the early theorists, including Eisenstein. The montage effect, which establishes relationships between images of objects and characters, is present when a scene is filmed in motion and without cuts. Mitry insists that editing can occur even in a single scene filmed from a fixed angle. It contains all the resources that provide context for isolated images. Through framing "the real can become an element of its own fabulation." In this sense, Mitry makes a comparison with the novel, in what is perhaps his most famous sentence: "The

---

[261] Ibid., 51.

novel is a narrative that organizes itself in the world, while cinema is a world that organizes itself into a narrative."[262]

His theoretical positions become even clearer when the author engages directly with some filmmakers and films. It is once again evident in these moments the importance placed on the presence of the world and the emphasis on formalist mediation. Additionally, there is the idea that meanings in a narrative should be portrayed as a "natural expression of things." A filmmaker selects specific elements of reality to construct his own cinematographic world. If he manages to harness the potential of his raw material, he can illuminate this world with meanings that extend beyond him. Great films share a complex world with us without ever preventing us from recognizing, in what we see, the reality we experience in our daily life. Mitry comments:

> There is no such thing as aesthetics in cinema if by that we mean a body of rules
> and regulations that govern the conditions of a film and the qualities that make
> it what it is. Interpreted in this way, aesthetic principles are conceivable only in
> terms of Art in the classical sense, that is, in terms of a form and representation
> whose elements, more or less stylized, are subject to laws and rules by reason
> of their own stylization or whose methods are constrained both by their object
> and by the processes they employ.[263]

Now, if no stylistic procedure can claim a natural privilege over the others, it would be expected that Mitry would also defend a broad pluralism with regarding cinematic structure and the legitimacy of all possible cinematic worlds and forms. However, that is not quite what happens. In fact, Mitry reserves some guidelines and limits for formalist activity. For him, the filmed events and their most immediate meaning should not be altered by analogies or metaphors. That's what Andrew summarizes so well: "Without this tension between a brute reality we always recognize and the human meaning it is made to speak anew in each film, the cinema loses its power."[264]

In this way, Mitry will critique any artificial construction that seeks to undermine the naturalness of the material captured by the camera. He will specially oppose expressionism and the French avant-garde. For Mitry, what is observed in these cases is an endeavor to adopt styles from arts forms other than cinema. The excessive preoccupation with creating an aesthetic world through framing obscures

---

[262] Mitry (1965, 354).

[263] Ibid., 453.

[264] Andrew (1976, 209–10).

the reality that these images, as analogues, should convey. The tension that Mitry seeks between the aesthetic and psychological aspects of the cinematographic image is diminished. In other words, the expressionists and the avant-garde would have abandoned the depiction of reality distancing themselves from the medium of cinema itself. Even Eisenstein will be put in check:

> *In a general way, as we have seen, Eisenstein based the meaning of montage upon an emotional shock produced by the collision of two images; and upon fragmentary representations whose sum and juxtaposition awakened in the audience's intelligence and emotions a final synthetic image, a symbolic idea, the very idea which obsessed the filmmaker himself. It is certain that the accidental juxtaposition of objects with no apparent association, the intensive nature of significations, and the condensation of ideas produced by emphasizing certain specific details exert a tremendous emotional influence. Nonetheless, though these poetic images become in a sense the 'emotional incarnation of the theme,' the idea must not mask the reality which generates and supports it; it must not be imposed by the arbitrary association of two images, by contrived relationships.*[265]

Mitry lists different types of montage and points out those that work against the vehicle, seeking abstract meanings without grounding them in concrete feelings. It is based on this conviction that he will attack the use of metaphors by the Russian filmmaker, particularly in *October* (*Oktyabr*, 1927). In this film, shots of a peacock are juxtaposed with those of Alexander Kerensky, the final prime minister of the Russian Provisional Government. This would be a purely abstract comparison for Mitry. It is what the author refers to as "defects of formalism in its excesses," which is curious: Although he is emphatic in his criticism of Bazin, Mitry also criticizes symbolism and thesis-cinema.

However, still on *October*, Mitry praises the juxtapositions of an equestrian statue and General Kornilov, the harpers, and the congress. The intellectual effect sought by Eisenstein is achieved immediately without compromising the logic of representation and the authenticity of facts. That is, it was not the principle that was wrong but rather its application. Bazin is aloof once again. At another point, Mitry considers the resources used in *Storm over Asia* (*Potomok Chingis-Khana*, 1928) acceptable. Vsevolod Pudovkin makes the scenes vibrate beyond a reasonable proportion by cutting them rhythmically in collages that add up to 100 shots.

[265.] Mitry (2000, 342–43).

This is precisely the kind of montage that Bazin condemned. For him, the use of this reflective montage would reduce the natural power of the image, subordinating the ambiguous natural meaning of the world to the abstract desire of the film-maker. Mitry, like Bazin, argues that cinema should constitute the presentation of a living reality that appears unfold freely. However, the author of *The Aesthetics and Psychology of the Cinema*, contrary to what Ismail Xavier points out, does not dwell on the notion of "ambiguity of the real." He does not attack it, but he also does not consider it as a center. For Mitry, there is no inherent sense of the world; instead, there are only the meanings we assign to our perceptions. Reflective montage, although it can operate in terms of a "biased" meaning, when used based on our perception of the world, can be as legitimate as any other technique. It can also collaborate in creating a more open and participatory cinema that engages freely with our imaginative faculties.

In this sense, Mitry's observations on the cinema of Jean-Luc Godard and Michelangelo Antonioni are intriguing. The author has his reservations about this modern cinema, but he appreciates the inclination of these filmmakers tendency to de-dramatizing and incorporate chance. It is the idea that the events represented do not occur as a result of a predetermined situation, following precisely what is written in a script. When dealing with the role of dialogues in a film, Mitry praises *Breathless* (*À Bout de Souffle*, 1960):

> *Thus, whether it is all-pervasive or otherwise, film dialogue must provide an impression of life which has been lived (or at least as it might have been lived in the given situation). Nothing is more irritating in the cinema than the 'author speaking' through the mouths of characters who would otherwise apparently be incapable of speaking in that particular way—at least in the given circumstances. This does not mean that film dialogue must be unstructured and banal: it must just be spontaneous. It must come out of the characters' mouths, not the actors' memories. Moreover, even in the most lively moments of conversation, characters must have the time to think about what they are going to say—as in real life [...] The so-called New Wave may be criticized for many things, but it must be admitted that the young directors have been able successfully to free themselves from the yoke of theatrical dialogue still in use in contemporary cinema. From this point of view, films such as Breathless are a step forward toward a complete abandonment of 'fabricated' text.*[266]

[266.] Ibid., 237.

This attempt to synthesize a formalist tradition, which was then in decline with the first references of phenomenology, the "openness to Being," and the notion that Being is only meaningful when I transform it, is very welcome. That does not mean that Mitry does not sometimes fall into the traps he intended to denounce—especially when it comes to Bazin. After all, while attempting to place all stylistic resources and procedures on the same hierarchy, Mitry ultimately establishes certain norms and limits and advocates for a particular type of cinema over others. It is a cinema that must respect my perception of the world, but also create another world, one that is more intense and offers a different perspective. For Mitry, reality only has the meanings I give to it: "Cinema doesn't allow the world's meaning to shine through. It shapes that reality and shakes it until it bears a human meaning, the only kind of meaning it can bear."[267]

In this way, when watching a film, I directly experience the filmmaker's worldview and become aware of a subjective and contingent meaning. Finally, cinema allows us to compare our perspectives and interpretations of the world, and to ascribe new meanings to our everyday reality, thereby enriching it. In a brief text regarding the impossibility of "reading" a film, the American essayist Tag Gallagher highlights the central point of the issue:

> I have no need of cinema to capture reality. There is more reality outside my window than in all the films ever made. What art provides is a sensibility toward reality. What is called Realism in cinema is not reality captured but the felt presence of the moviemaker, the dialectic between the subjective and the objective. A stone in a river has as much reality as the Parthenon in Athens. But what astonished me when I saw the Parthenon, what no picture of it had led me to expect, was the direct experience I felt of what is was like to be an Athenian in Pericles's day.[268]

What is once again glimpsed is the appreciation for the concept of experience. Mitry encourages me to immerse myself in a film, embracing the reality it creates and the experience it offers me. For him, the spectator does not learn to appreciate a film by comparing it to other films. "Like experiencing a person," says Gallagher, "Do I experience my wife Phoebe because she is Phoebe? or because of the ways she is or isn't like all the other human beings in the world?"[269] A film is both a representation and an event, at the same time. For this reason, it is

---

[267.] Andrew (1976, 210).

[268.] Gallagher (2001).

[269.] Ibid.

necessary to be careful when considering, for example, the conventions and aspects that form a genre, regardless of what it may be. Similarly, when I overestimate the interpretative frameworks we build around a film, I always run the risk of overlooking its artistic qualities. Mitry's great lesson, which he sometimes seems to forget, is that a theory valid for all films is useless. Following a film with a theory as a starting point would be like listening to music without rhythm.

These teachings are invoked when I encounter the seemingly impenetrable cinema of Hou Hsiao-Hsien. It is a form of realism that focuses on the phenomenon of experience, turning cinema into a space for organizing new sensory *stimuli*, shocks, and enjoyment. It aims to establish a search for a differentiated connection with reality. I am submitted, or led to submit myself, to a decoding of our perception, to a "revirginization" of the gaze, to a relearning of the very way of relating to a film. It is necessary to review the previous criteria of mise-en-scène, enunciation, actors' interpretation, audiovisual dramaturgy, and classifications such as documentary or fiction. Everything is in question and out of question. For the spectator, what is established is a relationship with the film that goes beyond cognition and becomes sensory as well. It is not, however, a matter of simply asserting the primacy of sensitivity to the detriment of the film's narrative or discursive functions. What is claimed is the recognition of a sensitive sense, of awareness of a perpetual cycle of movement, and of an ongoing quest that can never be completely fulfilled.

> *In the cinema, what must have priority is not the signified or the signification but the continuous passage from the nonsignified to the signified, the transition from the emotional to the intellectual through a constantly contingent signification. We have already expressed this essential truth in various diverse ways, considering it from different angles, and we cannot help but come back to it, since it is at the heart of every single aesthetic question in the cinema.*[270]

It would not be an exaggeration to go a few steps further and capture, in this excerpt, the conception of cinema as a celebration of the mysterious and tangible nature of visibility. More than just seeing an image, I see according to it, I see with it, through it. It directs the gaze toward what is not present. Things appear against the indeterminate background of the world, they are delineated from this background. What is not present, the invisible (an extremely important term for Merleau-Ponty's final philosophy), is the stuff of what is present, the visible.

---

[270] Mitry (2000, 239).

What is most interesting about Mitry is precisely the idea that the aesthetic process of cinema shares a powerful psychological reality and fulfills my desire to understand the world and each other in a necessarily partial way. For him, great films are those that manage to create meaning that goes beyond the surface level of the story or theme. Cinema is thus liberated from its connection with pure perception, also disconnected from a particular narrative, free to engage and stimulate my sensitive and imaginative faculties.

It is an extremely important lesson for this book, interested in walking through a contemporary cinema and its desire for the creation of a pre-logical regime. Hsiao-Hsien's work reveals a narrative awareness that presupposes a rather laborious composition. The starting point of his movies is almost always an unveiled, clear artifice. Although they propose conceptual experiences, his films emanate a sense of revelation and apprehension of reality that disarms me. They do not fall into the trap of believing in an immediate apprehension of reality; it must be reiterated. What is at stake is akin to embarking on an adventure with no guarantee of truth, a bending over things to listen to their silence and what is said in it. Look, how curious! Listening to the silence of things? Film is this wonderful form of a continuous overcoming of a paradox.

2.

Deleuze

Beyond Movement-Images and Time-Images

In the previous chapter, we explored a somewhat overlooked tradition of film theory. This tradition comes to my rescue when I find myself confronted with a certain contemporary cinema that avoids the most common modes of critical and theoretical approaches. It is precisely a differentiated way of looking at cinema that I encounter in the legacy left by authors such as André Bazin, Amédée Ayfre, Roger Munier, Maurice Merleau-Ponty, Michel Mourlet, and Jean Mitry. Each of these names, influenced by phenomenology, sought to understand how cinema connects us to the world and others.

The phenomenologically inspired film theory — recently resurrected, as we have seen, from various perspectives — offers me a mode of investigation that is based on the perceptive, sensual, affective, and aesthetic dimensions of the cinematographic experience. Critics influenced by phenomenology perceive cinema as a fundamentally new means of expressing the world in which I live and my own self. They reinforce the image as an amalgam of time and movement whose elements are absolutely interdependent and lose much of their significance when considered individually. They emphasize that the senses and meanings of a film do not solely arise from the narrative, dialogue, shots, and editing. Rather, they argue that these aspects are decisively shaped through a reversible, dialectical, and dialogical interplay between the film and the spectator, in a process of mutual constitution. That is what Bazin briefly evokes:

> *We can coldly isolate patterns in music or logic in dreams as does the psychoanalyst, but, more warmly, we can begin to live the rhythm of the music as an invitation to dance and to vibrate; and we can feel in it a sense, as an unveiling of the world expressed in the epiphany of the sensible.*[1]

[1.] Bazin and Agel (1973, 9).

We should make ourselves available to the cinema, says Bazin. Cinema has the power to move us from the detached rationality of logic into the realm of uncertainties and impermanence of experience. When I say "experience," I mean both the connection with reality and the ability to manage this connection. This is the cinematographic face favored by the authors discussed so far: cinema as a means of responding to the enigma of existence and the world through human, mechanical, and artificial creation. Since its inception, the seventh art has been regarded as a form of sensitivity and understanding. Film offers us moving images through which we can reconfigure the reality around us and our position within it. Cinema is not only a way of seeing but also a way of life.

Deleuze is nearby. After a long period of neglect, the French philosopher will revisit one of the central concerns of this tradition (he will pay, as we will see, a certain tribute to Bazin's thought, although he is tough in his criticism of phenomenology) and will become a watershed when he turns to film theory. His two books on the seventh art, widely read and discussed, have evolved from a somewhat dissenting view within the film studies community to a modern classic.

By setting aside epistemological questions about the image, the subject, language, and knowledge, Deleuze has certainly brought ontology back to the agenda, albeit with various criticisms and divergences in relation to some of the authors I have explored earlier, such as Bazin and Merleau-Ponty. Instead of thinking of cinema as a (misleading) epistemological practice that opposes true/false, appearance/being, and body/spirit, Deleuze envisions the seventh art as an integral part of life, open to the Bergsonian universe of energies, processes, becomings, and intensities. With Deleuze, cinema is essentially not about the production of meanings, processes of subjectivization, or identification, nor is it solely about the "representation of." Its objective is to contemplate movement and time beyond any subject/object or mind/matter division, as manifestations of life. It investigates the "gear," the operational logic of film-images.

Deleuze consistently engaged in a dialogue with diverse domains and objects, encompassing not only the philosophy of different eras but also the sciences and the arts. For him, philosophy is not about reflecting on cinema. Film is not a pretext for Deleuze. His philosophy does not aim to justify or legitimize cinema, but to promote intersections between both domains, always guided by a central question: What does it mean to think? The question of thought is not only found in philosophy, which does not hold exclusive privileges, but also in various arts and sciences. Cinema is then viewed as an internal and active ally. This is what Deleuze states when introducing *The Time-Image*:

> *In barren times philosophy retreats to reflecting 'on' things. If it's not itself creating anything, what can it do but reflect on something? So it reflects on eternal or historical things, but can itself no longer make any move. What we should in fact do, is stop allowing philosophers to reflect 'on' things. The philosopher creates, he doesn't reflect.*[2]

Philosophy is a creative process but a particular type of creation, because while science produces functions, and art creates sensations (affects and percepts), philosophy is carried out through concepts. These concepts often originate from other philosophers. This is evident in the case of Nietzsche and terms such as "will to power" and "eternal return"; Spinoza and "intensity" and "immanence"; and Henri Bergson and "actual," "virtual," and "duration." The metaphysics of the latter serves as a model for Deleuze's philosophy. In *The Movement-Image*, he explicitly refers to "Bergson's profound desire":

> *to produce a philosophy which would be that of modern science (not in the sense of a reflection on that science, that is an epistemology, but on the contrary in the sense of an invention of autonomous concepts capable of corresponding with the new symbols of science).*[3]

In this book, Deleuze also takes on and reorients the Bergsonian project:

> *a complete conversion of philosophy. It is what Bergson ultimately aims to do: to give modern science the metaphysic which corresponds to it, which it lacks as one half lacks the other. But can we stop once we have set out on this path? Can we deny that the arts must also go through this conversion or that the cinema is an essential factor in this, and that it has a role to play in the birth and formation of this new thought, this new way of thinking?*[4]

For Deleuze, cinema is a mode of thought. Film is not merely a platform for storytelling, where a universe unfolds as a world structured by the narrative, nor is

---

[2] Deleuze (1995, 122).

[3] Deleuze (1997, 60).

[4] Ibid., 7.

it a medium rooted in the materialist clash of montage, where the discrepancies of the world are replaced by the dialectical movement of immanent forces. Cinema is a way of thinking that is in tune with modern philosophy as it consistently explores two central themes: movement and time. Great filmmakers are akin to philosophers, as they think not through concepts but through images and sounds. Based on Bergson's philosophy of immanence and Charles Sanders Peirce's semiotics, Deleuze proposes a theory of moving images that can be interpreted as both a philosophy and a history of cinema. From Bergson, he emphasizes the primacy of movement, matter and time in the constitution of being and consciousness; and from Peirce, he incorporates a taxonomy and nomenclature to create a cinematographic map.

Deleuze's work is like an "essay in the classification of signs," resembling a "natural history." His goal is to create a taxonomy, which is a classification of cinematographic images and signs. He defines signs as "features of expression that compose and combine these images, and constantly re-create them, borne or carted along by matter in movement."[5] The signs are the components, the forming elements of an image. The concept of an image, on the other hand, is formed within a redescription of the ideas on movement found in *Matter and Memory*. An image contains the physical world of movement and the psychological world. It is not the double of things but the things themselves.

Unlike Bergson, who disliked film as an attempt to restore time through a succession of positions in space, Deleuze believes that, although movement is artificially produced by cinema, the spectator perceives it as "pure." If the means of recomposing the movement are artificial, the outcome is not. That is, the movement cannot be perceived as an addition to the image. It is always already in it. I perceive an image as movement, as a movement-image. "Image," says Deleuze, "is the set of what appears [...] Every thing, that is to say every image, is indistinguishable from its actions and reactions: this is universal variation,"[6] to be continued.

The images, or the set of what appears, do not merely support actions and reactions; they are inseparable from these actions and reactions in a world of universal variation. The universe is composed of moving images with eternal variation. This universe is material. Matter is the universe constituted by movement-images, acting and reacting among themselves, even before the distinction between bodies, qualities, and actions. In summary, starting from this identity, reinforced by

---

[5.] Deleuze (1989, 33).

[6.] Deleuze (1997, 58).

Bergson, between image and movement, Deleuze arrives at an identity between movement-image and matter: "This infinite set of all images constitutes a kind of plane of immanence. The image exists in itself, on this plane. This in-itself of the image is matter."[7]

The movement-image represents a cinema of perceptions, affections, and actions in which the sensory–motor scheme of the human body operates as a functioning unit. It is organized according to the logic of the sensory–motor scheme: an image conceived as an element of a natural chain with other images within a montage logic analogous to that of the final chain of perceptions and actions. For Deleuze, this is how classical cinema, especially Hollywood cinema until the 1950s, works. Classic cinema is made of movement-images because in it, the images act and react on each other, building an organic unit, a logical connection or, more specifically, linking perception and action through affection. These are, moreover, the three varieties of the movement-image.

In this way, the movement-image presents an indirect image of time according to a mechanism composed of perception-images, action-images, and affection-images. Deleuze points to a certain cinematographic shot for each of these types of images. The perception-image, which can be objective or subjective, implies the wide shot; the affection-image is the close-up, the foreground; and the action-image is marked by the medium shot. These images are always in a constant process of composition, connection, and agency. For instance, imagine character X spotting his enemy Y from a distance in a wide shot (image-perception). Y advances quickly toward X in a medium shot (action-image). I then see the face (affection-image) of X, waiting for the right moment to strike back. This is a common situation in classic Hollywood cinema, where action is fundamental, serving as the axis from which the other images are linked.

After presenting the three types of images that constitute the movement-image, Deleuze introduces the concept of another image whose relationship with thought is entirely different from the others: the mental image. "It is an image which takes as its object, relations, symbolic acts, intellectual feelings."[8] The philosopher credits Alfred Hitchcock as the main creator responsible for introducing the mental image in cinema, as in his films the action is characterized by a complex web of relationships that alter the theme, its nature, and its purpose. Hitchcock engages the spectator, who is always one step ahead of the characters, into the process of making the film. He takes a particularly shocking action and subjects it to a logical

---

[7] Ibid., 58–59.

[8] Ibid., 198.

chain of reasoning. Never mind how far-fetched some situations are (like the wind-mill turning the wrong way in *Foreign Correspondent* [1940] or the spray plane in *North by Northwest* [1959] appearing where there is nothing to be sprayed). Nor is the author of the action of interest, not even the action itself, but rather it is the set of relationships through which the action and its author are revealed. This new image serves as the culmination or realization of all the preceding images, framing and transforming them. "By including the spectator in the film, and the film in the mental image," underlines Deleuze, "Hitchcock brings the cinema to completion."[9]

At this moment, Deleuze begins to speak about a crisis of the action-image. In the mental image, perception no longer extends into action but is directly related to thought. It is no longer believed that a situation will lead to an action capable of modifying it, which raises doubts about the sensory–motor connections that make up the action-image. An announced crisis that encompasses social, economic, political, and moral dimensions: the war, the erosion of the "American dream," the growing awareness of minorities' issues, the pervasive influence of images in daily life, and the impact of new narrative forms explored by literature, the Hollywood crisis.

A new kind of image emerges, characterized by fragmented situations, in-tentionally delicate connections, and the awareness of *clichés,* which Deleuze identifies in post-war American cinema, outside of Hollywood, and particularly in Europe. However, Deleuze does not explain the new image using the five characteristics listed at the end of *The Movement-Image.* They are like external necessary conditions. If the crisis of the action-image is the negative condition for the emergence of the new image that requires more thought, the time-image only occurs with the emergence of pure optical and auditory situations:

> There is, therefore, a necessary passage from the crisis of image-action to the pure optical-sound image. Sometimes it is an evolution from one aspect to the other: beginning with trip/ballad films with the sensory-motor connections slackened, and then reaching purely optical and sound situations. Sometimes the two coexist in the same film like two levels, the first of which serves merely as a melodic line for the second.[10]

The so-called pure optical and sound situations are different from the sensory–motor situations, since they prevent perception from extending into action, directly

---

[9.] Ibid., 204.

[10.] Deleuze (1989, 3–4).

relating it to thought and time. These new situations arise with neorealism.[11] The films by Roberto Rossellini and Vittorio De Sica feature protagonists who register and observe more than they act. They are in contact with something intolerable and unbearable, a situation that is impossible to live with. It is too overwhelming, exceeding their sensory–motor capacities. The father and son in *Bicycle Thieves* and Karin from *Stromboli* (1950) do not know how to react and end up adopting a different perspective on the world around them. The character's perception, as well as our own, reaches a limit, capable of transcending the *clichés* that hinder us from forming a more direct relationship with reality.

I can hear Bazin between the lines. Deleuze values him. In a way, the philosopher provides the critic's intuitions and theoretical insights with a more theoretical foundation. By introducing pure optical and sound situations that no longer directly lead to action, neorealism signifies the emergence of a cinema of voyance or clairvoyance, which subordinates movement and presents a direct time-image. A visionary cinema that either replaces or enhances vision, as an exercise of the faculty of feeling, providing characters and us, spectators, with distinct, unpredictable, and revolutionary ways of resisting the world. We begin to realize, as is evident with the old man in *Umberto D.* and the bourgeois woman in *Europa '51* (1952), that sensory–motor schematics reproduce pre-programmed responses. For Deleuze, we exist in a world of *clichés*, and modern cinema can be seen as a quest for solutions.

> As Bergson says, we do not perceive the thing or the image in its entirety, we always perceive less of it, we perceive only what we are interested in perceiving, or rather what it is in our interest to perceive, by virtue of our economic interests, ideological beliefs and psychological demands. We therefore normally perceive only clichés. But, if our sensory-motor schemata jam or break, then a different type of image can appear: a pure optical-sound image, the whole image without metaphor, brings out the thing in itself, literally, in its excess of horror or beauty, in its radical or unjustifiable character, because it no longer has to be 'justified', for better or for worse [...] This was the problem with which Volume 1 ended: tearing a real image from clichés.[12]

Deleuze further explores the time-image by introducing the concept of the crystal-image. This is an image which pertains to the "order of time" and

---

[11.] Although neorealism is perhaps largely responsible for the dissemination of the new type of image, Deleuze draws special attention to Yasujirō Ozu, who first valued the importance of pure optical and sound situations, when the action-image disappears in favor of weak sensory–motor connections or a purely visual image.

[12.] Deleuze (1989, 20–21).

the coexistence or simultaneity of its elements. The crystal-image always implies a dynamic interplay between its two facets: the actual and the virtual, terms of Bergsonian origin. Deleuze argues that, unlike the movement-image, the time-image is virtual, or, rather, it represents a merging of the virtual and the actual. The image is no longer extended in motion and becomes an indivisible unit bridging its virtual and actual halves. They have different faces, but they are indiscernible. This is what the philosopher sees in a famous scene from *The Lady from Shanghai* (1947), by Orson Welles, when the multiplied mirrors absorbing the actuality of the two characters to the point that they can only reclaim it by breaking all the mirrors, ultimately finding themselves side by side and killing each other.

In the chapter "The Powers of the False," Deleuze distinguishes between the organic regime and the crystalline regime of the image based on description, narration, and narrative. An organic description assumes the independence of its object. The sets and exteriors must be placed independently of the camera's description. A crystalline description, in turn, is valid for its object, which simultaneously replaces, creates, and erases it. This is, for example, what we see in the films of Alain Resnais and Alain Robbe-Grillet, where descriptions of spaces give way to other descriptions that contradict, displace, or modify the preceding ones.

Moreover, unlike organic narration, where time is indirectly represented as a result from the action, crystalline narration involves a collapse of sensory–motor schemes. This collapse gives rise to pure optical and sound situations. Characters then become seers. The real in a feature like *Last Year at Marienbad* (*L'Année Dernière à Marienbad*, 1961) is no longer recognized for its continuity or coherence. The defining characteristic of the spaces depicted in this film is their inherently abnormal movements and non-localizable nature. Time ceases to be chronological; it becomes chronic. We cannot explain them in terms of space. It is no longer an indirect image of time in the prolongation of movement but a direct image from which movement results. "What aberrant movement reveals is time as everything, as 'infinite opening.'"[13]

Time then comes before movement. That is why Deleuze establishes a new status for narration: It ceases to be veridical, to aspire to truth, and to assert itself as falsifying. For Deleuze, it was the Nouvelle Vague that broke away from the concept of truth and instead emphasized the powers of life. This is because neorealism, in a certain sense, still maintained a connection to truth. The Nouvelle Vague, however, turns what Deleuze refers to as the "false" into the great character of cinema. It is no longer the criminal, the murderer, the hero, the powerful,

---

[13.] Ibid., 37.

the cowboy, the handsome, or the poor, as it was the case in the action-image. Instead, Deleuze talks about the faker, pure and simple, to the detriment of any and all action. It is the Robbe-Grillet principle that Deleuze is so fond of, "to avoid one of the true following consequences: either the impossible proceeds from the possible, or the past is not necessarily true."[14]

Falsifying narration evades the judgment system that organic narration still relies on. In other words, when confronted with the array of images from a Resnais film or the disarray of the judge's office in *The Lady from Shanghai*, it becomes especially difficult for the spectator to judge the characters. When the ideal of truth collapses, mere appearances will not be enough to imply a judgment. Deleuze explores Nietzsche's philosophy of truth and Bergson's concept of time to elucidate modern film narration. "What remains?" asks the French philosopher.

> *What remains? There remain bodies, which are forces, nothing but forces. But force no longer refers to a centre, any more than it confronts a setting or obstacles. It only confronts other forces, it refers to other forces, that it affects or that affect it. Power (what Nietzsche calls 'will to power' and Welles, 'character') is this power to affect and be affected, this relation between one force and others. This power is always fulfilled, and this relation is necessarily carried out, even if in a variable manner according to the forces which are present.*[15]

What interests Deleuze in cinema are those moments when we perceive the imperceptible, say the unspeakable, and think the unthinkable. This is what I see more specifically when Deleuze uses the expression "gestus" to account for filmmakers like Godard and John Cassavetes, who use the attitudes and postures of their characters as primary sources of intrigue, rather than the other way around. The term, coined by Bertold Brecht, does not refer to mere physical movements but rather a set of attitudes and postures. For the playwright, this combination of attitudes and postures that constitute the gestus should drive the story and narrative. Deleuze applies this idea to cinema. Gestus introduces time into the body, just as thought introduces life. It theatricalizes cinema images and undoes history, intrigues, and even space. " 'Give me a body then': this is the formula of philosophical reversal. The body is no longer the obstacle that separates thought from itself, that which it has to overcome to reach thinking."[16]

[14.] Ibid., 130.

[15.] Ibid., 139.

[16.] Ibid., 189.

At the end of *The Time-image*, we must ask whether one type of cinema could be seen as superior to the other. If we consider Deleuze's assertions that modern cinema is no "more important than the other, whether more beautiful or more profound,"[17] or that there is no hierarchy in terms of superiority between modern cinema and classical cinema, we can perhaps assume that the movement-image and the time-image equally pique the philosopher's interest. However, this is not my impression. There is a clear continuity between Deleuze's philosophy of difference and multiplicity and the modern cinema of which he was a contemporary. It is undeniable that Deleuze's time-image is much more suitable for expressing a philosophy of difference. Moreover, *the Time-Image* manifests sometimes a will that in *The Movement-Image* seemed restrained. Throughout the second volume, there is a noticeable overlap between philosophy and cinema. Classic cinema corresponds to classical philosophy, encompassing its modes of thinking, worldview, and great philosophers. In contrast, modern cinema reflects the revolution brought about by modern philosophy, represented by figures such as Nietzsche and Bergson.

Would it be more appropriate to consider the division between time-image and movement-image as a philosophical opposition? Jacques Rancière (2006) believes so. In fact, the very bifurcation between the two regimes of the movement-image and the time-image, which Deleuze links to the historical disruption of World War II, although clear in his statement, becomes somewhat obscure when we focus on the question of the relationship between an internal cut to the cinematographic images and the revolutions that mark the general history. It also becomes quite challenging to recognize in the actual films the evidence of this shift between two eras of the image. Rancière develops:

> The problem is no longer how to harmonize art history and general history since, strictly speaking, for Deleuze there is no such thing as art history or general history: all history is 'natural history.' Deleuze raises the 'passage' from one type of image to another to the level of a theoretical episode, the 'rupture of the sensory-motor link,' which he defines from within a natural history of images that is ontological and cosmological in principle. But how are we to think the coincidence of the logic of this natural history, the development of the forms of an art, and the 'historical' break marked by a war?[18]

[17.] Ibid., 270.

[18.] Rancière (2006, 108–109).

Deleuze forged an identity between image and movement. From there he arrived at an identity between the movement-image and matter. Finally, the philosopher reinforces that the material universe, matter, is light. That is to say, the combination of movements, actions, and reactions is like light being diffused. "The identity of the image and movement stems from the identity of matter and light. The image is movement, just as matter is light."[19] This reasoning is important because, contrary to Husserlian phenomenology, which saw consciousness as a beam of light illuminating things, Deleuze, following Bergson, believes that things themselves are already luminous. This is what Deleuze emphasizes every time he tells us that the "eye is in things"[20] or that "all consciousness is something."[21]

The Deleuzian perspective is highly original. Images are the things of the world. Cinema is another name for the world. Deleuze's taxonomy is actually a theory of elements about the diverse and historical combinations of beings. What constitutes the image is not exactly the gaze, imagination, mise-en-scène, or montage. The image is luminous by itself. It is matter-light in motion. As Bergson said in *Matter and Memory* (2006), photography, if it exists, has already been captured within the very essence of things.

Let us see, however, what Deleuze says about Dziga Vertov's cinema:

> *What montage does, according to Vertov, is to carry perception into things, to put perception into matter, so that any point whatsoever in space itself perceives all the points on which it acts, or which act on it, however far these actions and reactions extend.*[22]

Rancière identifies a complex contradiction in this passage. Now, why is it necessary to direct perception to things if, theoretically, it should already be there? First, the perceptive properties of an image are only potentialities for the philosopher. They must be extracted and removed from the cause-and-effect relationships that give rise to them. The true artist is the one who creates a plane of immanence that frees the bodies from the chains of action and reaction that mark them. Second, things lose their phosphorescence. The human brain is often the culprit, positioned between cause and effect, action and reaction, consistently asserting itself as the focal point of the world. In this way, the quintessential

---

[19] Deleuze (1997, 60).

[20] Ibid.

[21] Ibid.

[22] Ibid., 81.

cinematographic operation would be one of restitution, giving back to the world its essential and disordered multiplicity.

Would this operation not be present in both the affection-image and at the basis of the rupture through which the crystalline time-image is born? Just think of Robert Bresson. His "whatever-spaces," where pure events predominate, serve as an example in the affection-image chapter. Furthermore, in *The Time-Image*, Bresson is remembered for restoring the potential of spaces, for his approach to connecting them, and for redefining the relations between the optical and tactile. The films mentioned are the same in both books. That is, at times it seems impossible to separate the seemingly opposite properties of movement-images and time-images. This leads me to conclude, in agreement with Rancière, that the movement-image and the time-image may not be two opposing types of images, associated with two cinema eras, "but two different points of view on the image." *The Movement-Image* "analyzes the forms of cinematographic art as events of the image-matter." *The Time-Image* "analyzes these same cinematographic forms as forms of thought-image."[23]

It would be possible to analyze any film in terms of movement-image or time-image. The first concerns the materiality of the image, a specific mode of appearance. The second corresponds to the image as a subject of thought, from the perspective of its ideality. *The Movement-Image* presents us with the endless chaos of matter-light transformations that characterize the cinematographic image. *The Time-Image* demonstrates how thought can harness power amidst this chaos. Cinema, as a restorative and redemptive process, aims to reprint images in their original order. Thus, the elements that Deleuze lists as characteristic of the time-image, such as the false *raccord*, the aberrant movement, and the falsifying narration, do not precisely indicate a rupture between two image regimes (one governed by the logic of association, conceived according to the movement between action and reaction; and another where the gap predominates, in which each image departs from life and returns to it) but rather the different ways in which thought operates to equalize the chaos that originates it.

If we revisit Deleuzian thought, we find that the crisis of the movement-image is evident in Alfred Hitchcock's cinema with the emergence of the mental image. The master of suspense synthesizes movement-image cinema by privileging relationships over action, perception, and affection. With him, following Deleuze, the movement-image reaches a state of exhaustion. In other words, the epitome of the movement-image is equivalent to its exhaustion, to the moment when it enters

---

[23.] Rancière (2006, 112).

a crisis, disrupting sensory–motor schemes and imposing a world of sensations. Now, when Deleuze attempts to pinpoint the manifestation of this crisis in the tangible aspects of a work, he turns to a symbolic element: Jeff's paralysis in *Rear Window* (1954) or Scottie's vertigo in *Vertigo* (1958).

However, the motor issues experienced by Hitchcock's characters do not prevent the progression of images into a chain of actions and reactions. In contrast, Jeff's paralysis and Scottie's vertigo are narrative elements of the utmost importance for the stories being told. They are somewhat like prerequisites for the intrigue. We see Scottie suspended in the void. We see Jeff paralyzed. However, these images influence subsequent actions and reactions. They are integral to a grand scheme, enhancing the interplay of mental connections and sensory–motor situations that unfold throughout the films. "The only remaining alternative is to consider the paralysis symbolic," says Rancière, "these fictional situations of paralysis as simple allegories emblematic of the rupture in the action-image and its principle: the rupture of the sensory-motor link."[24]

What I understand from this explanation is a relentless effort of restore, pulling the bodies out of pre-established schemes and placing them in a realm of pure events, in the margin of the actual and the virtual, of non-specific spaces, and a non-linear concept of time. "The gesture that frees the potentialities remains, as always, the gesture that chains them up again. The rupture is always still to come, like a supplement of intervention that is simultaneously a supplement of disappropriation."[25] In this sense, one of the first examples of the crystal-image mentioned by Deleuze, in *L'inconnu* (1927), by Tod Browning, offers Rancière a peculiar allegory regarding the endless process of rupture of the sensory–motor link. The hero of the film hides from the police in a circus and pretends that he has no arms. He falls in love with an Amazon woman who has an aversion to the hands of men, and ends up having her arms amputated.

> *If L'inconnu is an emblem of the crystal-image, the exemplary figure of the time-image, it is not because of properties specific to the shots and their assemblage, but because the film allegorizes the idea that artistic activity is a surgery of thought: the thought that creates must always self-mutilate, amputate its arms, in order to thwart the logic by which it invariably takes back from the images of the world the freedom that it restitutes to them. Amputating the arms means undoing the coordination between the eye that has all the visible at its disposal*

[24.] Ibid., 116.

[25.] Ibid., 118.

and the hand that coordinates the visibilities under the power of a brain that imposes its centralizing logic.[26]

It is precisely an operation of restitution that interests me in a certain contemporary cinema. A cinema of actions, characters, and intrigues but which strips itself of the more traditional anchoring anchors of these terms, creating instead a more sensory form of audiovisuality. A cinema that explores the relationship between the body and the world within an experience of time as atmosphere, triggering a multiplicity of sensitive states. In a seemingly paradoxical blend of empirical savagery and devices with unique artistic properties, a certain lost paradise of the visible and audible is restored. When dealing, for example, with the cinema of Apichatpong, Oliveira Jr. resorts to a notion that precedes the concepts of scene, shot, or language: intensity "(an element not measurable except enigmatically, at the same time the first and the last possible link between the image and what it represents), the not-yet-instituted."[27]

Apichatpong creates a backdrop of immanence to which nothing is alien. A dog lying on the street. The strange smile of an acquaintance. A movie session. A truck ride. Fireflies illuminating a tree. They are like incompatible but coexisting pieces of life, removed from a specific and determining space-time, and placed in a plan before the action. There is an interdependence between narrative and the installation of sensory states. What is being sought is the world before my conscience deciphers it. This quest has reached a level where distinctions between terms and natures are no longer made, and images strive primarily to enchant us with their sensory power, portraying a continuous birth of the world. A search that, therefore, also requires creativity to articulate.

Deleuze is important to me because he challenges the traditional fable of the blind man and the paralytic: The filmmaker's perspective should be tactile, identifying with the blind man's gaze as he feels his way to coordinate the elements of the visible world. What is perhaps most intriguing in the philosopher's cinematographic work, beyond the division between the movement-image and the time-image, is the depiction of a primordial dialectic inherent in cinema between what is thought and what is unthought. Deleuze speaks of a "birth of the visible, which is still hidden from view."[28] Cinema has the ability to elevate the faculty of feeling to a certain threshold of intensity, freeing it from the schemes

---

[26.] Rancière (2000, 119).

[27.] Oliveira Jr. (2008).

[28.] Deleuze (1989, 201).

that create it and allowing us to imagine new forms of life and a new type of relationship between man and the world.

In the end, Deleuze is driven by the desire to restore faith in the world and re-explore the potential of the body. Deleuze, inspired by Antonin Artaud in particular, appreciates a certain powerlessness at the core of thought. It would be precisely this that compels us to think, marking our bond with the world. Cinema would reveal this powerlessness. Deleuze argues that it is essential to have faith in the human-world connection, to make treat this connection as an object of belief, something that was lost with the organic representation and the subsequent rupture caused by the time-image. This bond can only be re-established by faith, not in some transcendence but through a faith that is inherent in this world. For Deleuze, modern cinema revolves around the idea of restoring man's belief in the world. "What it produces," he says, "is the genesis of an 'unknown body' which we have in the back of our heads, like the unthought in thought."[29]

The question, as the philosopher explains through Jean-Louis Schefer and his *L'Homme Ordinaire du Cinéma* (1980), is not about the presence of bodies but rather about describing the ways in which cinema can restore the world and body from their absence. Cinema does not aim to recreate the presence of the bodies but rather to initiate and set in motion a fundamental genesis of the bodies in the pursuit of the visible that is not yet either figure or action.

What the late Merleau-Ponty seeks is not very different: a return to perceptive faith. From an unshakable commitment to sensitive certainties, he aims to suspend the instrumental view of the world, breaking with the philosophical tradition of the starting point and leading the philosopher to relinquish his sovereignty, in order to restore the experience as an initiation into the mysteries of the world. For the phenomenologist, painting does not reproduce the object perceived by the sense of sight but rather brings the invisible into visible existence, as per the well-known saying of Paul Klee, also cherished by Deleuze: "It makes visible," that is, it enables us to see the visible.

> *That there are no lines visible in themselves, that neither the contour of the apple nor the border between field and meadow is in this place or that, that they are always on the near or the far side of the point we look at. They are always between or behind whatever we fix our eyes upon; they are indicated, implicated, and even very imperiously demanded by the things, but they themselves are not things. They were supposed to circumscribe the apple or the meadow, but the*

---

[29] Ibid.

apple and the meadow 'form themselves' from themselves, and come into the visible as if they had come from a pre-spatial world behind the scenes. Yet this contestation of the prosaic line is far from ruling out all lines in painting, as the impressionists may have thought. It is simply a matter of freeing the line, of revivifying its constituting power; and we are not faced with a contradiction when we see it reappear and triumph in painters like Klee or Matisse, who more than anyone believed in color. For henceforth, as Klee said, the line no longer imitates the visible; it 'renders visible'; it is the blueprint of a genesis of things.[30]

So, how can we not notice several similarities between Deleuze and many of the phenomenologically inspired authors discussed here? It is no small thing: the intention to extract concepts from the films, being attentive to the questions and problems posed by the images; the development of a theory that maintains a search effect; the notion of restitution, valued by Roger Munier, Michel Mourlet, and the late Merleau-Ponty; the Bazinian idea of "mummification," which now seems absolutely Deleuzian to me; an image as a dynamic principle endowed with certain powers and potentialities that generate forms of life and thought; the image as an indivisible, undecidable amalgam that gives birth to the world, radiates it, reorganizing the concrete and the abstract, the animated and the in-animate, the actual and the virtual, the visible and the invisible, the general and the particular; and cinema as an art that makes the space and light speak, not an appreciation or a judgment of the world but belief and faith in its continued birth.

How can I avoid being swept away by the resonances between Merleau-Ponty and Deleuze? I can sense the presence of their philosophies and respective invest-ments in film theory throughout the affective and sensory upheavals that took the seventh art form by storm. I admit, however, that this assertion is far from obvious, not only because it contradicts Michel Foucault's well-known interpretation[31] but also because of the manner in which Deleuze himself described his con-nection with Merleau-Ponty specifically, and with phenomenology in general. Deleuze, in fact, rarely discusses Merleau-Ponty. In all of his books, there are only a dozen or so references, and they are almost always negative. Perhaps it is fair to say that the author of *Phenomenology of Perception* did not interest him very much. Furthermore, although Deleuze published his first text on Bergson in *Les philosophes célèbres*, edited by Merleau-Ponty, there was never, as far as

---

[30] Merleau-Ponty (1964c, 183).

[31] Foucault once claimed that Deleuze's *Logic of Sense* (1993) "can be read as the furthest possible book from *Phenomenology of Perception*" (1977, 170).

is known, any other significant contact between the two — nonetheless, another philosophical authority, closer to Deleuze, Paul Virilio,[32] said in an interview that the author of *The Movement-Image* had enormously appreciated Merleau-Ponty's last and unfinished book, *The Visible and the Invisible*.

In general, most authors, including some contemporary ones, bearing in mind, like Deleuze, only the first phase of Merleau-Ponty's work, usually reproduce the same argument. While Merleau-Ponty views sensation and affect as subjective phenomena that stem from an intentional and individualized connection with the world, Deleuze regards the sensational and the affective as material flows whose individuation and exchange are not based on subjective intentions but rather on the operation of an anonymous and non-organic force or life. However, does this criticism really stand up to scrutiny? Does Merleau-Ponty truly perceive time as the neutral framework that one must assume in order to contemplate the shift from one existentially established Gestalt to another?[33] Upon closer examination, is it not possible to identify moments in the cinema books where Deleuze himself adopts the phenomenological method and concepts?[34]

It is true that there are differences between them — especially regarding the philosophical principles that drive these authors' forays into the seventh art. Focusing on perception as an embodied and rooted experience, Merleau-Ponty identified a convergence between phenomenology and cinema, highlighting a shared goal of prompting us to relearn how to see the world. Deleuze envisioned cinema not as a mere reflection or reproduction of something that already exists but rather as the emergence of a visionary critical activity, open to the Bergsonian universe of energies, processes, and intensities. He sees images on an immanent plane beyond a perceiving subject. The image exists in itself as a luminous matter. Deleuze is absolutely right: A foundationalist face embarrasses Merleau-Ponty's initial phenomenology. It is true that the phenomenological approach emphasizes the interaction, continuity, and transition between the filmmaker, cinema, and spectator. However, Merleau-Ponty is always seeking a level where these terms become intertwined. That is to say: If, on the one hand, there are differences, on the other, it does not seem to me that the approaches

---

[32.] Virilio (1997, 42).

[33.] In an instigating work, Judith Wambacq (2017) brings Deleuze and Merleau-Ponty closer together through the intercession of Bergson, an author that both knew and quoted widely.

[34.] Boaz Hagin (2011) follows precisely this hypothesis: Phenomenology is not absent from Deleuze's Bergsonian taxonomy of images. Furthermore, he says: "Access to movement-images depends on the spectator's experience, not on the mere existence of strips of celluloid or a meditation on Bergson's philosophy of images in *Matter and Memory*" (Hagin 2011, 278–79).

and concepts that Merleau-Ponty and Deleuze employ when they engage with cinema are necessarily mutually exclusive. Quite the opposite.

The most significant argument in favor of the resonance between the two thinkers must be, at least initially, philosophical. In general, both thinkers could be united by the same project. Both of them examined the conditions of thought, indicating that their motivations are not strictly epistemological. Their main focus is not on the empirical causes of thought. Deleuze and Merleau-Ponty do not dedicate much time to discussing, for example, the principles by which thought operates, or should operate, to attain truth. The central question of his works revolves around what must be presupposed for a phenomenon such as thought to be possible. Their projects are both guided by immanence.

An ontological consequence of this is that if the condition is to be situated within the conditioned, it cannot belong to a being that is fundamentally different from the being of the conditioned. Thus, Deleuze and Merleau-Ponty reject the classical idea of the transcendental condition and its inherent dualism. The condition is no longer associated with the perfect, infinite, immutable, or original; nor does it continue to oppose the imperfect, finite, changeable, secondary nature of the conditioned. Both thinkers reject this dualism in favor of an immanent being, a being without hierarchy and fundamental differences. Judith Wambacq adds:

> Moreover, both understand the relation between the condition and the conditioned as a relation of expression: the essence, which is how the condition is often understood, is expressed by or in the conditioned. As we will see, this suggests that the ontological primacy of the condition is complemented by the epistemological primacy of the conditioned, and also that the ontological power is distributed over the condition and the conditioned.[35]

Neither Deleuze nor Merleau-Ponty view this immanence of being as the annihilation of difference. This is well known in Deleuze's case—he is, after all, the thinker of difference—but Merleau-Ponty, contrary to what Deleuze himself sometimes implied, is not far behind. There is no denying, for example, that Merleau-Ponty's ontology focuses more on immanence than on difference, as is the case with Deleuze. Their styles are also quite different: Merleau-Ponty's writing is smooth and poetic, especially when compared to Deleuze's more dry and polemical prose. It does not seem to me, however, that such variations in focus and style also encompass a more significant difference.

---

[35] Wambacq (2017, 3).

In fact, in *Foucault*, a book after his cinematographic volumes, Deleuze himself acknowledges some of the implications that the development of Merleau-Ponty's philosophy brought to phenomenology. Deleuze connects Foucault to Heidegger and Merleau-Ponty through the theme of the fold, and suggests that these philosophers went beyond intentionality by exploring the fold of being, or phenomenology as an ontology. "It is even this twisting which defines 'Flesh,'" says Deleuze, who even goes so far as to describe the problematic of the fold in Merleau-Ponty in the same way he had done when he explained it in Foucault: "An Outside, more distant than any exterior, is 'twisted', 'folded' and 'doubled' by an Inside that is deeper than any interior, and alone creates the possibility of the derived relation between the interior and the exterior."[36] For Deleuze, phenomenology—in order to exorcise the psychologism and naturalism that continued to mark it—surpassed intentionality as a relationship between consciousness and its object (the entity). In Heidegger and then in Merleau-Ponty, the overcoming of intentionality occurred toward the Being, the fold of the Being. Deleuze comments:

> *The surpassing of intentionality tended towards Being, the fold of Being. From intentionality to the fold, from being to Being, from phenomenology to ontology [...] It was Merleau-Ponty who showed us how a radical, 'vertical' visibility was folded into a Self-seeing, and from that point on made possible the horizontal relation between a seeing and a seen.*[37]

And so, another connection emerges: According to Deleuze and Merleau-Ponty, art is rooted in the invisible forces that shape our world. The first writes: "In art, and in painting as in music, it is not a matter of reproducing or inventing forms, but of capturing forces."[38] The second agrees: Painting, he says, "gives visible existence to what profane vision believes to be invisible."[39] It is noteworthy that they both reference Cézanne. For Deleuze, Cézanne does not depict the likeness of a mountain but rather the active folding force of a mountain. He does not even paint what an apple looks like but rather the germinating force of the apple. Merleau-Ponty, for his part, praises Cézanne for not painting an apple by simply determining its contours and fixing its essence but rather by considering the ideal contour or boundary to which the sides of the apple recede in depth.

---

[36] Deleuze (2006, 110).

[37] Ibid.

[38] Deleuze (2003, 56).

[39] Merleau-Ponty (1964c, 166).

These connections resonate everywhere regarding cinema. The philosophies of Merleau-Ponty and Deleuze and their implications for film theory are closely intertwined in many ways. Both Merleau-Ponty's phenomenology and Deleuze's transcendental empiricism dismantle epistemological systems that rely on non-corporeal acts of signification or cognition. The attempt to establish a distinct boundary between subject and world, perception and perceived reality, and subjective and objective experience is equally suspended and consequently undermined by both thinkers. Since both philosophies propose a continuity between the human body and the world, a sensational and affective approach to the world tends to replace the purely mental and visual methods of the disembodied cogito.

This is the kind of cinema that Deleuze envisions and that the late Merleau-Ponty, in his analysis of painting and vision, evokes for me: a cinema that expresses the longing to renew trust in the world and reencounter the potential of a body facing the unthinkable. Deleuze and Merleau-Ponty are interested in the cinema's ability to reveal everything that is presented to it and only what is presented to it. The seventh art suggests the possibility of a more consistent and enduring rediscovery of the world. It emphasizes the world as that which defies world-views, eludes theories and perspectives, and separates itself from any effort to depict it as a specific entity, confining it within a gaze, an idea, a theory. Cinema underlines this condition of the world and engages with it. In that sense, I say: Film is an ontological event.

It is true that the authors inspired by phenomenology who guided me through these pages, sometimes fall into various traps. They emphasize, at certain moments, the concept of representation, the belief in the possibility of an objective image of the world, and the supposedly more realistic nature of one aesthetic or strategy. The trap that the term "representation" imposes is something that really permeates the work not only of Bazin but also of Ayfre, Mourlet, and even Mitry. These authors, at times, seem to describe reality as a kind of second nature or the secondary nature of a film. However, the concept of representation employed, particularly as used by Bazin, ends up becoming confused with the thing it represents. What persists is the belief in the image as a constant antagonism between the unity of the thing represented and its countless potentialities, a duality between being and appearing, the concrete and the abstract, the immanent and the transcendent. These elements complement and combine each other, justifying themselves in a formal unit, that is, the image. This means that, in a candid confrontation with films, Bazin equips me with the necessary tools to overcome all these questions, envisioning cinema in its ontological bet, in the emergence of the image as a world. Is not that exactly what Bazin has in mind when he talks about *Umberto D.*?

> *The function of the subject is here no less essential than the story but its essence is reabsorbed into the scenario. To put it another way, the subject exists before the working scenario, but it does not exist afterward. Only the 'fact' exists which the subject had itself forecast. If I try to recount the film to someone who has not seen it-for example what Umberto D is doing in his room or the little servant Maria in the kitchen, what is there left for me to describe? An impalpable show of gestures without meaning, from which the person I am talking to cannot derive the slightest idea of the emotion that gripped the viewer.*[40]

Bazin ties cinema to the presence of the world in the immediacy of the instant. For him, it is through the experience of cinema and cinema as an experience, that is, it is through images — understood as the temporal mobility of the world and the process of reversible constitution that unites the spectator and the images in their unfolding — that the seventh art can put us in the same terms as reality. Bazin and the other authors who brought me here, each in their own way, bet on a return to experience. Experience is more than just a concept. It is also what is at stake. It has the power to open us up to what is beyond ourselves. It is an exercise in exploring what has not yet been subjected to subject-object separation. It is the potential for a promiscuity of things, bodies, words, and ideas. Cinema, therefore, is not simply a copy or an illusion of reality but rather its ever-present potential for a continued birth of the world.

With the assistance of Deleuze, Merleau-Ponty, and Bazin, I envision an ontological approach to cinema on the horizon that challenges all dichotomies and guides us toward a distinctive experience of disorientation at the core of the most familiar experiences. It is a meticulous and serious undertaking, always to be resumed. The image is an amalgam that fills the world, reorganizing the abstract and the concrete, the animated and the inanimate, the real and the virtual, the general and the particular, demanding a new classification of what exists, that is, a new ontology. The image as a dynamic principle endowed with certain powers that engender forms of life and thought. Cinema molds rather than reflects reality. Cinema does not shed light on a reality that already exists but rather illuminates a reality that is in the process of taking shape.

---

[40] Bazin (2005b, 77).

Ontology here means the possibility of restoring an original articulation of the sensible and the sense. Each image carries such potential. Every image may convey meanings and identities and spread similarities without meaning or origin. The image knows no structuring lack, no primordial division but a conflicting continuity. A film must be seen as the founder of its own reality. Each film demands from us a thought that does not retreat despite the uncertain and ambivalent experience that connects us esthetically, emotionally, and sensually, with the world.

It is this gaze that the contemporary cinema of Hou Hsiao-Hsien, Tsai Ming-Liang, Claire Denis, Pedro Costa, and Apichatpong Weerasethakul seems to require from me. It is a cinema that does not completely disregard the conventions and expectations that we are accustomed to when watching and contemplating a movie. After all, there are characters and stories that are often associated with concepts of film genre, pop music, and so on. In films such as *Goodbye South, Goodbye*, *The River*, *Good Work*, and *Tropical Malady*, bodies fade and disappear, illuminated and darkened, interwoven in fluctuating degrees of sounds, words, colors, and all sorts of fluids. They are distorted, impenetrable, phantoms, devoid of character, and sometimes even annoyingly gifted. These films compose bodies dynamically, in one movement, shot by shot, frame by frame, and scene by scene. They transition from a line of light to shape a volume, then a body, and, eventually, a character. At any of these stages, the process can be abstracted, revised, expanded, or distorted.

These elements, however, appear to have either dissipated or surged in the end. I constantly feel as though I am surrounded by paradoxes: a specular, carnal cinema, which works taking the shot as a unit of dramaturgy and as a practice of the gaze and which operates conceptually but also through fleeting affects, real and unreal, material and immaterial, truthful and fictional, all at the same time. Representation, for example, is not exactly denied. That is no longer the issue. Hsiao-Hsien, Tsai, Denis, Costa, and Apichatpong clearly operate within a certain radicalization of modern cinema and a distinct return to film origins and tradition, revisiting some fundamental questions such as: Why do we make images? What are they worth? What real can animate them? The French filmmaker Philippe Grandrieux, for example, speaks of a certain requirement, of a dynamic that seeks to return to the deepest and most obscure sources of the desire for representation. He says:

> *What do we seek, since the first traces of hands impressed in rock the long, hallu-*
> *cinated perambulation of men across time, what do we try to reach so feverishly,*

with such obstinacy and suffering, through representation, through images, if not
to open the body's night, its opaque mass, the flesh with which we think—and
present it to the light, to our faces, the enigma of our lives.[41]

Grandrieux refers to an image with no apparent face value, which preserves a
kind of fascination that cinema has not seen for some time and requires a different
attitude from us. Before understanding, one must see. This is not a decryption. A
film must achieve a consistency, insisting on itself, opening up, exposing itself,
and generating life. It is a certain opacity of the vision's thought that is under
debate: an experience that is irreducible to generalization, which, precisely
because it is beyond our possibilities, forces us to think.

In this book, I outline—still admittedly preliminary—a way of seeing and
venturing through cinema in its continued renaissance, as a creative experience,
of belief in the world, which differs significantly from analyses more centered on
notions such as narrative or mise-en-scène. In this way, instead of the history or the
structure of events, instead of a study of the shots and frames, the aim is to capture
the instituting as creation. In other words, something less "formal," since the starting
point is the bodies of characters, things and the relationships established between
them; less "visual," in the sense of not being limited by the search for meanings
and intentions in each visual arrangement; less interested in specific movements or
scenes, but more attentive to the ways in which films invent in the communion of
their elements, in a flux and reflux, a chain that corresponds to a kind of dawn of the
world. Nicole Brenez summarizes with a poetic verve that is very particular to her:

> *The image is no longer given as a reflection, discourse, or the currency of what-*
> *ever absolute value; it works to invest immanence, using every type of sensation,*
> *drive and affect. To make a film means descending, via the intermittent pathways*
> *of neuronal connection, down into the most shadowy depths of our sensory expe-*
> *riences, to the point of confronting the sheer terror of the death drive (Sombre),*
> *or the still more immense and bottomless terror of the unconscious, of total*
> *opacity [...] To confront the unknowable, precisely what we don't want to know:*
> *because cinema is based upon the linking and unlinking of images, it can risk*
> *this. Nothing is nobler than to shatter a film upon such an ambition, such belief,*
> *such confidence: the cinema can manifest everything, it can be vertiginous like a*
> *coma, pitiless like a Hobbes treatise, limpid like the spectrograph of a corpse.*[42]

---

[41] Grandrieux and Brenez (2003).

[42] Brenez (2003).

What I'm looking for is an adequate formal exploration of how a film's unique power of evocation can operate—that which, in Brenez's words, "rediscover its solidity, its fruitfulness, its fragility, its own density or possible opacity, in short, its problematic virtues."[43] It is a cinema that makes me recognize myself as a finite being in front of a universe of things whose possibilities are infinite. We are never truly able to apprehend these possibilities, but the films led me to admit their existence, beyond our hypotheses, arguments, and theories. How can one approach experience in the sense in which it resounds in this exclamation, that is, before being invaded by words that judge and distribute what belongs to the subject and what belongs to the object? It is, without a doubt, an adventure, and adventures do not usually go well with general assumptions. More than that. There is no adventure without risk!

The notion of plasticity, dear to Brenez, proves to be a useful consideration. A character is not a solid and definitive three-dimensional being. In some cases, like the contemporary cinema that interests me, you must look at it more as a silhouette, a project, a form. Everything is plastic in the cinema. People, plot, and meaning are discontinuous in a film. Emotions are plastic. Thought is a very plastic thing. "Plastic," as an adjective, means two things: on the one hand, being "susceptible to changes in shape" or malleable (clay is a "plastic" material); and, on the other hand, "having the power to give form, the power to mold," as in the expressions "plastic surgeon" and "plastic arts." Plasticity describes what is "plastic," being at the same time capable of receiving and giving form. Everything can be deformed, distorted, erased, and retouched. Everything is in a kind of formation process. It is up to us to pursue this process.

Now, it is time to go back to the films of Denis, Costa, Tsai, and Apichatpong. I walk with them with these previous pages in the rearview mirror, with the conviction that the cinematographic image asserts itself in the reversibility of its elements, figure and background, character and body, these and the setting, light and shadow zones, documentary and fiction, narration and installation, and so on. Without one, there is no other, and the absence of one raises the presence of the other. The body proves to be a useful guideline. I will be attentive to what it manifests, in an experience of a certain emptiness but also of excess. Denis opens up a path of transgression through sensation. Costa proposes aesthetic figures that assert themselves politically. Tsai makes the carnal exploration of the world his own thing. Apichatpong claims a certain nameless and privilegeless experience.

Come with me, my friends!

[43.] Brenez (2023, XI).

3.

A Certain Contemporary Cinema

3.1 Claire Denis

Transgression by Sensation

In the darkness of the night, a beautiful young woman lights a cigarette in a medium shot. She gives us a confident, somewhat challenging gaze. The slightly bluish image causes light and dark to fight. In the background, there is the trunk of a tree. We are in a forest. We hear a little of it. Off, a female voice: "Your worst enemies are hiding inside, hiding in the shadows, hiding in your heart." Black screen. Credits. An open, bright, and colorful shot, in stark contrast to the preceding image, shows us a customs booth. It is a border. An agent walks. Another reads a newspaper. The camera pans up to reach the French flag and continues without cutting to the Swiss flag. A car approaches and stops at the guardhouse. A close-up shot taken with a handheld camera. Another beautiful young woman questions the driver. A dog searches the car, seems to find something, and hears praises from the agent, who ultimately plays with the dog. Through a frontal view of a building, we see two windows of the same apartment are visible. Through one of them, we see a shirtless man at the top of a ladder painting a wall. The children babble on. One of them starts to cry. The shot brings us closer to the man who comes down the stairs and meets the children. As he leaves our field of vision, the camera tries to follow him, and he soon returns with a child in his arms. He goes back for the other one. This time, we follow him. He lifts the baby, who was wet. They are having a bath. The man wraps the child in a towel and takes him to the other child. He bottle-feeds both of them at the same time. Another handheld camera. The customs agent arrives at the house. She smiles. The man, her husband, plays with her, taking the gun from her belt and kissing her to the sound of babies in the background. Cut. She washes the dishes. Sitting behind her, he looks at her as if she was up to something. An erotic game begins between the two. He asks if she can hear his voice and paints a scenario for her to imagine. "A dark, hostile pine forest," he says. "You feel your belt weighing you down. Your gun is holstered on your hip. Your throat is dry. You're on a hunt." The woman drops the cutlery and sponge into the sink. The camera shows her hands and rises to her face. Her eyes are closed. He approaches from behind. A very close shot frames her neck and his mouth. Her breathing takes over the soundtrack. The frame opens. The camera floats. He whispers "one, two, three," unbuttons her shirt, and removes her pants. We see her bottom. He sits down and takes off his shorts. He asks her to sit down. She obeys. The two groan. Cut. She remains on his lap. One of the babies wakes up. We hear him. They laugh. A detailed shot of the baby monitor. A shot of the baby in the crib. With his eyes closed, he moves his arms, legs, and head. Cut. We tilt back down to the dark forest. A song wins the soundtrack with a minimalist mix of synthesizer and two guitar chords. A group of people is seen hiding. They run across the board, first horizontally and then diagonally. Cut. A directional light, similar to a headlight on a moving car, illuminates the title of the film: *The Intruder* (*L'Intrus*, 2004).

What do these images convey? What do they represent? What do they create together? Who are these characters? Where did they come from? Where are they going? What do they want? What are they thinking? They do not even show us the protagonist of the film. He will arrive already wrapped in a universe of things. The shots do not appear to be edited or arranged based on a practical requirement for the plot or a concern with the dramatic fluency of the whole. They do not articulate with each other in linear mechanics; instead, they emanate a seemingly random principle, in an assembly that engages sensitive states (colors, bodies, landscape) rather than revealing evolution. Some scenes always come to us after they have begun or are abandoned midway through. Others seem staged for our gaze. They are blocks of life. The attention is focused on the fulcrum of the moment, the power of movement, the magnetism of the bodies. There is a kind of disorder being claimed by the documented or orchestrated event itself—terms that may seem contradictory but, based on what I see, sound inadequate or perplexing. What is established in these first few minutes is an exercise in a wandering and dispersed gaze that dilutes the drama and prioritizes a sense of presence and mobility.

Claire Denis offers us a hypnotic experience. Bodies, landscapes, camera, cuts. The movie just happens. The images evoke a curious desire to be immersed by what they show, an impulse that overlaps the narrative layer by layer. In fact, it is not actually an overlay. This desire for immersion experienced while watching *The Intruder* is at the heart of this filmmaker's cinema: a unique approach to the cinematographic gesture, the embodiment and creation of sensorial narratives. From *Chocolat* (1988) to *Stars at Noon* (2022), the filmmaker and her collaborators (in particular photographer Agnès Godard, screenwriter Jean-Pol Fargeau, sound technician Jean-Louis Ughetto, and editor Nelly Quettier, not to mention the actors and musicians) embrace a seductive form of minimalism, characterized by ellipses, a camera in love with the skin of the bodies, and a melodious tone that harmoniously integrates all the elements into a single hierarchy.

Denis was a child of the decolonization era. She grew up as a girl in various regions of sub-Saharan Africa[1] and only moved to France in the 1960s. She was a teenager. Her experience is one of a double foreignness, whether on the African continent or in Paris, where she felt like an outsider. This feeling of rootlessness has been with her since and contaminates her cinema, which is filled with deeply disconcerting questions about identity and alienation, assimilation and rejection, desire and fear. The post-colonial malaise, always looming in the horizon of this cinema, has made it a rich subject, particularly for cultural and gender studies. *Good Work*, for example, tells the story of a sergeant in the Foreign Legion whose life is turned upside down with the arrival of a new recruit. This film has been the subject of numerous analyses focusing on the multiple identities of the characters and the "feminization" of the soldiers' male bodies. Insisting on "reading" this film from the point of view of the latent homoerotic desire among legionnaires is certainly an interesting and rightful yet easy path. This is because the fascination with the male body is not a fetish here. In addition to revealing the affective and erotic ambiguities that fill this community, Denis seems much more interested in the impenetrable reality of those bodies. *Good Work* is not a movie about the Foreign Legion. Nor is it a film willing to give voice to another marginalized character. Denis is not a naturalist. Her aim is not to denounce a certain state of affairs. The desire to understand a particular reality is met with an unsurpassable opacity. The gaze of the French filmmaker, as she herself underlines, is that of an intruder: "I have never felt like someone who has invaded, but I felt a bit like in Conrad: someone who enters lands to almost disappear; to enter something that he will perhaps understand."[2]

The notion of intrusion is extremely important for Denis' work in general and for *The Intruder* in particular. In this film, the intruder is, first and foremost, the foreign heart that needs to be transplanted into the chest of Louis Trebor (Michel

---

[1] Denis' father was a colonial administrator with stints in Haute-Volta (today Burkina Faso), Djibouti, and various regions of Cameroon. Denis describes him as someone who believed in the independence of African countries and who "asked questions about why we were there" (Denorme and Douin 2001, 21).

[2] Renouard and Wajeman (2004, 15).

Subor), and which, metonymically, spreads throughout the film. I feel this sense of intrusion from the beginning, when we see the character for the first time, naked in the forest, with his face turned to the sun and his body buried in the bush, sensually communing with his dogs. He swims in an icy lake, feels his heart, and climbs out of the water, holding his arm, and panting. The camera captures movements in the dark forest in the background and zooms in to provide a close-up view of an intruder. Trébor is never alone. When leaving the lake, a close-up shows his hand wringing the sand with force. A cigarette butt comes to the surface.

However, we know very little about Trébor. He is depicted at the beginning of the film living a lonely life on the French-Swiss border. Neither his lover, the local town pharmacist, nor his son, with whom he has a distant relationship, seem to know him, and the film offers few clues to unravel his mysteries. Trébor lives outside the law of men, clinging to the rawness of nature. He has Swiss and Russian passports. He has lived in many countries. He was trained to kill. He watches from a distance (while also being watched) the desperate advance of groups of illegal immigrants hunted by customs officials. He is also hunted and remains constantly alert, attuned to the heightened senses of his dogs. Now, Trébor needs a new heart, but that does not free him from his past, which haunts him and materializes itself in the form of a young Russian woman who follows him everywhere.

What is perceived in the first few minutes of *Good Work* is that the character's inner conflict is dissolved in the landscape as an expansive metaphor. I mean, Trébor is more than just a character; he is a kind of device. He is not merely a physical entity upon which the film constructs a discourse or a story. Trébor asserts himself as the conductor or executor of all recorded actions, almost like a hidden narrator, akin to the character of Denis Lavant in *Good Work*, albeit without the voice-over narration. Denis transforms the film into a physical entity confronted by intrusive presences—which include dreams, nightmares, memories—never underlined as such—and even images from another feature, in which Michel Subor acts, *Le reflux* (1965; Paul Gégauff). In an interview, the filmmaker states:

> *Michel is the flesh and the heart of the film, we should feel free to break up each scene as if even Michel wasn't needed in the image, as if every image came out of his mind. Therefore, we decided that he could be in the frame or not in the frame and also that he could be in frame sometimes but not as the main object, not as the centre. I wanted each image to convey a sense that it was generated by his mind.*[3]

[3.] Smith (2005).

The Intruder is inspired by a short essay written by Jean-Luc Nancy. The homonymous work by the French philosopher establishes an instigating analogy between the physical, psychological, and metaphysical implications of a heart transplant he had received ten years earlier. Nancy fears being invaded by an intruder—in this case, a heart that could save his life. If his heart was giving up, leaving him in the lurch, to what extent can he say that that organ was really his? Nancy no longer recognizes his own body. He now objectified a part of his body in his consciousness, something he has never done before. He is no longer whole, but rather an "assembly, a set of organs and functions."

> *I had (who is this 'I'?, that is precisely the question, the age-old question: who is the subject of this pronouncement, always alienated from his own utterance, always, inevitably, an intruder, and yet, inevitably, the driving force, the engine, the heart?), then, to receive the heart of another person nearly ten years ago. [...] My heart has become a stranger to me: a stranger precisely because it is inside me [...] A foreigner that reveals itself in the heart of what was most familiar to me, although the familiar term is insufficient: in the heart of what never made itself known as 'heart'.*[4]

Denis' film is a precise tribute to the richness of this metaphorical journey, avoiding simple conclusions and asserting itself in its opening. In this manner, I am not undergoing an adaptation or transposition. When discussing the relationship between her work and Denis' cinema, Nancy compares it to a creative form of "sonship," which intriguingly alludes to one of the central themes of the film: the concept of kinship or lineage, whether real or imagined. This affiliation occurs in the elaboration of a new set of metaphors on the themes of identity, alterity, and corporeity. Nancy highlights the rich connections and fertile starting points that the bodily allegory of transplantation creates in both formal and narrative terms. "Claire Denis didn't adapt my book," says Nancy, "she adopted it. [...] it is a natural and implicit relationship established through a purely symbolic lineage"[5]

The Denisian adoption takes place, above all, in what Jean-Sébastien Chauvin calls "perambulation-infiltration."[6] In Denis, everything is conveyed through the spectacle of a body in motion. The camera always seeks to identify this movement, emulating its characteristics. If a character rides a bicycle, I ride alongside them.

---

[4] Nancy (2000, 13, 17).

[5] Nancy (2005, 1).

[6] Chauvin (2001).

As he walks through the forest on foot, the camera follows him, fixed to the back of his neck, capturing even the scent of his surroundings. If you're sledding, that's where the photographer is positioned to incorporate the frenzy of the race. Throughout the film, we are taken to three completely different landscapes, from the mountains at the beginning to the crystal-clear sea at the end, and the bustling big city at night. We are transported and immersed in various atmospheres, light, and colors. Denis creates a world with uncertain boundaries: blending dream and reality, present and past, black and white, children and adults, silhouettes and landscapes, figures and characters, and human beings and animals. Saad Chakali (2005) rightly describes Denis' work as having an "oceanic impulse," where everything is caught on the borderline between emergence and immersion.

Gradually, *The Intruder* takes on the dark atmosphere of a thriller, with a plot that evokes the presence of an international mafia and organ trafficking. What is intriguing is that Denis does not just tell stories; she often does so within the framework of particular film genres. The synopsis of *The Intruder*, for example, suggests a transnational espionage film. The movie takes advantage of presenting itself as a story, negotiating our engagement in the narrative. The espionage genre already has its place in cinema, encompassing a complete imaginary world. If, on the one hand, Denis brings us closer, on the other hand, *Good Work* never forms a recognizable narrative structure. The filmmaker creates expectations but then defies the conventions of the genre by removing the need for each shot to be rooted in continuity, suppressing the narrative dimension whenever it shows itself in the process of being fully complete.[7]

At this point, one has to ask: should we still talk about mise-en-scène? The term, as identified by André Bazin and many others, is based on an aesthetic of centrality and a greater concern for maintaining the continuity of the scene. This was the primary goal of the mise-en-scène: to fill space and conceal the inability of the visual to portray it, infusing it with a physical presence. Is that what I see in Denis? The bodies that inhabit *The Intruder* are organized according to staging. The cinematographic frame does not seem to be her starting point. While it would be an exaggeration to declare the death of staging, it cannot be ignored that it is

---

[7.] Regarding the gaping aspect of the film, Denis reveals in an interview a very particular methodology, unusual and absolutely visible in his films:

Often we do a first draft that has no gaps and then I feel it doesn't sound musical or interesting to me. So then I cut, because I think it's important to cut before [starting in] the editing room. It's important to cut it already in the script. Maybe I'm wrong, but I do it because I think it's more dangerous, in a way. Then everyone is aware—the crew, the actors—that there is a gap, so they don't expect, 'Well, in the next scene, I will explain more about myself.' They know there won't be any explanations, so they act differently. (Smith 2005)

no longer as prevalent as scene management, and it remains more like a writing gesture and an exercise for the eye. Jacques Aumont elaborates:

> *Denis tells a story about which it is impossible to know which parts are 'real'*
> *and which parts are dreamed or fantastic; the film multiplies the ellipses, never*
> *identified as such and of variable durations, making it difficult and random to*
> *understand the story (many details are not clarified); finally, there is no staging*
> *in the sense of laying out the shot as a painting: the shots are almost always*
> *details — mainly the faces in close-up — which ends up preventing, almost perma-*
> *nently, mentally reestablishing the space-time relationships between characters*
> *and between shots.*[8]

It is definitely necessary to bet on a different perspective before *The Intruder*, on a different approach to the cinematographic gesture, not exactly interested in deciphering, dissecting, or analyzing it. What I was looking for in the previous chapters was precisely a certain vision of cinema. Authors of phenomenological inspiration emphasize cinema as the dawn of the world in eternal rebirth. They invite us to experience *The Intruder*, its rhythm, breathing, colors, shapes, and plasticity. It is curious: Denis asserts the prominence of bodies on stage, which serve as raw material for the conception of a cinema, not only according to Bazin but also by Michel Mourlet, although the filmmaker's methods and strategies do not exactly align with the ideas of these authors. Mourlet, above all, would have difficulties with the Denisian discontinuity, with the sensory intoxication she so inveterately seeks. Amédée Ayfre also mentioned a certain stylistic asceticism to be pursued. For him, cinema should focus on what reality already has at its most spectacular: the ordinary man in his everyday actions, at any time, on any day. Instead of deriving fiction from reality, the neorealist project began with the mundane meaning of small events captured by observation. For Bazin, as well as for Ayfre, the presence of the world in the image emanates when captured in blocks, in their entirety, for the spectator. The spectator, for his turn, constitutes a world from its original ambiguity, which then reveals the mystery of existence.

However, in Denis' cinema, "revelation" may not be the most appropriate word. She does not think in terms of fiction and reality. The filmmaker is exploring what makes the presence of others effective for the spectator. In *The Intruder*, we are definitely in the realm of an "art of the epidermis," of a "carnal universe," of the "reconciliation of man with his flesh" (expressions cherished by Mourlet).

---

[8] Aumont (2008, 179).

Nonetheless, the presence of a body is not solely guaranteed by the objectivity of the mechanical device. It is necessary to connect it to a sensation, to living an experience that seems forbidden and intimate.

This feeling of interdiction and intimacy often rises from the music. The filmmaker frequently points me in this direction in interviews: "It's true that music is the origin," she says, "it opens free space and I trust that. Music gives an opportunity."[9] The soundtrack is never just an "accompaniment" to Denis' film image. The music in films such as *The Intruder* and *White Material* (2009) emphasizes the sensual quality of the images, decenters things, avoids a sense of narrative and conclusion, and keeps me engaged and alert. In features such as *Trouble Every Day* (2001) and *Friday Night* (*Vendredi soir*, 2002), the sound and music possess an almost tactile quality, shaping the characters, defining the dramatic *tempo* and leaving us between suspension and sudden acceleration. They combine the melancholy of the music with the more violent passages in the former, and punctuate the emotional fluctuations experienced by the protagonist in the latter.

It's as if the sound waves were infiltrating my nervous system, penetrating my ears, and taking possession of my brain and body, immersing me in a rhythm and a particular state of mind. It is the inevitable tragedy of the score of *White Material*, the sweet and dangerous joy of *Nénette and Boni* (*Nénette et Boni*, 1996), the call of the world in *Friday Night*, the lost and now impossible love of *Trouble Every Day*, the uncontrollable sensuality of *Good Work*, the imminence of death in *The Intruder*, and the sad but hopeful longing of *35 Shots of Rum* (*35 Rhums*, 2008). Denis synchronizes, harmonizes, and intertwines visual and musical forms in a style that could be described as a fusion of architecture and music. This style favors optical and sonic elements over dialogue, psychological realism, scenic continuity, and other cinematic strategies and conventions.

Denis has a clear appreciation for music: from opera to beat music, not to mention contemporary traditional African music. She always works in close collaboration with musicians, has directed music clips (*Incinerate* [Sonic Youth, 2006], *Faites Monter* [Alain Bashung, 2002] and *C'est Déjà Ça* [Alain Souchon, 1993]), and a documentary (*Man No Run*, 1989) about a Cameroonian group on a French tour. She also assigns substantive narrative weight to pop songs (Bob Marley, The Beach Boys, Neil Young). Music is part of the gestation process of the films—Tindersticks, in the case of *Nénette and Boni*, Benjamin Britten in *Good Work*, and Johnny Cash in *The Intruder*. Denis writes while listening to

---

[9.] Romney (2000).

music. She films while listening to music. Dickon Hinchliffe, a former member of the British band Tindersticks with whom Denis has been collaborating since *Nénette and Boni*, describes a certain tension between sound and image in the French filmmaker's movies:

> *The music always emerges as a strong voice in the films—even more so because there is little dialogue. Dialogue is less important, and this opens up a poetic space in her films. So music and sound effects play a crucial role in affecting the audience. They become a more direct route to the unconscious than the visuals. There is a flow in much of the scores rather than a rhythm or a beat: it evokes a state of suspension, or a liminal state. Suspended chords abound, creating a sense of the unresolved. Cues start and die in a non-conclusive way—it creates an impression of the unfinished.*[10]

This impression of something inconclusive reminds me of Johnny Cash. The music contributes enormously to the characterization of the characters and to the relationship between them and their environment, often in terms of intensity, proximity, and distance. In an interview with the website *Senses of Cinema*, Denis revealed that most of the hints she gave to the actors of *The Intruder* were musical. Michel Subor, for example, listened to Johnny Cash:

> *He had read the script and I gave him those new songs to listen to because I wanted him to be inspired. I told him, 'Probably I will never use this as music for the film', but I wanted him to feel that death is coming closer, to hear that voice, that man in Cash's last two records whose life has been rich and full of love and emotion. And there is a trembling, as if the moment is coming. I could have given Michel a book to read but I thought it was good that it was Johnny Cash songs. And I think it was so great for him. You know, sometimes when people get older they surrender and they decide it's time to put everything in order and to be a good person. And I wanted the character to feel that and yet not to surrender.*[11]

Cash, the man in black, is actually a musical variation on Louis Trebor (Michel Subor). His body is sore, tired, and unyielding. His presence is fascinating, although perhaps not very pleasant. His deep, almost rough voice is disconcertingly sweet as he sings of his love and, most notably, his tragedies. Denis is specifically

---

[10] Vecchio (2014, 6).

[11] Smith (2005).

referring to the final albums of the American singer, the *American Recordings* series. In these albums, Cash, who was already ill and grieving the recent death of his wife, revisits classic American songs, leaving us with a captivating and endless lament that could only culminate in his own death — the last two albums in the series were released posthumously. Even though Cash was still alive when filming for *The Intruder* began, he died before the release of the film.

Music is, therefore, a more open sort of dialogue for Denis, punctuating her films with startling disjunctions and sudden breaks from one sensual event to an entirely different one. The use of rhythm as an irregular structuring device is evident in *Good Work*, where the filmmaker orchestrates sets of visual, auditory, and tactile rhythms that interact with each other. Laura McMahon (2014) highlights some of these unequal correspondences: "the percussive disco beat and play of pulsating light in the nightclub scene; the hum of voices and clatter of a train as it carries Djiboutian passengers through the desert; the quivering of tufts of grass in the wind; the rising murmur of *O heave!*; the almost imperceptible swaying of ceremonial bodies."[12] Bodies, objects, sounds, and movements emerge as intimately linked across divergent times and spaces, through what McMahon poetically calls "a non-metrical relay of corresponding rhythms that reverberate in excess of causal logic, engendering the kind of 'unforeseen connections."[13] *Good Work* is the result of a broader aesthetic endeavor focused on inter-rhythmic resonance.

This cinema project seems to be even more well executed in *The Intruder*, a film with an erratically structured narrative that is enhanced by Staples' musical piece. His composition is essentially made up of a synthesizer base that vibrates with a minimalist guitar melody. It serves as a leitmotiv or a signature, leaving a lasting impression on the images and piercing through the narrative, the past and the destiny of the protagonist. Denis engages in conversations with Staples about the film:

> Stuart decided that he was not going to work with the band [Tindersticks], that he would do it alone, and then he decided that he was in a brutal part of his life. Stuart knew Michel from Beau Travail and liked him very much, so he really wanted to participate in the film. But he wanted to be the 'drill' of the film: that is, to provide no melody. Every time I asked him to explain this idea, he said, 'No, don't ask me to be nice. I'm going to drill the film.' And very soon he came

---

[12.] McMahon (2014, 180).

[13.] Ibid.

to me and said, 'I think I'm going to loop it.' I was kind of surprised because
actually the film felt more like a ballad.[14]

Staples' guitar infuses the film with an intangible sense of strangeness, simultaneously intriguing and disturbing. It possesses a fascinating quality of something ethereal, suspended between an indefinable sense of threat and enchanted nostalgia. Music helps Denis to expand the gap between script, mise-en-scène, and editing, keeping these operations and their more conventional strategies in a state of suspension or self-doubt. This seemingly random, moment-by-moment inventiveness of Denis' style — her sense of constantly constructing, dismantling, and reconstructing figures, a world, a history — has led some American critics to draw a curious parallel with the *Free Jazz*[15] of Ornette Coleman and Charlie Parker[16] — an avant-garde subgenre created in the 1960s and characterized by collective improvisation, a break with traditional harmony, and great melodic and rhythmic freedom. This connection between Denis' cinema and *Free Jazz* successfully identifies a shared and expansive common ground that leads me to explore other avenues.

The improvisation that is at the base of the work of American saxophonist Ornette Coleman — who, incidentally, did not like the expression Free Jazz very much — prompts inquiries about the identity of a piece of music, the nature of composition and performance, and the very notions of creation and creator. For improvisation is between composition and performance. It is not something that precedes the composition or is excluded by it; rather, it is in opposition to the composition. Composers never create ex nihilo but "improvise,"[17] sometimes from songs that already exist but more often and more importantly in the tradition in which they work — and musicians realize very early on how much they speak on behalf of others and therefore how much they owe them. The composition is neither just an echo nor an original: it is both and none, something that escapes any simple opposition. Nor should improvisation be considered a "work or structure produced on the spur of the moment." Coleman expands the jazz vernacular in many ways, and while he may seem to work without the jurisdiction of lines and structures, he is definitely not playing aimlessly. Coleman operates within specific

---

[14.] Smith (2005).

[15.] Jones (2000).

[16.] Rosenbaum (2000).

[17.] It is known today, for example, that one of the best-known jazz albums, *Kind of Blue* (1959), was based on sketches brought to the studio by Miles Davis about half an hour before recording.

constraints and a certain kind of structure. These coordinates, however loose or subject to change a song may seem, establish certain limitations in advance.

This claim may not be intuitively obvious. Instead, it may simply seem fake. The almost immediate reluctance that this assumption awakens in me is much more associated with a certain traditional way of thinking about music, which is constantly contradicted by practice. Contrary to the perhaps still dominant paradigm in the field of music, where composers are seen as the true "creators" and performers merely fulfill their desires, Coleman's *Free Jazz* presents an innovative vision in which composers, performers, and even listeners are more appropriately regarded as "improvisers." In other words, *Free Jazz* suggests that the process by which a work comes into existence is best described as improvisational at its very core, not only in terms of the act of composing but also of the acts of performing and listening. The nature of composition, performance, and listening is improvisational, although in different ways and to varying extents.

Is not that what Staples means when he says that the music in Denis' films is not exactly composed but constructed? He continues:

> *Ultimately, it's not even music that's composed. It's a kind of music that's built. It's like grown from seeds. When I think of the word 'compose', I think of someone sitting in front of a screen, with a bank of sounds, and picking on themes and characters and putting these things together, whereas, for us, we experiment until it makes us happy. And we kind of learn what's wrong by doing it. Especially working on the last two films with Claire, I felt the shape you give to the music could be however you want it to be. It does not have to have a strong centre to it because, really, the strong centre is the image. A lot of times, I feel the image is the melody, you don't need to have a melody, you just need a colour, a feeling, to let that image sing.* [18]

For Staples, as for Coleman, making music is about creating a world in which music can happen. In this world, we all live side by side, composers, performers, and listeners. Improvisation (defined in a broad sense) is in this sense essential to the entire process that involves the creation of music. Making music is actually an ongoing process of creating and recreating music — a constant improvisation. A Coleman song is always a kind of improvised conversation, a free dialogue with a series of patterns and structures, drawing from the tradition that sustains it, and involving the musicians who accompany it, whether dead or alive, sharing

---

[18.] Vecchio (2014, 10).

the same stage, as well as those who listen to it. The creating of a song depends on an improvised translation: the influence of tradition on the composer, the development of ideas and musical fragments, and the act of listening that combines these moments and blends them together to form a whole.

It is not much different in a feature film such as *The Intruder*. The film impresses us with fictional moments—a murder, business meetings, and an escape—and a whole network of connections that gives *The Intruder* an undeniable aura of mystery. The montage, however, takes us on a strange "continuing wandering."[19] In its complex narrative structure, time rarely seems to be tied to the plot. Editing not only favors omission but also enables the narrative to diverge into a diverse array of digressions, creating a "porous" time, where the present is constantly visited by the past and the future. What is then established is a kind of continuum, an incessant production of sensible presences. There is a conscious option for the fragment, for rough stones. *The Intruder* is a film made of moments that are sufficient on their own. The montage materializes a paradox: each fragment of the film is simultaneously independent in its existence, detached from the story, and also essential for the construction of a whole. Following Martine Beugnet's lead, achieving the sensual fluctuation of the meanings in the French director's cinema requires surrendering to the textures, shapes and skins: "it is the materiality of the medium of the moving image that first comes to the fore here,"[20] says Beugnet, "the cinema of sensation is an approach to filmmaking (and, by extension, to the analysis of film) that gives precedence to the corporeal, material dimension of the medium."[21]

This is the true substance of Denis' cinema. The characters carry stories that the filmmaker just does want to clarify. The actors are replaced by their bodies, which are always in motion. The result is a kind of touch-camera that constructs the space gradually and appears to need to touch the objects in order to transform them into an image. To address this aspect of Denis' cinema, Beugnet uses the term "haptic visuality"[22]: "a mode of visual perception akin to the sense of

---

[19.] Beugnet (2004, 25).

[20.] Beugnet (2007, 3).

[21.] Ibid., 32.

[22.] The notion of "haptic visuality" was initially developed by art historian Alois Riegl (1985), who characterized the physical and tactile quality of ancient Egyptian art as "haptic," in contrast to the "optical" quality of Roman art, which was more abstract and associated with the birth of figurative space. Riegl's work influenced other thinkers, especially Erwin Panofsky, Walter Benjamin, and Deleuze. Although the latter used the expression "haptic visuality" in *The Time-Image*, Laura Marks developed it more systematically. She even proposes a possible definition: Haptic perception is usually defined as the combination of tactile, kinesthetic, and proprioceptive functions, the way we experience touch both on the surface of and inside our bodies. In haptic visuality, the eyes themselves function as organs of touch. Haptic visuality, a term contrasted to optical visuality, draws from other forms of sense experience, primarily touch and kinesthetics. (Marks 2002, 2)

touch, where the eye, sensitised to the image's concrete appearance, becomes responsive to qualities usually made out through skin contact."[23]

In this sense, the response that Denis gave to a spectator at the Toronto Film Festival who asked her about the subject of the film is very interesting: "My films, unfortunately, are sometimes unbalanced. They have a limp arm, or a shorter one, or a big nose, but in the editing room, when we try to change that, it usually doesn't work."[24] Denis' apology may seem insignificant, but her choice of words is remarkable. Some of her films are best understood when described in the words and bodily allusions that Denis employs: monstrous, misshapen creatures, intoxicated, light-drained, and colonized organisms. Furthermore, the comparison of an editing room to a Frankenstein laboratory seems particularly fitting in the context of a film like *The Intruder*. This movie not only aims to portray the vulnerability of modern man's identity through his body but also presents him as primarily a sensory universe, a body of sensations.

It is important to move forward with these allusions and clues in mind. Denis operates at the crossroads between a narrative as a gateway and access, the centrality of the body, and the sensoriality that goes along with all of this. In her cinema, sensation assumes the condition of primordial force of reality: There are only sensations and our awareness of them. A "sensationalist realism,"[25] to use the expression of Fernando Pessoa and Mário de Sá-Carneiro. However, it is worth emphasizing, it is nothing new to think of the seventh art as a dramaturgy of concrete and gestural actions. The body, as previously underlined, has always been the raw material of cinema. Several filmmakers have invested and continue to invest in different forms of representation focusing on skin and surface issues. In *The Time-Image*, Gilles Deleuze dealt with many of these directors, grouped under the name "filmmakers of the body." He says:

> *The scenery is often made according to the attitudes of the body that it demands and the degrees of freedom that it allows them, like the flat in Le mépris or the bedroom in Vivre sa vie, in Godard. Embracing, striking, intertwining and bumping bodies animate major scenes as in First Name Carmen again, where the two*

[23.] Beugnet (2007, 66).

[24.] Denis (2004).

[25.] The term sensationist is defined by Fernando Pessoa (1966) as the substitution of thought for sensation. To be sensationalist is then to express a sensation in such a way that it evokes the greatest possible number of sensations and that the whole produced seems organized. He says: "To feel is to create. [...] Only what one thinks can be communicated to others. What you feel cannot be communicated. You can only communicate the value of what you feel. You can only do what you feel" (Pessoa 1966, 216–17).

lovers attempt to grab each other in doors or windows. 'Not only do bodies bang into each other, but the camera bangs against the bodies, in Passion each body not only has its space, but also its light. The body is sound as well as visible, all the components of the image come together on the body.[26]

According to Deleuze, the Nouvelle Vague pushed the boundaries of this cinema of attitudes and postures. These have drained the characters of heroism, intelligence, and psychology. The camera did not dramatize the action but instead tried to de-emphasize it. In this way, only the raw state of beings and objects remains. Therefore, any adjectival notion is omitted as evidenced by the title of another film by Godard, *A Woman Is a Woman* (*Une femme est une femme*, 1961). Serge Daney even spoke of a Godardian pedagogy and defined *Here and Elsewhere* (*Ici et Ailleurs*, 1974) as a "painful meditation on the theme of restitution, better: reparation. To repair is to return the images and sounds to those from whom they were taken."[27]

This focus on the physicality of everything was an important aspect of a certain project of modern cinema. Godard's films and many other filmmakers emerged from a widespread crisis of the concept of representation. The image should now appear as an immediate presence. This conviction was born at the same time from a theorization of the real in cinema that comes from Bazin, but also from the certainty that the image is always an element of a discourse, an evidence to be deciphered. Godard, for example, explores a certain despair in relation to the idea of reading images and deciphering the world. Although it nurtures an appreciation of the sensitive presence of bodies, its images are entirely bound to discourses, and intended to be interpreted. Let's see what Rancière says: "This in Godard is completely contradictory…a practice where all images are compelled to be put into discourses, to emit a discourse if we place them in front of any other, in the presence of no matter what."[28]

This, however, was not the only answer to the dilemmas that troubled cinema in its modern age. Maurice Pialat, for example, would inscribe the problem of representation in another way, in a kind of primitivism. In *Naked Childhood* (*L'enfance nue*, 1968), Pialat's first feature, he portrays the daily life of an orphan boy who constantly moves because he does not fit in with any family. During filming, Pialat deliberately omits parts of the script in favor of situations

---

[26.] Deleuze (1989, 193).

[27.] Daney (2007, 114).

[28.] Carlin et al. (2000).

he observes or hears from members of his amateur cast. Pialat does not mitigate the violence of the cut through the meaningful organization of a narrative. His movies just seem to accumulate, piling one shot after another. At a certain point, François (Michel Terrazon) screams his anger and discomfort toward his adoptive mother. In the next close-up, he declares: "If anyone touches Mama's hair, I'll kill him!" The energy of these moments, emanating between the actors and the filmmaker and constituted during the cinematographic experience, is more valuable than the logic of a character or even the main plot.

Pialat's cinema is of the order of shock and impact with what is immediate. Pialat is an action director. His characters are what they do. No loop comes before or explains them. Narratives are always broken, discontinued, and filled with ellipses. It is quite hard to tell when a take begins or ends. A Pialat shot is always characterized by the here and now. Always. The montage maintains a continuous flow between the images, even though the cuts consistently miss both ends of the shot, their influx, before it is smoothed into a stable form. The framing, lighting, performances, and camera are unstable, as if they were elements on the verge of combustion. The plastic beauty of a well-framed shot or the skillful performance of an actor is only meaningful if they successfully convey the emotional intensity of that moment—otherwise they will be overlooked by perhaps potential shaky, poorly lit and/or framed shots. This is his guideline: "the force of a moment, the inspired presence of an actor, the singular energy of an action."[29] In the end, what we see is an implosion, a return to a kind of original chaos.

To Our Loves (*À nos amours*, 1983), for example, reveals the possibility of what Luiz Carlos Oliveira Jr. (2005) called the "aesthetics of Stonehenge." The image does not appear to convey a hidden discourse or reveal a world. Pialat seeks the production of a pure meaningless presence. It is a portrayal of the irreducibility of affection. It's no wonder that when asked about his influences, Pialat curiously did not mention the Nouvelle Vague, of which he was a contemporary and with which he shared some values and references, but instead cited the Lumière brothers. That's what he looks for in each scene: that magic that overflowed from the first Lumièrian views. In other words, modern cinema's counterattack on representation not only focused on the endless construction of language but also on the self-affirmation of a sensitive presence.

Well, Denis is much closer to Pialat than to Godard. Attention to the *gestus* (which Deleuze placed at the heart of body filmmakers) remains important as the starting point of a story, but the primary focus is to dissolve them into the

---

[29.] Oliveira Jr. (2014, 78–79).

landscape, into the sensitive matter of the world. In *The Intruder* I feel compelled to explore the restitution of a certain primordial gaze that, despite being able to identify the terms, is incapable of completely separating them. This ambivalence also concerns Douglas Morrey's diagnosis: "Claire Denis's films have, for some time now, been tightly focused around bodies, but seem precisely to pivot around an undecideable point on which the body balances between its thick, inscrutable materiality and its diaphanous, symbolic sense."[30]

Over the body, layers and layers of discourses were successively placed. Godard undresses this body and then dresses it again, repeatedly as if caught on in a kind of vicious cycle. In Denis, however, the body is neither naked nor completely covered. The body draws attention to itself, but appears to exhaust its senses and capacity for meaning. He is a complex combination of forces, flows of energy, and desire. When dealing with this topic, Morrey draws another parallel between Denis' cinema and Nancy's philosophy:

> *Nancy's discussions of artistic meaning have frequently centred around images — both painterly and filmic — as the phenomena whereby the real, in manifesting its presence, is granted a certain sense. Claire Denis, in common with the vast majority of live-action filmmakers, necessarily deals in images and bodies — images of bodies — but her frequent refusal to provide the traditional cinematic signifiers of psychological depth often means that the spectator is brought up short before the strangeness of these bodies as bodies, which in turn opens up an interrogation as to the sense of her images.*[31]

This strangeness concerns the dual nature of the body: it is in the middle of things, it is a thing among things, but it is also endowed with reflexivity. The body is the visible that sees, the visible that becomes a seer within visibility. Not only is he counted among things in the fabric of the world, but also he keeps them as extensions of himself, inscribed in the same fabric. Maurice Merleau-Ponty, as we have seen, coined the term "flesh" to express the primordial unity between the body and the world, "the indivision of this sensible Being that I am and all the rest which feels itself in me."[32] This undivision, however, is also the fission that gives birth to the sensible mass of the body within the sensible mass of the world.

[30.] Morrey (2008, 21).

[31.] Ibid., 10.

[32.] Merleau-Ponty (1968, 255).

The concept of chiasm underlines the essential reversibility between the body and the world, obscuring the phenomenological distinction between the sense of interiority and the sense of exteriority, while also rejecting them as separate or separable. Merleau-Ponty borrows this concept from the field of rhetoric (chiasma is a figure of style comprising four terms whose relations are the opposite of what symmetry would suggest, such as being rich in defects and poor in qualities) and introduces it to think not about identity or difference, but identity in difference, or unity through opposition.

Both terms, flesh and chiasm, help me understand Denis. She seems to work precisely on this intertwining of the visible with the invisible, on a presence that, as Deleuze said, asserts itself from an absence. To go beyond oneself is to delve into oneself: this is the dialectical requirement that *The Intruder* imposes. The seer cannot possess the visible (which withdraws in its transcendence) because he himself belongs to the visible and "is in it." Seer and seen, sign and meaning, interior and exterior, each of these terms is only what it is when compared to the other, in a relationship that indeterminates them without confusing them in an undifferentiated mass. Trébor is a body that does not say "I think" but "I can." However, this "I can" or "I want" materializes only in relation, acting, performing an experience, and being the experience itself.

Denis challenges the privilege of discourse as the sole source of meaning, allowing for alternative ways of understanding. "Watching *The Intruder*," says Denis, is "like a boat lost in the ocean drifting."[33] I am encouraged to feel the images. What exists are the sensations and my awareness of feeling them. I feel immersed to the point where I cannot clearly see the contours of the events, always filled with vague edges. It is definitely a different perspective on cinema and the world. What is established is not a mechanism of identification or empathy with the characters and/or the situations in which they are involved, nor is it a relationship based on intellectual reasoning or on the transmission of a discourse. *The Intruder* reproduces, as it were, a baby's typical perception of the world: sensory confusion typical of everything that comes into the world as an entirely new, singular, and different event. The impact that this film has on me is akin to that of a dream, where thoughts, feelings, and sensations have not yet coalesced into a well-ordered and logical grammar.

Denis never relinquishes the plasticity of the image or the narrative, instead revealing in them an affective power, a sensitive force, which seems to erupt in a manner similar to the pictorial process through which Francis Bacon's bodies

---

[33.] Smith (2005).

and Cézanne's landscapes pass. The primary focus is on the constitution of an "openness-to-things without a concept," exploring the ways in which the image and its various elements can "present us with things, forests, storms—in short the world…as a particular case, with a more ample ontological power."[34] What I experience in a Denis film is that a sensation is felt the most wildly and intimately only when I do not understand it, that is, when I do not immediately dress it up with whatever it is and let myself sink into all its possible names and paths. "Each sensation, being strictly speaking, the first, last and only one of its kind, is a birth and a death,"[35] as Merleau-Ponty beautifully describes. A sensation is created by or belongs to a birth and a death.

What is at stake in Denis is a transgression of representation through sensation. In front of a film like *The Intruder,* I feel affected by something that my coordinates cannot fully capture. Her cinema embodies and fosters an interrogative stance that falls between yes and no. This is Denis' delightful mystery: referring to the things of the world before they become part of a world. The filmmaker aims to describe what Merleau-Ponty refers to as "Brute Being." It is "the world which precedes knowledge, of which knowledge always speaks."[36] It is the world to which we are open in perceptive faith, untamed because it has not yet been shaped by my idealizations, my syntax, or a set of manageable, accessible meanings. *The Intruder* emerges within the cinematographic experience of a spectator; it embodies this experience, directed at the blend of the world and us that comes before reflection. Denis, in other words, evokes, or rather, attends to a Bazinian kind of posture: to let oneself to drift, to be an integral part of an atmosphere, to live in a certain rhythm. In her cinema, she rediscovers the cinematographic potential that once frightened Roger Munier. She has the power to infuse a kind of magic into the most ordinary bodies and situations, re-enchanting reality through the cinematographic experience.

At the end of *Good Work*, we see the protagonist lying down with a gun on his chest, where the tattoo reads as follows: "Serve the good cause and then die." The camera captures the character's pulse, a pulsating vein, while the beats of music gradually rise in the background. We are then taken back to the nightclub at the beginning of the film—or at least that is how it seems to me. This time, instead of the African pop music to which the soldiers and women danced, the club looks empty. Galloup is alone and without his uniform. He dances to

---

[34] Merleau-Ponty (1964c, 172).

[35] Merleau-Ponty (2002, 250).

[36] Ibid., X.

The Rhythm of the Night, a hit by the electronic group Corona. He dances alone, frantically, out of control. That is all. The scene is violent in its depiction. The real is much more communicated here than captured or frozen. Denis employs a self-conscious, exhibitionist form of seduction and blasts the real out of the screen at me. Galloup's body is looked at, and it looks back at me. I look with a groping gaze, immersed in the realm of sensation. This realm, in fact, seems to reveal a whole universe of things (in addition to Galloup, his body, and me): the lights, colors, mirrors, reflections, music, movement, and so on. This is how the film ends, with this opening gesture, placing a new bet on the potential of the body and cinema.

3.2 Pedro Costa

The Body and its Powers

A distorted image with dark edges. The darkness poses a threat, encroaching upon the frame, not only from the sides but also from above, seeping through a small visible patch of the sky. A darkness that not pertains to the night but also appears to be a sort of backdrop against which the image reaches us. The shot is fixed at a slightly low angle. We see some houses poorly glued to each other. Something like a slum. Time has left its mark on them, seemingly abandoned. The distortion is most likely caused by the digital camera. The exploding pixels on the screen, the surviving pastel tones amidst the black, and the fixedness of the image give us the impression of a painting depicting a medieval wall. The soundtrack, however, populated by an indeterminate series of noises, reveals the humanity that inhabits that space. Behold, suddenly through the window of one of the houses, in the center of the frame, someone starts throwing objects to the floor: a cupboard, a chair, a door, and so on. Cut. A woman with a knife in her hand. She looks serenely furious. It is difficult to locate her in space. Maybe she's in the middle of a ladder. The shot, still under threat from the darkness, is on the verge of being erased. The angulation goes from top to bottom, with a clearly defined diagonal. The woman speaks as if reciting a monologue. The tone is somewhat theatrical, a sort of stylized naturalism. She remembers her childhood days, when she was fearless and swam among sharks, like a fish, to the astonishment of the men of São Filipe, in Cape Verde. They shouted her name and asked her to come back. Her name is Clotilde. If her appearance is somewhat untamed, resonating with the surrounding space, her speech is noble, flowing through her body, and aligning with the aesthetic beauty of the composition.

Her gaze, which was once directed toward the left diagonal of the frame, now looks thoughtfully downward at the right corner. Clotilde remembers Jójó, who cried when she went swimming. She stops, takes a deep breath, and resumes the more aggressive and imposing posture from the beginning of the shot. With wide eyes, she begins to walk slowly backward until she reaches a wall at the back of the frame. We only see a part of her body. She lowers the knife. Cut. *Colossal Youth* (2006).

The two scenes will be "explained" in the following one. Clotilde, whom we will not see again throughout the film, although her presence keeps being felt, threw her husband out of the house and his belongings out the window. It is a scene that, for me, as a Portuguese speaker, adds another layer of imagination to what we see: Here, between Cape Verde and Portugal, between communication and poetry, between script and improvisation, Portuguese is displayed in all its vibrant diversity. The language, alive like everything else in this film, actively contributes to the dynamic and ever-changing universe. Language does not belong to anyone. It reflects, creates, and contaminates reality. Language is at the origin of everything.

Ventura, a Cape Verdean immigrant, retired civil construction worker, is portrayed as a symbol of a class and elegance that no longer exists. Throughout the film, he wanders through the neighborhoods of Fontaínhas, which are on the verge of demolition, and Casal da Boba, where residents are being relocated to popular houses built by the government, with small rooms and white walls. Ventura visits his children, real and imaginary, and tries to help Lento, a bricklayer friend, in memorizing a letter to his beloved — despite the fact that we just never know If Lento is dead or alive.

Does this brief description help me in any way? Pedro Costa's cinema is the representation of a thing and an event. Both things at the same time. Costa chooses a group of people totally abandoned to their fate. They build unexpected emotional bonds and ways of continuing to live even in the most inhospitable conditions. He approaches victims of the development of contemporary capitalism who have lost their place, been dispossessed of their experience, history, and language. However, Costa never portrays them from the perspective of exclusion. His films not only reject the sociological approach but also diverge greatly from the tone of social criticism. It is not that these perspectives do not make sense but rather that they are simply insufficient.

Perhaps the most important or useful aspect to consider from a critical and theoretical standpoint is the tonality that these two opening scenes establish in the film. I can see glimpses of a poetics of light and shadow, of appearance and disappearance, where the bodies always reach us in their undeniable concreteness, but under a constant threat, living and dying between one moment and another. It is sometimes difficult to identify what comes from the beauty of the shots and what comes from the singularity of the bodies, their movements, and speeches. History and fiction are presented simultaneously at the beginning of *Colossal Youth*. The rest of Costa's feature reverberates and echoes this first blow — something that perhaps differentiates this cinema from the vast majority of modern films, from Godard to Antonioni, in which the film is put on hold before the question is posed by fiction.

These two opening scenes are completely alien: their rhythm, duration, rawness, atmosphere, plastic richness, and staged spontaneity. None of this implies an exhibitionist exercise in originality. It's as if they expressed an internal need for the film, a way of engaging with reality. Costa is like a craftsman. His cinema is his work! It requires a level of expertise from us. In front of his films, I am captivated by the intensities and flows, as if the screen is directly connected to my nervous system. I have submitted, or allowed myself to submit to an analysis of my perception, to a "revirginization" of my gaze: mise-en-scène, enunciation, acting, audiovisual dramaturgy, documentary, fiction. Everything is in question and out of question. As we saw in Denis, a new and different gaze is necessary. This is what I envision in phenomenologically inspired authors; and, with them in mind, I fully accept Costa's invitation.

Blood (*O sangue*, 1989), Costa's first film, already pointed to a different kind of cinema, although much has changed since then. Costa reinvents himself with each film. After experiencing the tale of love and death in Lisbon, the filmmaker traveled to Cape Verde, where he filmed *Casa de lava* (1994). This film can be seen as a reaction to the cinephile references and sentimentalism of its predecessor. It was his first experience working with non-actors. On the last day of filming, the set was invaded by Cape Verdeans. They asked the team to take letters and gifts to emigrated family members in Lisbon. Costa, back in Portugal, visited some of the poorest neighborhoods in the capital, including Fontaínhas:

> *I would go to Seu José's house and tell him that his daughter sent him a letter, that she was missing him a lot, and then I would by immediately invited to come in the house, drink the grog, eat the soup or stay a little or invited for the following Sunday, when someone's daughter would get married. It is clear that this immediately gives birth to a mot de passe, a password, and this gave rise to the film Bones. I stayed there to have a drink, I started to like it, I felt part of that*

place, aesthetically or plastically, I liked the place, the spatial organization, the colors, it wasn't just the sense of community, which evidently impressed me a lot, but above all the characteristics of that limited, small, ghetto place.[37]

From this encounter, the desire to create another film was born. *Bones* (*Ossos*, 1997) tells the story of a young couple living in a deteriorated neighborhood. It is Costa's first film featuring Vanda Duarte and her sister, Zita. Something, however, still bothered the filmmaker: dealing with the numerous film crew and all the technological equipment that a feature requires. Does it really? Who said that? Now, it was necessary to reconsider the methods and goals. Behold, on another exhausting night of filming, Vanda turned to the filmmaker and spoke:

'Cinema cannot be just that. It can be less tiring, more natural. If you film me, simply. Shall we continue?' This was a dream. It was the little 'fiction' that I arranged to make this 'film-documentary'. So I went to her room, to be with her and wait with her for the 'bulldozers' that would come and ravage Fontaínhas. Everyone has a place in the world. This is Vanda's place. And this is Vanda's sister; Zita. And that is her mother. And the one who goes there is Pango, a homeless boy. And so on. I mean, in this horrible society, it's good to have a place, a center, otherwise we're robbed within ourselves. And I could start filming because I found a place, this center that allowed me to look around, almost 360 degrees, and see the others, the inhabitants, friends. And I began to see how the neighborhood came and went in Vanda's room.[38]

Still on Vanda, Costa continues:

During the filming of Bones, Vanda didn't want to speak, she refused to say the dialogues I had written. She wasn't focused the way you need to be on a classic shoot. It's not that kind of concentration that I want today in a shoot, but in the recording of Bones, that attitude seemed scary to me. Instead of saying 'good morning' she said 'good night'. Instead of laughing, she cried. Instead of entering a room, she didn't enter. She asked a lot of questions and didn't feel like saying the right phrase at the requested time. It wasn't even that she thought the script was silly, she just didn't feel like it. She said: 'since I'm not an actress, I can't

[37.] Guimarães and Ribeiro (2007).

[38.] Ferreira (2001).

lie'. So it was a problem for me and the team. I've always had trouble forcing people to do what they don't want to do. I was told that one day Rossellini had a fit of laughter while directing a scene in one of his latest classics—like Voyage to Italy—in which two actors were supposed to say 'I love you'. At the end of ten minutes of repeating 'I love you', he had this crazy fit of laughter. You have to be very strong and, deep down, a bit of an idiot, as Truffaut said, to believe all this. I can't do eight weeks of 'I love you, I don't love you'. There is something profoundly ridiculous and pathetic about film footage. 'Bones' had to do with it. to believe it all. I can't do eight weeks of 'I love you, I don't love you'. There is something profoundly ridiculous and pathetic in a film shoot. Bones had to do with it.[39]

In Vanda's Room (*No quarto de Vanda*, 2000), his following film, was born from these questions and confrontation with Vanda. Costa reduced equipment and staff to a minimum, adopted a small video camera, and started visiting the neighborhood every day for about two years. In the end, there were a total of 130 recorded hours of scenes and conversations based on events in the lives of some residents of Fontaínhas. Right at the beginning of the film, we are informed that we are in a neighborhood that is slated for demolition. The camera then captures what happens in front of it. People take drugs, sell vegetables, smoke cigarettes, watch television, and listen to music. Vanda, who had already been the protagonist in *Bones*, assumes her own name, and, in a complex blending of documentary and fiction, throws in our lap a character that is difficult to define.

Michel Mourlet comes to mind several times. What seems extremely inter-esting to me is the probable fact that Mourlet perceived Costa's intervention as excessive, as well as his "phenomenological perspective" on things being somewhat vague. From the Mourletian perspective, the Portuguese filmmaker would fail both in the "mise" and in the "scène." Costa seems equally interested in exploring how to access the presence of things, the feeling of the being of things, as advocated by the French critic. This access, however, is only possible in a negotiation with the world that unfolds in equal measure in an openness to the impermanence and imprecision of things, and in an obsessive, millimetric rigor of shapes, frames, and gestures.

Costa positions the camera at a specific and consistent angle in each environ-ment, establishing a fixed direction with minimal deviations. He positions his characters in front of a stationary camera, using a unique angle and avoiding

---

[39.] Duarte (2010, 25).

any cuts, thus eliminating the need for internal editing within the sequences. It is just that. But it is too much. Vanda is in the center of her room. She has been there for a long time. Nothing is done to dramatize or even to "mean" or "tell" anything. It is from there, however, that a world unfolds as if by itself, as if the meticulous precision of this style, which is never interested in erasing its features, were necessary for reality to show its face.

It is from this bewilderment that the beauty of a scene in which Bach reaches towards Vanda and Zita. There is no melodrama or even a hint of lyricism. Vanda and her friend converse as they leaf through the yellow pages in search of traces of heroin. They smoke with the help of aluminum foil. They cough, move toward Costa and his camera, and tell different stories. What I see and feel is perhaps just a state of mind, a certain spirit that comes from the characters, but that seems to be in everything. *Colossal Youth* repeats and accumulates these fragments devoid of greater purposes or meaning—a film inhabited by absences. It is a plastic bottle in the middle of a table, a bicycle in the doorway of a house, a chair in ruins, an empty soccer ball, and an open window. It is Vanda's shadow on the floor of a bar where she orders a martini. They are ephemeral, contingent and self-evident presences. "Everything is," sums up Paolo Spaziani. "Everything is Vanda."[40]

It is worth insisting once more: would it be an exaggeration for someone to think of a hyper-Bazinian cinema, with the minimal intervention of the long take, the "open window" to the everyday world? André Bazin advocated for the use of techniques such as the long take and depth of field, as well as the preservation of the spatial and temporal unity of the recorded event. These procedures would lead cinema to a more accurate representation of life as we live it. Costa does not meet all of Bazin's prerequisites. In fact, what I see is a fully edited film, complete with a certain amount of violence. This paradox is strange: a strong enunciation, producing in the spectator the most vivid feeling of freedom and a deep respect for things.

It is something similar to what Jean Douchet diagnosed about Kenji Mizoguchi's cinema: "an impression of truth, of authenticity, which is evidently due to the maximum of artifice."[41] A cinema with modern roots (Jacques Rivette, John Cassavetes, Jean Eustache) in which a particular mise-en-scène is rejected, in the sense of rejecting the desire for absolute control over every aspect of the film. A cinema concerned with preserving not just ambiguity, although the term is not unfamiliar in this context, but rather dyssynchrony and diversity. Costa

---

[40] Cabo (2009, 188).

[41] Douchet (1990, 184).

radicalizes this movement. If Bazin sometimes seems to advocate in the name of a more equitable portrayal of life, viewing reality as a sort of second nature of film, the Portuguese filmmaker refuses to think in these terms.

This radicalization seeks a working method, an ethical stance, and a distinct style of mise-en-scène. If this cinema effectively provides us with the most tangible sensation of the being-there of things and bodies, it is because its enunciation is at the same time, and not contradictorily, strong and without origin. It is a highly committed cinema, created within the context of social reality. Yet it never sacrifices itself to the desire to explain, to denounce. Instead, it allows forms to speak for themselves. Perhaps this is what differentiates *In Vanda's Room* and, later, *Colossal Youth*, from Costa's previous films. He himself says:

> *One of the criticisms I made of myself was that, in the film, I saw more of myself than of the people I wanted to film. This happens to many filmmakers and artists. Now I'm going in the opposite direction. It is not exactly an erasure, in which the thing becomes anonymous. But who knows? My films are very grounded in reality. I feel that if I film it the other way around, I might lose my footing. I can pass a kind of border that is not reality, but an invention.*[42]

This is what attracted the Portuguese critic João Bénard da Costa to certain shots of *In Vanda's Room*. A Cape Verdean woman is hunched over, sitting facing the open door of what appears to be her home. The camera is positioned behind her. Shortly after, a girl appears. She enters and exits the frame until she finally stops in the doorway. She turns to the lady, shifting her weight from one foot to the other and presses the horn of a small bicycle. The girl honks non-stop, as if she wants to grab the attention of her "scene" companion, as if they were engaged in a game. They do not speak. I also do not know what the relationship is between them. At a certain point, as happens in almost every scene of this film, a strange *malaise* begins to take hold. A swift and abrupt cut takes us to the next shot, significantly shorter, where we catch a glimpse of a document from a funeral home. Did someone die? Who? "In this film with very long shots, this is the one that lasts the longest. In this ritual film, this is one of the most ritualistic shots. In this mystery film, this is one of the more mysterious shots,"[43] says Bénard da Costa.

It is something like the intention of the absence of intention. The filmmaker still has an initial intention, but this must not imply a stifled project. A feature

---

[42] Faria and Gontijo (2009).

[43] Bérnard da Costa (2010, 64).

film is always a collaboration between the artist and reality. Costa, like Robert Bresson, adopts Corot's formula as his own: "One must not seek, one must wait." What remains is not an answer to some question, the resolution of some problem, but powers, hypotheses, possibilities, and doubts. What matters is the movement that unfolds over time, not its purpose. Waiting but never expecting, because expecting is already associated with a representation and its represented object. Waiting, however, does away with that. Or, as Martin Heidegger says, "in waiting we leave open what we are waiting for [...] Because waiting releases itself into openness."[44]

Something different happens in *Colossal Youth*. Costa's cinema reappears in a different light, thanks to a new relationship that requires discovery, this time with Ventura. A relationship that is of a different nature but no less intense than the one maintained with Vanda. The film is born through this examination of a character; it is this examination itself. Costa explains:

> For me it was more like a day job. Before starting each day at work, what mattered most to me was how to really get to know that man, that big man I spoke to and who accepted my proposal to make a film. Then came the moment, within the first few weeks of filming, when I had to figure out how I could I match him with my camera—words are not enough. The camera had to go down and down and down because I couldn't stand up to him. I needed to be below. It wasn't instinctive, but in the first few weeks of filming I adopted this height, this positioning, this respect perhaps—that's how it came about and how it stayed. Sounded good to me. It looked good on him, especially for the picture, and it looked good on him in space. He was more or less the designer of the space.[45]

The filmmaker then positions the actors' bodies in front of a fixed camera, constantly "looking up," with a very rare inclination, and a light directed most of the time toward the lower central part of the screen, creating an unusual play of light and shadows. The bodies are apparently freer to enter and leave the frame. Frame, by the way, is an important concept for this film, as it gives the impression that I am constantly seeing paintings. The deliberate use of these elements merges with the pixels of the digital camera, along with the unique and un-repeatable authenticity of the Fontaínhas neighborhood, and the impenetrable opacity of those bodies. This combination gives rise to a peculiar and seemingly contradictory

---

[44] Heidegger (1959, 68).

[45] Duarte (2010, 29).

equilibrium between a sense of monumentality and a profound intimacy, between the subtlety of gestures and the magnificence of angles, lighting, and composition.

This impression of constantly being confronted with an image, a composition, a painting, does not in any way indicate a desire to create distances. Costa's dominance has nothing to do with exercising power over the spectator. A work of art is based on distance, artificiality, style, and what Ortega Y. Gasset (2005) referred to as dehumanization. However, this distance and dehumanization do not separate us from it; instead, they bring us closer to the world, or, rather, it immerses us in it. Although Costa's films employ a strong device of enunciation, everything happens as if it were impossible to determine this device by an insistence that would function as the origin and address of this enunciation.

Costa takes and is taken by characters and places, and insinuates something beyond the visible — it is there, and it is not. It is in this sense that Costa reconnects with a filmmaker like Bresson, who emphasized the use of his models as a way of embracing a certain mystery. "The thing that matters is not what they show me but what they hide from me and, above all, what they do not suspect is in them."[46] The model is the character. He does not add anything of himself but "opens himself up," disinterestedly to something that can occur and be captured. Both Costa and Bresson share a common preference for a particular understanding of encountering reality, which the Frenchman refers to as a "visible way of speaking" about bodies and the world. It is something that certainly brings both of them closer to Bazin and even Roger Munier's cosmophony. For it is the actual cosmos, whose visible face is mystery itself, that manifests itself in such encounters. For this manifestation to take place, work is needed, a "writing," in the case of Bresson. What sets Costa apart from the French director, in addition to his distinctive tone and inclination toward stylized naturalism rather than the automated neutrality of Bressonian models, is his desire to share the mise-en-scène, the dialogues, the script, with his characters. The Portuguese director comments:

> I make my films for Ventura, knowing that he — or others as well — probably won't want those films. [Ventura's] letter is a bit like that, it's the things he wants and the things I want, combined. And also things I don't want but have to accept, and things he doesn't want but has to accept. This is important: there are things in the film that Ventura himself doesn't like. That's why it's not documentary at all. It's good sometimes to have things you don't agree with.

[46.] Bresson (1977, 2).

We are very limited, me, you. It's always you in relation to something else — and that's what's difficult.[47]

What emerges is a unique kind of cinematographic portrait. I am not exactly invited to accompany the dramatic unfolding of a character, nor am I led to decipher the means and ways of approaching that character. I am standing in front of bodies, or parts of bodies, under a powerful light that cuts them out, that illuminates and darkens them. Costa tells us a story, gives it a body, while also imbuing it with an ethereal or ghostly quality, almost real, almost fictional. As Felipe Bragança rightly underlines, what is perceived then is a certain sense of dramaturgy and film narrative in which the question, "Who is the character?" is annulled and replaced by the problem of, "What can this character do?" It is from what this body can or cannot do, that the film will be designed. I guess I could even say that there are not exactly any characters. I don't see an actor wearing an idea or a character, but a body that is, in itself, an idea and a character. Ventura is a body with interference and inference capabilities. In the case of *Colossal Youth*, it was necessary to match Ventura. Before composing a pre-established sense of drama, the body does not present itself as a dramatic element or function but rather as a "geometric location of expression," as Felipe Bragança says, "it exists because it acts, it does not act to exist [...] The body exists, then the body is filmed — not the character yet."[48]

In *Colossal Youth*, nothing is more real and capable than a body. After all, who is Ventura? A Cape Verdean worker who immigrated to Lisbon in 1972. A former bricklayer who worked on the construction of the Gulbenkian Foundation museum. He was evicted by the government. He has been abandoned by his woman. He treats friends and neighbors as if they were his children. This brief description, however, does not allow us to define the character. Costa is not interested in working on a knowledge of the reasons that produce this life but rather diving into the direct confrontation between a life and what it can be, between what I would generally expect from this character and the freedom that the film grants him. Ventura is a type of fable-double that spreads through the desire for affirmation, imagination, and narrativity. Jacques Rancière helps me:

The often silent Ventura utters now and then an imperious command or lapidary sentence, and sometimes loses himself in his narrative or in the reciting of his letter. The camera portrays him as a strange animal, too large or too shy for

---

[47] Butcher (2010).

[48] Bragança (2007).

the set, whose eyes sometimes shine like those of a wild animal, and whose head is more often bent down than held up: the distracted gaze of a sick man. The point with Ventura is not to gather the evidence of a hard life, even if it is in order to figure out who cinema can share this life with, and to whom it can give it back as his or her life. The point is rather to confront what cannot be shared, the cracks that have separated a person from himself. Ventura is not an 'immigrant worker,' a poor man entitled to be treated with dignity and to share in the pleasures afforded by the world he has helped build. He is a sort of sublime drifter, a character from tragedy, someone who interrupts communication and exchange on his own. [49]

Ventura is the king in the diegesis of *Colossal Youth*. His posture, elegance, and distinctive gestures make him stand out in the images. He changes his mind frequently. He resists my judgments in each and every image. He goes back and forth in time. He is framed as if he were a walking work of art. The sequence of Ventura's visit to the Gulbenkian Museum somewhat condenses this enigma. Ventura reigns supreme as he sits on a Louis XIV style sofa to look at a Rubens hanging on a wall that he may have constructed. This scene transcends both the "present" and the "past," and encourages us to reconsider the temporality of the film and the nature of Ventura. His body is a conductor of narrative hypotheses, provisional and changing condensations of possible multiples, circulating among different layers of times. In another moment, a band around Ventura's head designates a series of sequences set in the past when he was working in the construction of the museum he had just visited. What time do these sequences belong to?

Ventura's body responds to me. It is he who generates time, space, and the world he occupies. Where he is, is here. What is within his reach is close. The moment he experiences is now. In other words, time is not merely a flow of events in which we find Ventura. Time is "a dimension of our being." It is born from the relationship of this body with things in the world, both sharing the same fabric. Time is the only source of heterogeneity. It is differentiation that accounts for all differences, itself being nothing more than differentiation. It is this diverse conception of time that Maurice Merleau-Ponty approached toward the end of his life. The sense of time, instead of being constituted by a series of intentional acts that would demonstrate the connection between the past and present as a merging of the consciousness of the past with the consciousness of

---

[49] Rancière (2009, 62).

the present, actually generated from the differentiations that take place within the spatializing/temporalizing vortex itself (the flesh). Now, the walls and plaster textures of *Colossal Youth* are also integral parts of Ventura. His eyes raise objects, indicating variations in light and space reception. To be a body is to be in relation. Costa does not even seem to acknowledge the materiality of the body. On the contrary, bodies are akin to zombies, transcending materialism and idealism. Man, as a corporeal individual, is neither matter nor spirit, nor any kind of entity or substantial form. I can resort here to the Nietzschean perspective: man is like a game of forces in continuous dynamism, a collection of impulses in constant flux, a process of perpetual creation.

In *The Visible and the Invisible*, amidst radically rejecting dualisms, Merleau-Ponty dwells precisely on a plane of sensitive communion between undivided bodies, which have not yet been subjected to the differentiations that frame them. The flesh is that thickness between what is seen and who sees it. There is a cohesion around flesh that is not solely connected to its visibility but rather to both its visible and invisible aspects, which shape the interconnectedness between beings. Costa echoes these statements when he portrays life as a continuous process of interaction between bodies, an ongoing dynamic in which organisms and the environment, rather than being postulated as independent and external to one another, are intertwined in a process of reciprocal constitution. Things are not simply neutral objects that I contemplate in front of Ventura; each of them symbolizes and evokes a certain behavior from Ventura, provoking favorable or unfavorable reactions from him. Ventura's tastes, character, and attitude toward the world are read in the objects he chooses to surround himself with.

Ventura possesses an opaque and unbreakable monumentality. Silence is what imposes itself as a response to him. A silence that does not paralyze us; on the contrary, it stimulates various speculations and demands creativity from us. Ventura's world is situated in an antepredicative instant, where objects interact and collide in a state of "original presence." Costa appears to be intrigued by capturing the precise moment of contact between one body and another—intercorporeity, as Merleau-Ponty would say. For his films reveal a perceptive faith that goes beyond perceptions and subjectivities. Ventura maintains a carnal relationship with his surroundings. It is possible to rediscover in each thing a certain style of being that reflects Ventura's behavior. There is no relationship of distance or domination between Ventura and what surrounds him but a less clear dialogue, a vertiginous proximity that prevents me from apprehending the character separate from things, or from defining things as pure objects without any human attributes, hence the fear that characters have of the whiteness of the poorly made walls of Casal da Boba. "When we are given white walls, we will stop seeing things. Then it will all be over," says Bete. Merleau-Ponty is quite close:

> *What I 'am' I am only at a distance, yonder, in this body, this personage, these thoughts, which I push before myself and which are only my least remote distances (mes lointains les moins éloignés); and conversely I adhere to this world which is not me as closely as to myself, in a sense it is only the prolongation of my body10—I am justified in saying that I am in the world.*[50]

Costa's work asserts itself in the exploration of the potential of a body. *Colossal Youth* constantly reminds me that the burden of uncertainty carried by a body is inseparable from it. It closely aligns with it. A body in time, in motion, never coincides with itself. He is tied to his own transition, his own variation. That is, a body is in an immediate and extended relationship with its non-present potential to vary. This relationship, to borrow a phrase from Deleuze, is real yet abstract. Real, tangible, yet incorporeal. Inseparable, coincident, yet disjointed.

With each image, Spinoza's famous question is repeated: "What can a body do?" It is necessary to bear in mind that this question ("What can a body do?") does not exactly refer to the activity of the body but to its powers. Spinoza proposes a new model of reflection. He claims that we know nothing about what the body can do. This declaration of ignorance is provocative. I speak of conscience and its decrees, of the will and its effects, of the various ways of moving the body, of controlling the body and managing the passions. However, I don't even know what a body is capable of. Ignorance of the power of the body, highlighted by Spinoza at the beginning of part III of the *Ethics*, attracted Deleuze's attention in numerous passages, and became the driving force of a series of reflections on the importance of ceasing to discuss the body and instead allowing it to express itself. Deleuze insists: "It is a matter of showing that the body surpasses the knowledge that we have of it, and that thought likewise surpasses the consciousness that we have of it."[51]

The centrality of the body and its potential is also evident in Costa's fundamental choice for the use of the foreground. The filmmaker is arguably the most celebrated portrait artist in contemporary cinema. The close-up, in general, suspends the narrative, abstracts its object from space-time coordinates, and makes

---

[50.] Merleau-Ponty (1968, 57).

[51.] Deleuze (1988, 18).

it independent of a specific space-time. For Deleuze, the face, the soul of the foreground, has two aspects: It is reflective or qualitative, and intensive or potent. It is reflective when his traits remain within the confines of a fixed thought, without evolving. The face is typically the gateway to subjectivity, inviting us to enter the realm of dramatic figures. But it can also be intensive, when its lines escape the outline, forming an autonomous series, pure power, unleashing a range of intensities. The philosopher is interested in exploring the various methods, across different art forms, of disrupting the usual functions of a close-up. After all, by abstracting the face from its spatio-temporal coordinates, the image opens up to the possibility of what Deleuze calls "any-space-whatever"—a tactile, singular, non-homogeneous, disconnected, and pure place of the possible.

This is precisely what the philosopher observes in Francis Bacon's painting. Bacon privileges the body, but the body experiences a sensation: "to give the sensation without the boredom of its conveyance. And the moment the story enters, the boredom comes upon you."[52] Bacon never lets go of the image but rather reveals an affective power in it, a sensitive force, which seems to erupt into figuration, in a movement that goes from the optical to the haptic. In Deleuzian terms, this represents a logic of sensation. Bacon himself, in an interview, exposes the crux of the issue:

> The other day I painted a head of somebody, and what made the sockets of the eyes, the nose, the mouth were, when you analyzed them, just forms which had nothing to do with eyes, nose or mouth; but the paint moving from one contour into another made a likeness of this person I was trying to paint. I stopped; I thought for a moment I'd got something much nearer to what I want. Then the next day I tried to take it further and tried to make it more poignant, more near, and I lost the image completely. Because this image is a kind of tightrope walk between what is called figurative painting and abstraction. It will go right out from abstraction but will really have nothing to do with it.[53]

For Deleuze, Bacon is a painter of heads and not faces:

> There is a great difference between the two. For the face is a structured, spatial organization that conceals the head, whereas the head is dependent upon the body, even if it is the point of the body, its culmination. It is not that the head

---

[52.] Sylvester (1999, 65).

[53.] Ibid., 12.

lacks spirit; but it is a spirit in bodily form, a corporeal and vital breath, an
animal spirit. It is the animal spirit of man: a pig-spirit, a buffalo-spirit, a dog-
spirit, a bat-spirit.... Bacon thus pursues a very peculiar project as a portrait
painter: to dismantle the face, to rediscover the head or make it emerge from
beneath the face.[54]

Is not this what happens in Costa's close-ups? Ventura's initial shots are driven by pure affection and sensation. What I see is an exploration of the intensive strength of that face, in a relationship of serene tension between the eyes, the mouth, the hair, and the entirety of the form. That is to say, the body as a certain vibration that goes from the face to the global space of the landscape, and vice versa. Both as surfaces serve as inscriptions of the other. Both absolutely open, permanently outside of themselves without ever coming out of themselves. It is the sensitive, "the one who watches at the doors of our life."[55]

This brings me back to the artistic craftsmanship of the filmmaker. Costa never misses the opportunity to transform the scenery of these miserable lives into artistic objects: a bottle of water, a knife, a glass, a hut, a furniture store, the work of backhoe loaders, and so on. The artistic aspect and the beauty that emanates from these buildings are what make the lives within them visible showcasing both their strength and despair. For this reason, Rancière sees the relationship between great art and the art of living of the poor as the central focus of the film. Because in this relationship, a way of nurturing the other emerges without conflating it with a specific method control, an inventory of idiosyncrasies, denunciation agenda. What interests Costa is not to show or denounce the "misery of the world" but to restore the richness and beauty of that particular world, "like a love letter whose words and sentences they can borrow for their own love lives."[56]

It is the emergence of another type of political cinema that appears on the horizon. Ventura is black; his body carries a whole story. Costa never denies these categories ("black," "immigrant," "poor"), but he seems to view them as contextual and dependent. The filmmaker rejects the idea of focusing on the big story, psychological motivations, and the general tendency to naturalize the experience. Ventura is not the result of a clearly defined identity, tied to a specific territory or social status, but rather a nameless singularity. He is the indistinguishable common. An indefinable character. Ventura is, indeed, poor, proletarian, black,

---

[54] Deleuze (2003, 20).

[55] Chauí (1999, 273).

[56] Rancière (2009, 60).

and an immigrant, but that does not define him. He resists any ties that precede or explain him. His role is always being defined. As the film progresses, it is constructed gesture by gesture, word by word. Costa, in turn, does not ignore his privileged place in the social distribution of powers, but he does not intend to speak "for" those from whom this privilege has been withdrawn. He does not want to make them "access" to that place either. As Jean-Louis Comolli says, the most important thing is not exactly the imperative of "how to film," "but rather how to make a film."[57] Costa comments on Ventura:

> *As soon as I saw Ventura, I felt that he could be an ancient figure like Henry Fonda, who, at the limit, can disappear among the extras, without ceasing to be a wandering character who carries a whole past—Ventura, so to speak. I mean, he carries the whole neighborhood with him [...] There is faith in Ventura in the film...I don't know if it's in the character or in the person. I don't even know if he and the others are really people or ghosts—or if it's the same thing. What I do know is that every day I felt like I had to live up to Ventura.*[58]

It is an ethical distance that is manifested in his films—a sense of detachment and, at the same time, a sense of closeness. Costa inaugurates a place that is both political and affective, where a body of a very peculiar order is staged. What I have before me is not an individual who recounts his life but an aesthetic figure who asserts his power. *Colossal Youth* does not explain the social roots that give rise to these neighborhoods. He decides to ignore the entire chain of reasons for attributing the sensible potency of a body.

In other words, cinema is not political because of the messages it transmits, nor because of the way it represents social structures, political conflicts, or social, ethnic, or sexual identities. Cinema is political in the way it configures a space-time sensorium that determines ways of being together or apart, outside or inside. It operates a "sharing of the sensible." It is a policy characterized by the rupture of the cause–effect relationship. What this policy aims at is not the transition from ignorance to knowledge, or from passivity to activity. The aesthetic experience is emancipatory to the extent that a worker forges a new body, "separating his gaze from the arms that work for the boss."[59] Through aesthetic experience, I create the body and constantly invent the scene in which it will

---

[57.] Comolli (2008, 169).

[58.] Guimarães and Ribeiro (2007).

[59.] Rancière (2005b, 5).

have visibility. This is how it happens with Vanda and Ventura. They do not pre-exist the conflict of politics, but they name themselves and the world they want to be part of. From this perspective, the political character of this cinema is understood as an aesthetic practice. Costa asserts Ventura's political dignity by associating it with his aesthetic integrity.

Costa's cinema expresses the inseparable co-belonging of intention and gesture. It is curious that Merleau-Ponty advocated this when he distanced himself from his earlier works and moved toward a new ontology. The search for what he came to call the "Wild Spirit" and the "Brute Being" is expressed in a beautiful work note from *The Visible and the Invisible*: "Being is what requires creation of us for us to experience it."[60] The phrase goes on to unite art and philosophy: "for art and philosophy together are precisely not arbitrary fabrications in the universe of the 'spiritual', but contact with Being precisely as creations."[61] What is at stake is not the claim that everything is art indiscriminately but rather that everything, in its uniqueness, has the potential to be art. It is not a question of banalizing but rather about the presence of life in the relationship with art. This involves Ventura, Costa, and me as the spectator. That is to say, we are not only encountering an artistic form but also something that can be experienced and explored through boy and mind, breaking into the visible and the sayable and creating sensible things. About his project—his and Ventura's—Costa elaborates:

> *Ventura is a sophisticated man. Not high-heeled sophistication, but up-and-down sophistication. He is a more elegant man than the Portuguese middle class in general, for example. He wanted to register that sophistication. I'm going to sound nostalgic or reactionary, but Ventura is from a time when there was greater family solidarity, some kind of community, something that has completely ceased to exist. Ventura's world will end with the white walls of his new home, that kind of whiteness without a past. You can no longer see anything on those walls. The working class can no longer find work, but unemployment has its good aspects. The people we argue with in the film are unemployed. There is idleness. They are always looking for a job, sometimes they find it, but two days later they are fired. With the discipline that I impose on filming, which is a bit tough (it was two years of work, six days a week), they not only make money again but, I think, they start to think again, to reflect. When they are working, in such heavy jobs (they are bricklayers, etc.), it is such hard work that it is difficult for a person to stay*

[60.] Merleau-Ponty (1968, 197).

[61.] Ibid.

alive. A film, as it is something more aerial at times, is an excellent moment for
people like that to feel things again, to have that sensibility that I think is dying
out. And I think they convey that very well, a sensitivity that is not common.
With my films, I wanted to try not to let a human sensibility disappear. I want to
document her at a time when she might disappear.[62]

The Portuguese filmmaker evokes tradition but wants everything to look anew, "like the first things to appear in the world." He reminds us that the most important thing is not the talent, the mastery of a technique, but rather how much of him is in it. Costa, like Denis, rediscovers the raw energy of early cinema and revives the evocative power of this art of recording. It is a return to the origins but not to a tabula rasa. Costa does not deny the legacy of a century of cinema, painting, literature, and so on. Merleau-Ponty sees something similar in Cézanne's search for another kind of depth: "it is, rather, the experience of the reversibility of dimensions, of a global 'locality'—every-thing in the same place at the same time, a locality from which height, width, and depth are abstracted, of a voluminosity we express in a word when we say that a thing is there."[63]

3.3 Tsai Ming-Liang

Duration, Body, Holding

Movie title. *The River* (1997). Cut. A static shot of two escalators. They cut the frame diagonally. One goes down. The other one is up. In the background, there is the facade of a department store. A meticulously calculated frame with shallow depth of field, emphasizing the two-dimensionality of the cinematographic image. After twenty seconds or more with no one in sight, only the screeching noise of the stairs in the soundtrack, a young woman begins her descent on the left side, while a boy climbs on the right. As they pass each other, they recognize themselves and turn, but the stairs insist on separating them, pushing their bodies away from each other. Upon reaching the lower level, the woman immediately turns around and climbs back up to where her friend is waiting. Now, both of them are in the upper right corner in the background, with the stairs and their noise in the foreground. They are old friends who haven't seen each other in a while. She asks what he is doing. "Nothing much," he replies. "Do you want

---

[62.] Butcher (2010).

[63.] Merleau-Ponty (1964c, 180).

to come with me?" she continues. They descend the stairs and exit the frame. Cut. They are riding a motorcycle. She is on his back. The camera follows them closely. The shot is over. Everything indicates that they are going to the same place they visited at the end of the previous shot. However, the duration of the scene momentarily suspends this deduction, as if it initially denied being part of a specific chain. Cut. An open shot of a movie set situated on the banks of a sewer channel that empties into the river—presumably that is the river from the title. At the director's command, assistants attempt to position a doll floating in the water, as if representing a dead person. It doesn't feel real. It doesn't look like a dead person. A few minutes pass. In a medium shot, an assistant pulls the dummy out of the water. The doll is broken. The clothes are torn. It is necessary to fix it. Actions are filmed in their entirety. Cut. We see the doll being thrown into the water. A tilt goes to the camera crew. It doesn't work. Cut. They try once more. Now the shot is even closer, with another tilt to the camera crew. "What's the problem?" someone asks. "It looks fake," says the director. The young woman who accompanied us in the first two scenes of the film appears in the upper right corner of the frame. The film seems to explore the notion of imprisonment. The camera reframes her. She says, "Lunch is ready." The director interrupts the work. "Let's have lunch."

Thus begins Tsai Ming-Liang's third feature film. The first scene, which is paradigmatic of this cinema, depicts an encounter between two bodies/characters that are paradoxically separated and reunited through the technological landscape of the contemporary metropolis. A scene about a serendipitous and apparently pleasant encounter. In a world of flooded apartments, anonymous sexual encounters, mysterious and painful illnesses, and desperate solitude, Tsai begins one of his most acclaimed films by affirming the possibility of a rare and difficult, yet still possible encounter. The following sequences forces us to confront a radical form of realism, an inundation of the narrative, and a desire for something beyond mere storytelling. In each shot, Tsai is exploring the potential forces of a frame, either delineating, obstructing, or unleashing them. This exploration prompts us to notice the smallest details, such as the bodies on the scene and their movements, creating a blend of transparency and opacity. Montage cuts by associating or associates by cutting. Tsai warns us that the framework for this story, if it needs one at all, will be up to us. In just under five minutes, the filmmaker establishes the ambiguous dynamic that is characteristic of his cinema, oscillating between unity and disunity, connection and disconnection, and character and body.

This can be seen as the central theme of Tsai's cinema. In terms of the social and behavioral impacts of Asian modernization, Taiwanese cinema has revealed filmmakers of the great importance (especially Hou Hsiao-Hsien and Edward Yang). Tsai figures in a peculiar and lonely way in this cinematography. His movies are the result of a strange mixture between a clinical fascination for observation/contemplation and a very particular mythology, in which social interaction only serves to intensifies loneliness. He appears to disregard the conflict between tradition and modernity, creating an urban and detached perspective that is temporally dilated. This perspective combines irony and anguish, comedy and tragedy, conscience and hypnosis. At times, it adopts a "minimalist" approach, while at other times, it features moments characterized by a certain histrionics, as seen in the unusual musical scenes of *The Wayward Cloud* (*Tian bian yi duo yun*, 2005).

From *Rebels of the Neon God* (*Qing shao nian nuo zha*, 1992) to *Days* (Rizi, 2020), Tsai works based on the same material. Some features are openly placed in the continuation of others—as is the case with *What Time Is It There?* (*Ni na bian ji dian*, 2001) and *The Wayward Cloud*. There appears to be a mysterious, fluctuating connection that links the characters' disappearances and reappearances, as if all of Tsai's films were part of the same, very long feature. It is a Truffautian film project, starring Lee Kang-Sheng, who always plays the role of Hsiao-Kang—the actor/model/fetish of the Taiwanese director does not appear only in the documentary *My New Friends* (1995), in the short film *Fish, Underground* (2001), and in the *Aquarium* (*segmento de Bem-Vindo a São Paulo*, [2004]). Regarding the actor, Tsai says:

> *I just want to film him even if he gets fatter and older. And now we get to the question of 'What Is Film?'. For many people, film is just a consumption article, something you buy. But in my opinion, when you think that is true, you are selling film short. Film has the potential to also be a lot of other things. And for me, Lee Kang-Sheng is a bridge towards that question: 'What Is Film?' Through him I discover what film is and what it can possible become.*[64]

Lee Kang-Sheng is "art cinema's most unlikely superstar."[65] As a prominent Chinese actor in today's globalized film culture, Lee is a remarkably ordinary body, always busy with predominantly mundane actions: sleeping, smoking, drinking, eating, urinating, and masturbating. However, he also embodies irregular,

---

[64] Vijn (2010).

[65] Hu (2005).

unforeseen, and extraordinary movements. Lee Kang-Sheng is simultaneously unique and representative, extraordinary and ordinary, a revelation or discovery that can easily be overlooked. His stardom illustrates an intriguing juxtaposition of exceptional and commonplace, the real person and the star, and beyond heterosexuality and homosexuality. He represents "an unexpected kind of (post) modern sexual subject that is yet to appear fully."[66]

Lee Kang-Sheng serves as a curious kind of metonym for Tsai's cinema. What the filmmaker obtains from the actor is something that is very difficult to achieve through more conventional methods of directing actors. What stands out in his performances does not seem to depend on the order of interpretation but rather on a bodily action, a movement oriented and exposed in front of the camera in the most direct way possible. Tsai remembers when he first worked with Lee Kang-Sheng and regretted having chosen him. His "infinite slowness," which was not "natural," exasperated him. "It's my way of being natural,"[67] replied Lee Kang-Sheng. Gradually, the filmmaker learned to embrace his slowness, incorporating his pace into his cinema. As in the films of Truffaut and Jean-Pierre Léaud/Antoine Doinel, we witness "a slow biography of the character (Hsiao-Kang), the story of the evolution of a face."[68]

The impression that we would always be seeing the same feature film results not only from the existence of an extremely coherent universe but also from a cinematographic style that is at the same time very characteristic and variable. This includes a preference for medium and more open shots of long duration, still camera shots, expressive entrances and exits of frames, the study of rhythms, physical humor, delicate variation of focus from background to foreground, and direct sound without a track. Not to mention the solitary characters and the frequent symbolisms, starting with water in all its facets, "(rain, river, lake), social (bathroom, sauna; bottled, polluted, rationed water), physiological (fluids entering or leaving the body),"[69] which can refer to both purity and pollution, life and stagnation, comfort and danger, and the emotional and the biological. "The absence or blockage of water can lead to absolute catastrophe (*The Hole* [*Dong*, 1998]) or to a complete regime of watermelon-perversion (*The Wayward Cloud*)."[70]

[66.] Martin (2003, 166).

[67.] Reynaud (1997, 36).

[68.] Panozzo and Schanton (2004, 32).

[69.] Martin (2008, 223).

[70.] Ibid.

At the beginning of *The River*, the film director convinces Hsiao-Kang to enter the river and play the role of the dead man, rather than using a puppet. Diving into polluted waters constitutes a kind of narrative starting point, establishing a causal relationship between the character's participation in the filming and the pain in his neck that he will feel throughout the film, as a certain common thread. Another narrative line is drawn, which is also related to water: an infiltration in the apartment where Hsiao-Kang and his parents live. These two stories form the problem that the characters are trying to resolve through the film. Hsiao-Kang applies creams and plasters, consults a shaman, a doctor, two homeopaths, an acupuncturist, and a Buddhist temple, without ever referring to an ultimate cause.

What is then perceived is an emphasis on the behavior of the characters, on how often their physical actions, almost always in silence and alone, dominate the frame. From its first moments, *The River* follows a very precise and particular logic in developing its characters. After Hsiao-Kang freshens up at the hotel, his friend arrives bringing clean clothes and some food. Soon after, they both engage in sexual activities. A cut interrupts the action and takes us to an unknown space, where a naked male body wrapped in a towel rejects the advances of another man. After going to the bathroom and washing up, he goes home to take care of his household chores, only to be seen having a snack at McDonald's. Then, we see a woman operating an elevator. She keeps some food, enters a man's car, and feeds him by hand. Tsai hardly provides us with a close-up. The idea is to observe the characters in wide shots without fragmenting the scene or directing the spectator's attention. A certain distance is preserved, underlining the significance of silences and ordinary actions against a larger backdrop.

These actions and behaviors do not seem to be combined according to a narrative progression or dramatic order. Cláudio da Costa stresses, for example, that the conversations between the characters mainly consist of practical dialogues: "eat this," "take that," "try this." The characters "wander aimlessly through the streets even when they have specific goals like those of Hsiao-Kang and his father who seek a cure for the disease."[71] They go to the doctor, the temple, the restaurant...none of these actions are dramatic. Even the incest scene between the father and the son is depicted throughout the film as inconsequential in terms of the narrative.

It is quite curious that, once the initial discomfort of prolonged action is overcome, the comic inevitably emerges, as seen in the scene where the father urinates for more than a minute, restarting twice. It is about "a relationship

---
[71.] Costa (2005, 188).

between temporal distension and the burlesque of situations. What makes one laugh is the irruption of reality within the film, which imposes itself on it, but which is not thought of as an effect."[72] Ultimately, not even Tsai's team could have anticipated that the actor would take such a long time. Humor is inherently linked to the duration of a shot, opening up to the improbable and allowing for the development of a certain "program of the lurking absurdity."[73] This is also due to the loneliness of the characters.

> *That is way I often choose the moments when my characters are alone, because the way they behave in relation to others is often influenced by politeness, an things which I don't feel are true [...] That is why I like to film bodies in these solitary situations so much, because I think that a person's body only really belongs to them when they are alone.*[74]

The River is a strange and disconcerting film yet extremely immersive and captivating. A film of silences, of desolation, depicting a universe fragmented by long and fixed sequence shots. Each character seems involved, trapped in his own and eternal solitude, completely disconnected from those around him. Over time, we will understand the connection between these three characters. They are a family. They live in the same house. As Jonathan Rosenbaum explains, the urban alienation that pervades virtually every scene in this film also "affects this film's narrative structure, so that at least half an hour passes before it's clear that the son and his two parents are even related."[75]

Tsai's world is certainly filled with constant and inexplicable disjunctions. His filmography describes a failure of affective expression and physical interaction, consistently portraying the characters as islands. It is not for nothing that many critics describe the Taiwanese filmmaker as a poet of urban solitude, in a line that comes from the aimless youth of *Rebels of the Neon God*, followed by the empty apartments of *Vive l'amour* (*Ai qing wan sui*, 1994), and the characters who wander aimlessly across *The River*. Like Michelangelo Antonioni, Tsai would be "an artist of uprooting," of the incommunicable, of the upcoming apocalypse, of an existentialist humanism in crisis.

---

[72] Frazão (2009, 77).

[73] Ibid.

[74] Joyard et al. (1999, 100–103).

[75] Rosenbaum (2000).

It is impossible not to mention Antonioni and his trilogy of incommunicability (*The Adventure* [*L'Avventura*, 1960], *The Night* [*La notte*, 1961] and *The Eclipse* [*L'eclisse*, 1962]). Antonioni's cinema is not solely about boredom or alienation, as many have suggested, but rather about a fresh perspective on seeing and feeling the world. A cinema in which the idea of solitude unfolds in a detained thought about the construction of the shot and the montage, of the associations of man and the setting, or rather, in the incongruity of this connection. Antonioni insistently reflects on the objects, color, width, and thickness of the walls. His camera does not dramatize the action; instead, it seeks to empty it of any emphasis (be it psychological, moral, or dramatic).

The Adventure, for example, is a type of road movie in which the focus shifts from the foreground to the background. A film about a disappearance. However, it is a disappearance that gradually loses its significance and depth, tainting the narrative structure of the film. As Pascal Bonitzer (1989) once said, we are dealing here with the disappearance of a disappearance. The adventure that names this movie forces durations and spaces inside the characters, excavating them from within.

His characters are looking for freedom. Imprisoned, they struggle in a useless search, living in a frozen and repetitive situation. In *The Night*, this condition has its ultimate consequences: the beginning and end of the film are absolutely identical, with the characters repeating themselves. With each film, this theme evolves into the realm of the object, the raw and unprocessed, within time and space. This is the case with the famous final sequence of *The Eclipse*, in which, for seven minutes, the film abandons the fictional characters we had followed until that moment, and, like a documentary, shows us images of an eclipse.

Tsai walks very clearly through the doors opened by Antonioni in the 1960s. The characters in *The River* are involved in minimalist scenic performances, wandering through spaces that are sometimes small and claustrophobic, sometimes large and aligned to bodies that are striped of personality and psyche. Although the influence of the seminal Italian filmmaker is undeniable, would it not be a reduction, as Adrian Martin (2008) tells us? Rosenbaum summarizes:

> *Ever since I first encountered Tsai's work in Vive l'amour, I've tended to regard it as a kind of update on the urban melancholia Michelangelo Antonioni used to specialize in, especially during the 50s and 60s—a reference point that can only take one so far, as it does with another Taiwanese modernist, Edward Yang. One of the main differences may be that Antonioni is a master of alienated moods, but atmosphere tends to be more a given than a creation in Tsai's movies, which*

conjure up more mysteries in relation to what the characters tend to be inartic-
ulate and confused about—sexuality most of all.[76]

I think of a movie like *The Eclipse*. Right at the beginning of the feature, Monica Vitti's character opens the curtains of the house in the middle of an argument with her boyfriend. The view that emerges from the window is that of a strangely futuristic and disconnected space. The film's movement is established from the interior to the exterior. This movement is always born from a sense of subjective homelessness, from a feeling of self-loss. Antonioni uses the scenery and the objects in contrast to the characters, creating a dynamic where the object come to life through the vulnerability of the characters and the passivity of man himself. The scenery devours man, because man has abdicated the space around him, given up on living as a being in action. The streets, lights, bedroom walls, ashtrays, and fans seem to march on, while human bodies seem to be in constant motion, in sequences of pure despondency and emptiness.

Tsai also remains undecided between telling and presenting. But for him, the path seems to be the other way around. The atmosphere tends to be more of a given than a creation. Silence does not signify incommunicability but rather seeks more concrete meanings. In *The River*, immersion in everyday life and in the most intimate bodily processes, which involve basic affections and feelings, such as pain, fear, melancholy, and desire, appears without the weight of the existential stigma that besets Antonioni's characters. What we see on the screen are opaque, manipulable bodies that are open to the exploration of the world. Space can no longer be seen as a mirror reflecting conflicted interiorities. It is more intuited than constructed. The location already contains the scene to be staged. For Tsai, the location imbues the movie with a certain existence. In an interview, he commented on the issue of space, describing it as something that exudes a form of life: "Every location holds a certain form of life. I try to simplify the locations as much as possible and point out its traces of life. In my various scenarios, it works somewhat the same way. I want to define the essence of the matter, the main point of a place."[77]

Antonioni is also a poet of the body, capturing attitudes and postures devoid of conscience. In his films, bodies are captured while feeling something, but they struggle to articulate what they feel. This struggle is there some unforgettable scenes, such as the end of *The Adventure*, when Monica Vitti strokes Gabriele

---

[76.] Ibid.

[77.] Leopold (2002).

Ferzetti's head. In this sense, Deleuze describes a perfect "double composition" in Antonioni's work, highlighting the interplay between a cinema of the body and a cinema of the brain, and showcasing their distinct rhythms. For the French philosopher, the body "is never in the present," containing only "the before and after," producing and expressing enormous anxiety and anguish. These feelings are inscribed in the body and move through space. He elaborates:

> *Tiredness and waiting, even despair are the attitudes of the body. No one has gone further than Antonioni in this direction. His method: the interior through behavior, no longer experience, but 'what remains of past experiences', 'what comes afterwards, when everything has been said', such a method necessarily proceeds via the attitudes or postures of the body. This is a time-image, the series of time. The daily attitude is what puts the before and after into the body, time into the body, the body as a revealer of the deadline.*[78]

Things are slightly different in Tsai. The long take is a kind of return to the origins, reflecting a certain primitivism. One always seeks the eruption and clairvoyance of the present, of duration, of awareness of this present and this duration. His films are marked by the "cinematic fact," by the immersion in the experience of a concrete world, where actions are based solely on what one sees e hears. The present as rupture. The present as an impasse. If a good part of modern cinema sought to create aesthetic effects of transgression and denial, threatening an alienated reception of reality, today, this kind of denial has become somewhat unproductive. In a film such as *The River*, the event disrupts linear progression, engulfing the story by the urgency of experiencing a seemingly banal situation. The banal, however, happens and is happening with such force that the opposition between the internal and the external, between cinema and the world, between viewer and film, seems outdated, revealing a plane of immanence in a reception that dismantles the representative premise. It is the feeling so well described by Adrian Martin:

> *Even when Tsai makes use of compositions consecrated by Antonioni—accompanying a character alone through an urban and architectural frame, moving without hesitation along a line or vector, climbing an escalator, walking down the street or crossing the platform of a station—there is a feeling that the planes have less of atomization, the pulverizing of a solitary individual inside the concrete and*

[78.] Deleuze (1989, 189).

crystal arches, than the possibility, at the same time invisible and impossible,
of bodies and lines meeting/clashing, creating a delicate suspense. Each image
vibrates with a latent connection that can manifest at any time.[79]

In Tsai, as in Denis and Costa, a specific form of realism is established, distinct from the realism of the Italians who inspired Bazin and Ayfre. A form of realism that does not aim to create an illusion of reality. Instead, it follows the desire to relate cinema and art to a certain reality from which it emerges, incorporating this reality aesthetically within the work and situating the oeuvre itself as a transforming force. We are talking about a type of realism that is "referential," without necessarily being representative, and, at the same time, "engaged," without adhering to any political agenda. A form of realism that blurs the line between reality and fiction, refusing to see reality as a kind of second nature of a film. Authors of phenomenological inspiration, despite being involved in some of these quarrels, guide us in pursuing the idea of image as an ongoing conflict between the unity of the thing represented and its countless potentialities, a duality between being and appearing, between the concrete and the abstract, and between the immanent and the transcendent. By celebrating the aesthetic experience as a sensitive call to action in the encounter with cinema, the previously investigated authors point us toward alternative paths.

Narrative in Tsai's cinema, in turn, as suggested by Jean-Pierre Rehm, is abandoned "to the actors' bodies. To their opaqueness. However, this opaqueness is two-fold."[80] The Taiwanese filmmaker is obsessed with actions that apparently have no purpose other than filling time (watching television, riding a motorcycle, sitting still), calling our attention to the fact that the characters have a body: eating, masturbating, drinking water, sleeping, having sex or a shower. Tsai wants us to feel intimate with his characters. Their most banal gestures are thrown into our laps. Chris Berry analyzes this curious equation of intimacy and opacity and concludes: "We are with the characters, but they are still alone."[81] Watching a film by Tsai involves adjusting to the inexplicable behavior of his characters. Most of the time, they engage in activities that may seem strange to us, either because they are somewhat absurd or simply silly, or because they align with a fantasy that we do not have access to. In fact, we know little about Hsiao-Kang's family. The mother works as an elevator operator at a fast-food restaurant and has

---

[79] Martin (2008, 221).

[80] Joyard et al. (1999, 11).

[81] Berry (1999, 160).

a lover who sells pornographic video tapes. The father engages in homosexuality in secret. After all, who is Hsiao-Kang? He resists the word. He is an enigmatic character but not exactly mysterious; it is as if he was governed by different laws.

Hsiao-Kang has something "Bartlebian" about him. Bartleby, the clerk who replies that he "would rather not," is a character from the novel of the same name by Herman Melville (1997). He appears one day, out of the blue, in the solicitor's office in response to an advertisement. He is hired shortly after a brief exchange of names. Bartleby is a character with no past and whose motivations are inaccessible. Deleuze (1998) suggests that the defining characteristic of this character that he lacks specificity. He is just an ordinary man, lacking essence, who refuses to commit to some stable personality. Bartleby and Hsiao-Kang share the same claim: that of a subjectivity that is always to come. The formula of "I'd rather not," as Deleuze says, "germinates and proliferates," making the narrative to revolve around the same negation. Here, the characters are different. Hsiao-Kang is a reserved, timid and silent presence. He is a face, a body, a space, and a routine. Nothing to reveal. Nothing to hide. No rebellion. No refusal. He only displays a humble and serene acceptance of his conditions and an incorrigible approachability.

However, as tempting as it may be to interpret the characters' attitudes as passive or to define them as aimless wanderers and vague dreamers, their true essence, as I am trying to argue, lies elsewhere. The body is not a "blind mechanism" or the sum of independent causal sequences. It does not play a role of passivity and inertia but rather connects us with others and with the world. The actors in Tsai are malleable, adaptable, open bodies, they are always in a constant state of availability, always on alert. Eating, having sex, walking, sitting on a chair, turning on faucets, opening doors, all these everyday actions become sensory and emotional experiences. Hsiao-Kang touches objects like a child, fully available to the world and open to every sensation.

In this sense, drawing a comparison with comedians like Buster Keaton and Jacques Tati may be more fruitful. It is an association that extends far beyond the portrayal of characters and the physical comics that are so common in the works of these three filmmakers. Buster Keaton's cinema, for example, values a kind of subordination of the narrative to comedy, consistently exploring the influence of twentieth-century modernity on the human body. In many ways, his films focus on characters who need to master new technologies, objects, and environments. This is the case in *Electric House* (1922), in which Keaton mistakenly receives an electrical engineering degree and tries to adapt to his new profession—the engineer who should have graduated in his place, of course, will seek revenge.

The technology, however, is not there to emphasize the alienating properties of the machine as seen in Chaplin's *Modern Times* (1936). Keaton, on the contrary, celebrates the machinistic nature of cinema and embraces a certain artificiality without illusionism. The sun rises quickly at the beginning of *The Scarecrow* (1920), creating a magical effect that is consciously false. More than that. Unlike Chaplin's lovable tramp, Keaton never cries out for sympathy. He is a completely unimpressive character. The viewer is not invited to identify with him.

Keaton is always at the mercy of chance, completely indifferent to the forces around him. It is precisely this impassivity and adaptability to these forces that allow him to survive and triumph. Keaton always finds a way. He sees the objects around him not only for their inherent properties but also for their potential. For him, all bodies (living or inanimate) are capable of assuming only temporary identities, and everything is always in a state of flux. Then, a car can, for example, turn into a sailboat (*Sherlock Jr.*, 1924). Keaton has faith. He believes in the universe, even when it does not give him reasons to do so. It is kind of his secret. Keaton seems to grasp the logic of chaos.

In relation to Tati, mentions to Chaplin are also common and inevitable. However, French cinema operates according to a different mechanism than the gag. Carlitos invents the gag on the spot and in a way that catches everyone off guard. Hulot never invented anything. He does not create the gag, nor does he alter the course of the events. He is merely a witness. In *Monsieur Hulot's Holiday* (*Les Vacances de Monsieur Hulot*, 1953), in the cemetery sequence, the character's car breaks down. He opens the trunk. An air tire camera falls to the ground onto a heap of leaves. The leaves adhere to it, forming a wreath. Hulot did not do it on purpose. Quite the opposite. Tati reverses the comedy equation. In his films, there is no standout hero, someone who is funnier, kinder, or more naive than the others. Hulot could be any man. His psychology is reduced to a technique of behavior. There is not a clear distinction between the real world and the world of the comic character, as is the case with Chaplin, polarizing the comic virtualities of the world. Hulot, on the contrary, is the most ordinary of characters. The world becomes comedic precisely because of Hulot's lack of comic ability. In an interview with Bazin and Truffaut, Tati explains:

> *What I tried to do from the beginning was to convey more truth to the comic character. There is a school of comedy in which the character comes to us already with a kind of label: 'You'll see that I'm the court jester, that I can do an enormous amount of things, I can sing, dance, I know how to be funny'. It's a tradition that*

comes from the circus, from the music hall. I come from this school, but what I've always tried was to prove and show that we're all potentially comical.[82]

In *Monsieur Hulot's Holiday*, Tati's character is the only adult truly happy. He is a character thrust into the world, bound to the present moment, and immersed in the flow of time. In this sense, it is noteworthy that the only characters in his films who are both likable and funny are children. The image of children and dogs, whose poetry, running through the streets, opens and closes a movie like *My Uncle* (*Mon Oncle*, 1958). Neither animals nor children know melancholy or boredom. There is a certain coincidence between the animal, the child, and the passage of time. The present fascinates them.

That is to say, Hulot embodies a certain disorder, a childish and animal spirit that perpetuates itself ad infinitum after his passing. If Carlitos is an end in itself, Hulot is more like a catalyst. Before making us laugh, Tati creates an entire universe. A world ordered around Hulot but without him. Hulot spreads out among the other characters. "He may be personally absent from the more comic gags because Mr. Hulot is nothing but the metaphysical incarnation of a disorder that perpetuates itself long after his passing."[83]

This is what we see in a radical way in *Playtime* (1967). It is a film without any close-ups, no protagonists, and very little dialogue. A film where the action is always happening in the background or on the periphery of the frame. In most scenes, we don't see one, two, or three people but fifty. *Playtime* starts with Hulot and continues in a euphoric series of encounters between people and things, where the functionality of modern life seems to be renounced in the name of a certain notion of beauty and experimentation. An airport terminal, an office lobby, a hotel, an exhibition, an apartment complex, a modern restaurant, and so on. Sound is an important part of this game. Sound guides our gaze. Sound stimulates our imagination. It's so intriguing. Sound is something Tati finds and builds. It's something between the artificial and the realistic, which we observe and discover. The dialogues are either meaningless or do not appear to be situated in a dramatic context. Noises are a cacophony of completely identifiable elements.[84] *Playtime*, as the name implies, is a kind of amusement park. No

---

[82] Bazin and Truffaut (1958, 2).

[83] Bazin (1992, 51).

[84] Tati filmed without sound and composed his soundtrack separately. Perhaps it's fair to say that he directed his films twice.

wonder David Bellos describes the film as "an expression of amazement at the human capacity to create."[85]

Something similar happens to Tsai's characters. *The River* is grounded in a profound faith in the world and a commitment to the experiences lived by the characters. Hsiao-Kang (model-protagonist-body) performs actions that are almost symbolic of a state of affairs, and the shots serve less as unit of action and dramaturgy and more as an exercise for the eye. He maintains a curious attitude toward the world. For Tsai, the best way to understand human beings is to examine how they engage in the practice of their existence. The shot becomes a field for phenomenological observation. Hsiao-Kang feels constantly drawn to the outside world, and his body fully embraces this call, immersed itself in an adventure that allows him to discover a little more about a world that never ceases to surprise him:

> Hsiao-Kang drinks water from a bottle as if for the first time, tests the temperature of his bath, moves around in front of a window to catch the breeze, smells his food, touches objects like a newborn child. He is completely available to the world, open to sensation throughout his body and ready to adapt to things, to all the challenges of the real, at the risk of hurting himself.[86]

I am not in the world as someone who contemplates it from a distance. Phenomenology presents itself as an incredibly versatile collaborator: It serves as a philosophical method aimed at accessing to the essence of objects, reflecting on the experience of perception, and as a theory of being, opening the door to questions of manifestation and the presence of things. In Merleau-Ponty's conception, "truth does not 'inhabit' only 'the inner man', or more accurately, there is no inner man, man is in the world, and only in the world does he know himself."[87] He continues: "The world is not what I think, but what I live through. I am open to the world, I have no doubt that I am in communication with it, but I do not possess it; it is inexhaustible."[88] This is Hsiao-Kang's adventure. He does not feel paralyzed despite the contradictions of the sensible world. He defines himself through this exploratory movement and a somewhat irresponsible attitude toward the world. Tsai demonstrates a phenomenological attitude,

---

[85] Bellos (2001, 236).

[86] Joyard et al. (1999, 53–55).

[87] Merleau-Ponty (2002, XII).

[88] Ibid., XVIII–XIX.

conducting his own philosophical investigation into being and consciousness through an extraordinary exploration of the body's possibilities and reversible and chiasmatic vision. Like a phenomenologist, Tsai strives for a somewhat "return to things themselves":

> *What interests us is not the reasons one can have to consider the existence of the world 'un certain'—as if one already knew what to exist is and as if the whole question were to apply this concept appropriately. For us the essential is to know precisely what the being of the world means. Here we must presuppose nothing—neither the naïve idea of being in itself, therefore, nor the correlative idea of a being of representation, of a being for the consciousness, of a being for man: these, along with the being of the world, are all notions that we have to rethink with regard to our experience of the world. We have to reformulate the sceptical arguments outside of every ontological preconception and reformulate them precisely so as to know what world-being, thing-being, imaginary being, and conscious being are.*[89]

In philosophy, the pursuit of this "return to things" required a departure from purely abstract and an engagement with the world—as Merleau-Ponty used to say—"in flesh and blood."[90] Tsai's approach involves a narrative devoid of causes or effects, without psychological, moral, or ideological emphasis. He focuses on a hyperbolic accentuation of the materiality of bodies, on space and the characterization of his characters. His movies vibrate at each image with the possibility of a latent connection. Until now, I have used references to painting, Cézanne, and Bacon, but I could also use the "non-language" of dance, because, as José Gil explains, dance creates "a plane of immanence. Dance, therefore, does not express meaning; she is the sense, (because the movement is the sense)."[91]

Gil and dance help me understand that the body in this cinema is neither a thing nor an idea, but spatiality and motricity, dwelling an exploratory power. It operates on an "I can" basis. The physicality of bodies is a kind of barrier which consciousness encounters in its journey into the material world. Tsai's return is a return to the body. Merleau-Ponty reinforces at all times that it is through transitivity that we see and touch each other. Our senses operate in chiasmatic manner: the eye feels, the hands see, the eyes move with touch, and

---

[89] Merleau-Ponty (1968, 6–7).

[90] Merleau-Ponty (2002, 318).

[91] Gil (2001, 79).

so on; in other words, the crucial point is how the character's body absorbs the exteriority of the experience. There is a dilution at play here between reflective reasoning and subjective intentionality, the outside and the inside. The visible is a transcendent to which it is only possible to achieve through an experience that is also transcendent, entirely outside of oneself, yet without losing touch with one's own self.

Let us go back to dancing. Dancing once again reinforces the theme of the body and movement. Dancing embraces the transient nature of movement, which may seem aimless but is, in itself, a process and a form of progress. "Dancing is not signifying, symbolizing or indicating meanings or things," explains Gil, "but tracing the movement thanks to which all these senses are born. In danced movement, meaning becomes action."[92] In fact, considering a film like *The River*, I feel compelled to introduce another term into this equation. After all, is it possible to conceive a body without an intrinsic connection between movement and sensation, where each one immediately evokes the other? Starting from this intrinsic connection between the body, movement, and sensation, even the smallest and most literal displacements summons a qualitative difference, bringing to light a sensation that, in turn, has a tendency to fold itself, resonate, and interact with other sensations. These sensations intensify each other in unquantifiable ways, capable of unfolding again in action in unpredictable ways. In this sense, film highlights the logic of the world: the passage of meaning or meaning as passage.

We must then reconsider some adjectives commonly linked to Tsai, such as "apocalyptic,"[93] "melancholy,"[94] or "morbid."[95] This is the question Martin asks himself: "why do some people only see despair, emptiness, tears?"[96] Let us look at the last shot of *Vive l'amour*: a six-minute long sequence-shot in which we see one of the central characters, Mey, in a close-up, sitting on a street bench, with a destroyed amusement park in the background. She cries uncontrollably, pulls herself together, smokes a cigarette, and succumbs to tears once more. Why is Mey crying? Maybe it's the "perversely lucid regret of a bleary morning-after."[97] Perhaps "sadness has nothing to do with feeling lost or misplaced in modern

---

[92] Ibid.

[93] Veríssimo (2000).

[94] Costa (2005).

[95] Moriconi (2010).

[96] Martin (2008, 222).

[97] Lim (2001).

society, but rather with feeling all too much a part of it."[98] Tsai goes so far as to suggest that the scene would be a kind of delayed effect of the episode that occurred the night before, while she was taking a shower: if she died, who would care? She then becomes aware of her loneliness.

In fact, all of these readings add explanatory explanations to what we see. Because events do not link up with each other according to a psychological motivation, nor do they converge toward an end that provides meaning to what lies behind. The physical actions that we see on the screen are not configured dramatically, they do not promote the progress of the narrative through the drama. Even when the characters have certain goals, when we know that Hsiao-Kang and his father leave home to visit a doctor, in *The River*, the characters seem to wander aimlessly. What we see then is a lament that has no specific history, past or present.

The experience of the world is the world itself, detached from an organizing principle and the conditions of its representation. This is what Jean-Luc Nancy summarizes: "wanting the world, but not wanting a subject of the world (neither substance, nor author nor master)."[99] It is a question of thinking about the world anew but also of enduring the perception that this thinking about the world will not lift us above or bring us closer to it. It is a thought that prefers to participate in what it thinks. The world holds us and abandons us at the same time, all at once, in a single glance. Thought already proceeds under this demand, under this pressure, under the aegis of a world that always shows itself above and beyond our gaze. It is a question of thinking about a certain absence in its openness and evidence. It is also, therefore, a question of going beyond without going beyond the world.

Then I feel closer to Martin, who wonders if the tears represent sadness and despair or the possibility of a new beginning. Tsai's films do not provide answers or clues. No illness or inner neurosis, no trauma or loss can explain Mey's lament. What happened before the movie is irrelevant, and what happens after that is unknowable. Of course, as spectators, we can certainly relate to the sadness and despair of modern life, and the alienation and inhumanity of the third world metropolis. However, there is, ultimately, little or no social analysis in Tsai's work. When discussing "the breakdown of the traditional family," "alienation from life in the big city," "vacuity of relationships," expressions that are frequently mentioned in articles about the director, don't convey much. For Martin, we should take Tsai's words literally when he emphasizes considering his

---

[98.] Jones (2008, 48).

[99.] Nancy (2007, 49).

characters more like plants that need water than like three-dimensional subjects in a conventional drama.[100]

It is evident that Tsai works simultaneously on different levels of ambiguity and reversibility while focusing on elements such as mise-en-scène, character, plot, and the impenetrable thickness of bodies. At times, his style could also be describes as having a "heavy hand," with great rigor regarding framing, where the elements within the shot compose a spatial geometry meticulously calculated to the millimeter.[101] This may be a structural contradiction. The worst and the best of this cinema are found in this dilemma, between the appreciation for a freer cinema, for a realism more focused on a pre-predicative dimension of experience, and the insistent desire to talk about the ills of the contemporary world. In a way, like Bresson, Tsai reminds us that the "bad" filmmaker, that is, the one who imposes his will on the visible, is very close to the "good" one. The difference between the two is always on the verge of indiscernibility. Although the Bressonian models are entirely submissive to the filmmaker's will, when they do what they are told, they also end up doing something else, something unexpected. Bresson, like Tsai, represents an encounter between the active and the passive, the voluntary and the involuntary, the thought and the not yet thought.

What Tsai, Denis, Costa, and Apichatpong aim to celebrate life by re-empowering the body, reaching it before language, before it can be identified as a thing among things, reclaiming this state to evoke diverse thoughts and feelings in the spectator. *The River* wants to open our eyes and ears. It is less psychological and more physiological, not to mention physical—at the end of the session, we feel Hsiao-Kang's pain. There is a certain pedagogy in this desire: a didactic approach that only reveals a method and not an outcome, a journey and not a

---

[100.] Not to mention that *Vive l'amour* is, in fact, a film with two endings. Just before Mey's crying scene, Tsai offers us another long shot that closes the participation of the other protagonists of the feature, Hsiao-Kang and Ah-Jung. The first one comes out from under the bed, where it was hidden. He lays down next to Ah-Jung, who remains asleep. Hsiao-Kang enacts a romantic scene, wide-eyed, apprehensive but excited about his own game. He kisses Ah-Jung's cheek, covers himself with the boy's arm, and closes his eyes. In a sense, the strange fullness of this scene works as a counterpoint to what will follow.

[101.] I see myself far from the notion of "slow cinema," a fairly recent phenomenon in conceptual terms that has gained unprecedented critical value in film studies over the last two decades. One of the first to coin the expression "slow cinema" was the French film critic Michel Ciment in 2003, citing, as an example of this trend, directors such as Bela Tarr, Abbas Kiarostami, and Tsai. Supposedly based on a central dichotomy between slowness on the one hand and action on the other, "slow films," according to Matthew Flanagan (2008), are those based on the "employment of long shots, decentered and underrated ways of telling stories, and a pronounced emphasis on stillness and the everyday." Since then, many other filmmakers have been associated with the trend, and various film critics and authors have discussed this concept, expanded its theoretical application, and paved the way for its popularization (mainly) in the Anglo-Saxon world. I see myself far from these analyses because the idea of "slowness" seems misleading to me; it is much more a symptom than a cause. This devotion to stillness and contemplation explains, for example, how it was possible for this aesthetic to be so easily categorized, routinized, and reproduced (very rarely with the same potency as Tsai) as a kind of standard international artistic style. However, what bothers me most is precisely the emphasis on contemplation and almost absolute neglect of composition.

final destination. Tsai does not offer any solution or decree about the world. He does not show any definitive picture of the state of affairs but instead leaves us with the impression that we know nothing and that we live in the unknown. However, Hsiao-Kang manages to instill in us, through each image, a certain faith in the world.

3.4 Apichatpong Weerasethakul

To the Indeterminacy of an Opening

A black screen. There is some background music playing: something like Erik Satie's "furniture music," which blurs the line between melody and texture. It aims to create a certain atmosphere but in a quite serene manner. After almost thirty seconds, the credits roll. Cut. Trees sway in slow motion in a gentle *contra-plongée*. The image lingers for some time, combined with the music. A close-up of a man in uniform. He looks down. Cut. Another close-up. Another man in uniform. He also looks down. Music gives way to noises between the rural and the urban. A woman's sweet voice, out of frame, asks if the man in front of us has a degree in pharmaceuticals. He lifts his head, looks in our direction, and says that he only did it for two years, finding it rather boring. Then, he went to study medicine. What follows is a job interview of sorts. The frame remains fixed on the face of the interviewed character, and the rhythmic succession of questions and answers takes unexpected turns. "Do you like circles, squares, or triangles better?" she asks. "Circles," he replies. "What is your position in basketball?" she asks. "Central." After almost two minutes of a close-up shot, a more open shot situates us in the space. We are in an office. In the foreground is the man of the initial close-up, sitting on a sofa in the right corner of the frame. There are huge windows in the background, overlooking a forest. The woman inspects the hand the man uses to performs surgeries. He does not appear to like her very much. The interview ends. He has to go to the hospital emergency room. He gets up and says goodbye. A counter-shot takes over her point of view. The man is leaving the office. She then greeted the other man who was waiting for her and apologized. He looks shy. He brought her a gift: pork. The person who was interviewed returns to the office. It's his first day, and he does not know how to get to the emergency room. Another doctor appears at the door. The doctor conducting the interview is expected to be in a different department. She grabs her belongings and walks toward the door. In a close-up, we see her closing her office door against the light. She is now a silhouette. In the background, we can see a sunny green field. As she exits the frame, the camera initiates its first tracking movement and, in a reframing, replaces the hospital for the countryside landscape. The conversation continues out of frame, but now we the forest out there through a window. Blank credits appear over green. The shot lingers. As if I were under hypnosis, I hardly notice (what about you, dear reader?) that, at the end of the conversation, still off-screen, the characters meta-linguistically discuss about the numerous takes of that scene.

The opening sequence of *Syndromes and a Century* (*Sang sattawat*, 2006), Apichatpong Weerasethakul's fourth feature, establishes a specific harmony and a deliberate atmosphere to which characters, landscapes, and various objects seem absolutely connected. What I see and feel is a unique perception of time, an innocent portrayal, a simplicity in recording, which invite us to another type of fruition. A kind of praise of the ephemeral, and, at the same time, a crystallization of time, with shots floating above this flow. Apichatpong places the spectator in a constant state of awe before the world, elevating the apparent simplicity of its naturalistic staging to complex layers of meaning and an openness to the mysteries of existence, to a constant parallelism between the naturalism of the scenes and a spiritual, magical, metaphysical whole. This is something omnipresent in all of his works, something that contaminates each frame and projects itself within and beyond the filmic matter. Apichatpong demands from us to fully commit to its melodic and dramatic proposition.

Apichatpong immerses his images in a certain disarray. His cinema expresses an atmosphere or tone rather than a mode of thinking. A method has been developed in which the most unpredictable elements, such as the environment on the day of shooting, become dominant. Apprehending or representing an object is less important than experiencing "a kind of aesthetic intoxication."[102] One always perceives the pre-existence of a concept. *Syndromes and a Century* does not try to hide its "construction" traits. Shots are the outcome of a "conceptual operation of which they are both access route and result."[103] The filmmaker confronts reality with the intention of imbuing the images with a certain flesh, to transforming them into a world.[104]

From *Mysterious Object at Noon* (*Dokfa nai meuman*, 2000) to *Memoria* (2021), the Thai filmmaker transforms the most ordinary objects and landscapes

---

[102] Oliveira Jr. (2010, 124–25).

[103] Oliveira Jr. (2008).

[104] An example of this approach: on working with non-actors, Apichatpong wants them to also portray an element of their acting. He aims at a state somewhere between the natural and tense. The actors must know what he wants them to do.

into ineffable and enigmatic images, creating spectral zones where everything is fleeting and mutating. In these spaces, stories metamorphose, change direction, or begin anew, transitioning from fact to fiction and from fantasy to documentary. The characters undergo transformations, shifting from male to female, from human to animal, and from earthly to extraterrestrial. What they say and what they do are not enough for us to entirely grasp them.

An Apichatpong film starts and we may only see its opening credits after more than half an hour, as seen in *Blissfully Yours* (*Sud sanaeha*, 2002). His stories can either repeat themselves endlessly (*Mysterious Object at Noon*) or start over abruptly with slightly altered characters and settings (*Tropical Malady* and *Syndromes and a Century*). Apichatpong consistently gravitates toward the natural world (especially the forest) and a sense of serene ecstasy. The filmmaker continues to embrace a curious departure from rationalism, as James Quandt rightly states: "They [Apichatpong's movies] are among the most sensual, tender, and bewildering films in contemporary cinema."[105]

Apichatpong frequently dilates time and makes movies as if he is intuiting a mood. He is usually credited not with the traditional "directed by" but with the slightly pretentious "conceived by." It is indeed an unusual description, but it is completely justified. Although his movies are rigorous conceptual experiments, they exude a sensuality from each shot, creating an almost religious sense of revelation. This is what Tony Ryans succinctly describes:

> It's hard to write about Apichatpong's films without relying on the vocabulary of doubt: 'seeming,' 'apparently,' 'enigma,' 'opaque' and so on. There's certainly something evasive at the heart of Apichatpong's work, something beyond the modernist reluctance to commit to banal, clear-cut significations and signifieds. But there's also a serious engagement with the surrealist tradition, a confidence that irrational juxtapositions can yield unexpected insights, and it's lent extra potency by Apichatpong's interest in Buddhist thought—most especially by the quest for 'voidness' as the essential step towards enlightenment: the Barthesian retreat from "authorship" meets the Buddhist abnegation of 'self.'[106]

Cinema is seen as an act of generosity, extending a certain empathy and a sense of brotherhood with all things. It is a vision of cinema as an aesthetic experience of the world in its perpetual renew. Something we could already feel

---

[105.] Quandt (2009, 14).

[106.] Rayns (2009, 138–39).

in *Blissfully Yours*, his second feature—a film about three characters enjoying a free afternoon in the paradise of a forest. In its final third, the duration of the film nearly aligns with the diegetic time, in an experience of temporal flow that is not that common in cinema. This flow, however, does not prompt us to think about the image, nor does it cause any discomfort. The characters lie down by the river. The sun is like a character, just as the green of the forest is. The sound creates a tranquil sleep mise-en-scène. The young woman, in a close-up, looks at the sky. It is a quite long shot. A single tear trickles down her face, descending vertically from the camera, almost imperceptible. It is as if she were aware of the fleeting nature of that moment, of the impossibility of returning to it. I cry with her, seduced by the overwhelming melancholy of our memories.

Tropical Malady intensifies this sense of fluctuation, flow, and rupture that characterizes *Blissfully Yours*, extending the strangeness of the latter into a realm of shamanic mystery. As the director himself likes to say, *Tropical Malady* is like the "evil twin" of *Blissfully Yours*. The film consists two halves, two separate but interrelated narratives, each with its own set of credits.[107] Keng (Banlop Lomnoi), a soldier on leave in a small country town, woos Tong (Sakda Kaewbuadee), a shy boy who works at a local ice factory.[108] Suddenly, while we become familiar with the story of these two boys, Apichatpong breaks the chain and recontextualizes everything in a sweeping aesthetic effect.[109] We are then thrust back into that same opening scene, featuring the same two actors, but now in a completely different setting and mood.

A soldier (perhaps the Keng of the first part) seeks for the ghost of a tiger, which is the mystical incarnation of a shaman who "lives in the memories of others" and inhabits the body of the actor who played Tong—although it is unclear that are dealing with the same character. *Tropical Malady* is "a tale of love and metamorphosis in which a man must enter the underworld to retrieve his beloved,

---

[107.] The first screenings of *Tropical Malady* at the Cannes Film Festival were marked by confusion. After the end of the first half, the ten seconds of black screen and the initial set of credits, many believed that the reels had been changed and rose to complain to the organization of the event.

[108.] The two halves are marked with literary references. Right at the beginning of the film, the Japanese novelist Ton Nakajima, whose real name is Atsushi Nakajima, famous for his "elegance of language, erudition and pessimism" (Quandt 2009, 64), sets the tone for the first part of *Tropical Malady*: "We are all wild beasts by nature. Our duty as human beings is to become trainers who keep our animals in check, and even teach them to perform tasks far from bestiality."

[109.] The second half of *Tropical Malady*, entitled "Spiritual Path," is inspired by short stories by Noi Inthanon, one of more than thirty pseudonyms of the Thai writer Marlai Choophinit, "sometimes called the Hemingway of Siam…, celebrated for his regionalist fiction and his adventure stories about a hunter and his villager sidekick who venture into the Thai wild" (Quandt 2009, 64). At one point, a monkey addresses Keng: "The tiger follows you like a shadow. Your hungry, lonely spirit. I see that you are his prey and companion. He can smell you from mountains away. And soon you will feel the same. Kill him to free him from the ghost world. Or let it devour you to enter its world."

free him from 'the ghost world,' only to find him transmogrified into another creature."[110] A love story told in two tones, through a sensoriality that varies from one half to the other, from youthful and shy relationships to wild and spiritual passion, from the brightest spaces of urban everyday life to the dense darkness of the forest, its animals and myths, from fleeting encounters to fabled persecution.

Apichatpong inscribes a fissure in the middle of *Tropical Malady* ("Siamese brothers, non-identical twins," or "a mirror in the center, which reflects both sides.") He materializes in the structure and montage of this film the very concept of reversibility. One half cannot be done without the other. They are absolutely interdependent, like extensions of each other. A closer look reveals that the first half of the film presents a magical apprehension of the world. The filmmaker establishes an atmosphere, a rhythm, and brings it all in: trips to the cave, the dog found on the road, the local music scene, going to the cinema, a group of soldiers taking pictures with a corpse, and so on. The sensoriality that exudes from each of these shots seem to fill the gaps. Apichatpong does not separate the virtual from the real, and the fable is not there as a way to escape from reality. What is perceived is something like a game between these dimensions and regimes, intertwined and hiding within one another.

In the end, the soldier and the tiger face each other. The soldier, his body bathed in sweat and trembling with fear, could shoot at the enemy. The tiger, perched high in a tree, might attack. None of that, however, happens. Conflict is set aside in the presence of the rustling of leaves, the sound of the wind, and the dark green of the forest. What we see in this scene, in the dark of night, is an aesthetic experience that transcends the boundaries of the visible. *Tropical Malady* does not distinguish between men, trees, or machines. All share the same state of sleep. The forest, in its boundless darkness, is the quintessential space where we truly exist. Objects and beings recede, losing their visible and significant stability, and unveiling themselves in their fundamental fragility and transience.

Apichatpong makes no distinction between the permanent things that appear in our gaze and their fleeting way of appearing. His quest is the same as that of Cézanne: "matter as it takes on form the birth of order through spontaneous organization."[111] This does not imply a crude or primitive art, nor a disconnect between the senses and intelligence, but rather a longing to reconnect logic, ideas, and theory with the world. *Tropical Malady* reveals the background of the inhuman nature on which man settles. I am compelled to acknowledge this

---

[110] Quandt (2009, 76).

[111] Merleau-Ponty (1964b, 13).

fundamental reality to which Apichatpong's cinema refers, a realm populated by thick, open, and fragmented beings.

This is a somewhat wild cinema that thrives on fascination: its images seem to emanate from the things themselves, as if demanded by them, and existing within them. It is no longer just about discussing space and light but about allowing the space and light that are there to speak. It is an endless question since the vision it addresses is itself the question. Apichatpong's goal is to encapsulate and project what is contained within it. This is exactly what Klee evokes when he confesses:

> *In a forest, I have felt many times over that it was not I who looked at the forest. Some days I felt that the trees were looking at me, were speaking to me…I was there, listening…I think that the painter must be penetrated by the universe and not want to penetrate it…I expect to be inwardly submerged, buried. Perhaps I paint to break out.* [112]

In other words, nature is an enigmatic object that is not entirely an object. It does not lay before us. It is our soil. It sustains us. Apichatpong wants to involve the spectator at all times in a sensory experience that reconnects them to the world. Aligned with the Merleau-Pontian mission, the Thai filmmaker seeks a layer of being that exceeds my perceptive capacities. This position disarms the most radical skepticism, which suggests that perhaps nothing is known about the nature of reality itself.

It is no coincidence that, at times, Michel Mourlet seems close, particularly because I do feel entering a state of hypnosis maintained by an enchantment of gestures, voices, gazes, movements, and temporalities. Apichatpong, however, distinguishes himself from the French critic by focusing on a reduction of the narrative, immersive installation experiences, and meaningless contemplation. Apichatpong, as phenomenologically inspired theorists assert, aims to establish a connection with the world through cinema. This search yields terms that are reversible and inseparable. Believing in an image, contrary to André Bazin's assertion, is believing in the world, and vice versa. The relationship between reality and cinema is no longer solely defined by the presence of lines in the image or the objectivity of a mechanical impression, although these aspects remain extremely important. *Tropical Malady* asserts itself as a world by operating in terms of intensity and immanence. Roger Munier, for precisely investigating a kind of sensorial and sensitive intensification of the world through filming always

---

[112.] Klee and Merleau-Ponty (2004, 22).

comes to mind when I encounter Apichatpong. However, the Munierian concept of self-expression of the world through the cinematographic image does not apply to the Thai filmmaker. The theorist reflects on "the trembling of the leaf is enunciated insofar as it is a trembling, in its nudity."[113] The notion of naked-ness does not encompass the first and most fascinating shot of *Syndromes and a Century*. The trees that swaying in the wind and to the music do not represent a silent discourse of things. This image carries not only the nudity that Munier talks about but also an enormous amount of memories, narratives, myths, and fantasies. This image creates with our help a certain space-time ambience where we can all exist. In Apichatpong, the concept of mystery, which is so important to Amédée Ayfre, remains popular. Perhaps the distinction arises from the fact that in *Tropical Malady*,[114] I become intimate with the mystery. The filmmaker comments:

> *Living, breathing, is a joy. And that I believe. I try to make my work reflect the way I live and feel life, that is, the way my pleasure relates to images. It is not always possible because cinema is not life, and it is full of small technical com-plexities. That's why somehow I want my films to at least reflect the 'joy of being able to film and being filming', as if in reverse looking into the films. It's a way of combining and putting into dialogue my life without films and my life while I'm filming. It's the closest I can get to the truth. A double interaction between these two ways of being alive, this double.[115]*

For these and other reasons, it is challenging to find comparable instances in the history of cinema. The time that flows in *Blissfully Yours* is not, for example, the dead time of Michelangelo Antonioni. It is more like a "purification of nature by itself,"[116] as highlighted by Luiz Carlos Olveira Jr. The (non-)events are pre-sented to us in almost their entire duration, but this never amounts to a substantial experience. It is also distinct from Andrei Tarkovsky's cinema, where, contrary

---

[113] Munier (1962, 91).

[114] The list of acknowledgments in the end credits of *Tropical Malady* is quite curious: Brian Eno and Pierre Huyghe. Brian Eno created the term "Ambient Music" in the mid-1970s. His idea was to name a type of music that was more interested in creating a certain atmosphere, leading its listener to a different state of mind. "Ambient" comes from the Latin *ambire*, that is, to surround, involve, and be around. When laying the cornerstone of the genre, *Ambient 1: Music for Airports* (1978), Eno attached a short manifesto in which he explains: "Ambient music must be able to accommodate many levels of listening attention without enforcing one in particular; it must be as ignorable as it is interesting" (Eno 1978). Pierre Huyghe is a French video artist who made a remake of *Rear Window* (1954; Alfred Hitchcock) on video, scene by scene, with non-actors.

[115] Bragança (2006).

[116] Oliveira Jr. (2010, 87).

to popular belief, time is not stretched out. "Time is dense, a compact mass, without sponginess or dispersion," says Oliveira Jr. "It is the sum of what has passed, what will pass (maybe), but it is never what is going through,"[117] he adds.

Apichatpong is clearly a contemporary filmmaker. He tends to fragment narratives and delegate them to bodies, creating a disjoined relationship between the actor, character, and plot. However, this disjunction, fragmentation, and delivery glimpses a certain unity and evokes a resonance and vibration that runs through it. The spectator is invited to a heightened state of perception, attentive to the smallest visual and auditory elements — a surprising experience given the strangeness of Apichatpong's cinema. In that sense, Andy Warhol is closer. The Thai filmmaker says:

> *Andy Warhol is a combo of Einstein and Buddha because he changed my way of looking at time. Apart from having the same initials as me, he showed me the importance of scenes (such as an old man walking his fat pug), which in fact, can be any moment when you are just aware of your existence.*[118]

Apichatpong, however, is more akin to a blend of Warhol and a certain notion of romantic drama. The filmmaker does not invest in an annulment of the plot, in the shattering of the drama. On the contrary, Apichatpong, as Quandt likes to say, is a "compulsive storyteller."[119] Narratives swarm in his films, overlapping in consecutive layers that do not necessarily require an internal logical order. The sense of dramatic confrontation, heroism, and tragedy, of a serious world of problems and contradictions, is certainly absent. What is proposed, as in Costa, Denis, and Tsai, is a dramaturgy in which the question "who is the character" has lost its centrality. The body comes to the fore, not exactly in its exploratory potential, as in Tsai; nor as an esthetic figure, as in Costa; but rather as the stuff of the world, the woven from things, in a carnal communion with everything that surrounds it, whether visible or invisible.

A film like *Tropical Malady* also brings to mind the unique experience of watching *Hiroshima, mon amour* (1959), *Last Year in Marienbad* (1961), and *Muriel* (1963). In these films by Alain Resnais, the objects serve as a different kind of link with reality. Images are physical presences. Slices of thought in its eternal becoming exist while being seen. Beyond that, they fall into emptiness,

---

[117] Ibid.

[118] Quandt (2009, 15).

[119] Ibid., 100.

absence, or, as it is described in *Marienbad*, into a "marble silence." André S. Labarthe used to say that if Marienbad exists, "it is like an object: like Rorschach stains."[120] Resnais dissects and captures reality through a series of camera movements. We walk through corridors, halls, galleries, framed paintings, marble, mirrors, columns, statues, doors, and so on. We are invited to live these fragments in their own space-time. The shot is absolute. The representation of love in these movies reveals this aesthetic. Whether on the streets of Hiroshima or along the corridors of Marienbad, love encounters always begin with the abstract. Love unfolds between formal layers. It is not the protagonists, their appearance, movements, gestures and exchange of looks that convey the idea of love. Resnais objectified everything. Although easily discernible from each other, man and object seem to be on the same level.

Marienbad distances itself from the tension between man and the world, annulling character, man, present, past, and future. A land where everything is allowed. Resnais spreads imagination everywhere, freeing it from certain mechanisms and traditional hierarchies. What is seen in this film without formal antecedents is the search for a new description. The literary project of the Nouveau Roman by Robbe-Grillet and Marguerite Duras was also founded on a new approach that could trigger another subjectivity. Down with the idea that man could only have a subjective knowledge of the world! No more using man as justification for everything! Therefore, it was about challenging a conditioned mechanism that leads us to identify subject and object, man and nature. Similar to the Nouveau Roman, these early films by Resnais appear to blur the boundaries between things, denying all anthropomorphism and allowing reality to emerge in its opacity.

Watching an Apichatpong film is akin to experiencing the effects of a similar centripetal force. His cinema is very close to Resnais' proposal when he de-hierarchizes the past, future, and present, rejecting anthropomorphism and a humanist conception of nature. The films by Resnais and Apichatpong are characterized by a raw presence and take on various forms of evading the realm of representation. At the same time, the directors showcase different sensibilities in relation to the values of the world and cinema. As we have observed, the Thai filmmaker presents a on the surface state of affairs, drawing the spectator in and requiring a sort of cinematic innocence from us. It is no longer necessary to reflect on language in order to reflect on the world.

The world described in films like *Blissfully Yours*, *Tropical Malady*, and *Syndromes and a Century* is primarily a physical world, in its microscopic

---

[120.] Labarthe (1961, 30).

and permanent movement. This physicality is intertwined with the sensorial aspect of the characters, whose bodies interact with the landscape and all bodies of nature. To watch an Apichatpong film is to become part of a shifting geography that melds into a depiction of an absolutely physical world, where all things identify with each other. The filmmaker refuses to make any distinction between the subject and the object. Apichatpong captures the world in a moment that precedes the separation and differential organization of its objects. He does not identify the "Being" with one of the beings (God, man, or Nature), and rejects a way of thinking that is based on the cleavage between God, man, and creatures.

Tropical Malady doesn't spread man everywhere. It does not focus solely on showing the distances between subject and object either. Instead, Apichatpong blurs every boundary, treating everything indiscriminately. Looks, characters, love encounters, and the sweat running down the body are described on the same level and narrative hierarchy. A physical narrative that emphasizes the unity of all things: a sort of cosmos. The sensorial transforms narrative and nature into one. It is no longer nature or objects that are humanized; instead, it is man himself who loses his humanity. Man appears as a part of something much larger than humanity.

Consider *Cemetery of Splendour*. The original Thai title literally means "Love in Khon Kaen," referring to the film's location, the director's hometown in northern Thailand. The feature is inspired by a real incident and revolves around a hospital ward that is still under construction and already filled with soldiers affected by a mysterious sleeping sickness. The protagonist is a middle-aged local woman named Jen (Jenjira Pongpas). She volunteers at the infirmary, which is being built on the site of her former primary school. Walking there is like stepping back in time for her, to a period when things were simpler and happier. In the infirmary, she approaches a sick soldier named Itt (Banlop Lomnoi) and a young woman named Keng (Jarinpattra Rueangram), whose purported psychic abilities have drawn the attention of the FBI. An unusual treatment method is being tested on soldiers. Light poles are installed next to their beds to soothe their troubled minds—at one point, we learned that the unusual technique grew out of a neurological study conducted at MIT, which successfully created artificial memories in rats by exposing their neurons to flashes of light. These poles are constantly changing colors, influencing the mood in the ward, while the windows are closed, blocking out the outside world. When the poles glow and the soldiers are enveloped in darkness and color, it is as if we are witnessing a peculiar piece of art installation or perhaps a fascinating inversion of Plato's allegory of the cave.

Cemetery of Splendour is overwhelmingly serene and entirely uninterested in disruption or shock, yet at the same time driven by an unmistakable sense of social urgency. The film is set in a timeless real world, yet captures the present in its smallest details.[121] As the film progresses, we learn that there is a reason for the illness. The hospital was constructed on the grounds of an ancient palace where kings were buried thousands of years ago. In another world, these kings are still at war, draining energy from the soldiers. Everything indicates that they will never wake up — and this impression is packed with a somewhat pessimistic feeling, highlighting the state of a nation that has been governed by a military junta since a coup d'état, in May 2014, took over the country. Only a certain facet of this reality is visible on the surface of a film that seems smooth and serene. *Cemetery of Splendour* then explores the story of two worlds, one visible and one invisible, both existing simultaneously. Apichatpong creates a universe where humans and non-humans, "past and present, dreams and reality, life and death constantly commingle, yet which is always grounded in a palpable now."[122]

Cemetery of Splendour always seems to be on the verge of some kind of epiphanic outburst. At one point, we observe people strolling around a lake. They sit down and stand up. They switch positions with one another. A scene meticulously staged, choreographed, and seemingly gratuitous. In another moment, quite unexpectedly, we are presented with a CGI of an amoeba floating in a bright blue sky. Apichatpong discovers the extraordinary within the ordinary. He is a compulsive storyteller, although most of the time it feels like no real story is actually being told. He can be both funny and tragic. *Cemetery of Splendour* is both a melodrama and a spiritual film. It is a conceptual and sensory experience. Realism is both dry and magical. It is political yet not explicitly militant.

Apichatpong is a pantheist. His films are not a means to dilute the experience but to relish and expand it indefinitely. *Cemetery of splendour* is made of open (Apichatpong always avoids close-ups), long and static shots that enable us to see the characters inserted in the space of the frame, suffering the influence of other actions, objects, and characters. Everything matters. The presence of immovable elements such as objects, plants, lakes, earth, grass, and buildings serve to contextualize in a broader way the diminished presence of the characters in

---

[121] Kong Rithdee brilliantly describes the subversive tension between tranquility and anxiety that lies beneath the calm appearances of Apichatpong's cinema: *"Cemetery of Splendour* is the first Thai film that responds to the uncertainty — political, personal, historical — of military-ruled Thailand. It's all the more astonishing because this dark prophecy is done in the gentlest and most civilized, yet clear-eyed and unflinching, way" (Rithdee 2015, 48).

[122] Koresky (2016).

the grandeur of the world. I can return to the sequence described earlier, where characters, landscapes, and various objects appear to be completely intertwined. These disconnected yet sensually and visually coherent shots all work to suspend time in an atmosphere of compassion. It is like a floating, ethereal stream of actions and objects. Understanding or representing an object is less important. I find myself intoxicated by the objects of the world. Objects exist beyond any possibility of complete presence, yet they are rooted in a carnal environment where my body encounters the voluptuous textures of all things.

I am deeply drawn to contemplating an image as a repository of unfolding presences. The camera always reveals a vision that is not yet complete—the vision of an object that is only partially revealed and exists beyond its mere appearance. Objects seem to have intention—to have "a mind of their own." They appear to be aware and they use this awareness as a way of drawing attention to their own being-in-the-world. It is as if Apichatpong captures and makes accessible to us the nameless spectacle of which we are part without realizing it. In a movie such as *Cemetery of Splendour*, I am constantly being compelled to acknowledge the integrity of things, completely independent of myself. These encounters alter the parameters of the world, disrupting "the fabric of meaning" and diverging from all consensus. *Cemetery of Splendour* does ontology.

There is a problem here. Phenomenology needs help when we go beyond the question of the human being and the world. To unravel the mysteries of this cinema that fascinates me so much, I must go even further into the decentralization of humanity. I must enter non-human territories. I must give all objects and their interactions equal attention. While it may be impossible to understand what it is to be a non-human thing, a film such as *Cemetery of Splendour* seems to show me that it is possible to gather certain metaphysical insights beyond the human without accessing it directly. This is a cinema that persistently demands a more object-oriented analysis of the world.

This idea of an object-oriented analysis is part of what has been termed speculative realism, a recent trend in contemporary philosophy characterized by its opposition to what Quentin Meillassoux referred as to "correlationism," that is, the idea that "thought cannot get outside itself in order to compare the world as it is 'in itself' to the word as it is 'for us,' and thereby distinguish what is a function of our relation to the world from what belongs to the world alone."[123] Philosophers of speculative realism affirm the existence of a reality independent of human access, and reject the Kantian thesis that the meaning of the world

---

[123.] Meillassoux (2008, 3).

depends on the way our minds (or our languages, or our cultures) work to structure it. Along this path, they challenge us to consider the world beyond our narrow vision of it, acknowledging the difficulties of thinking the unthought (the outside of thought, or the "absolute," according to Meillassoux) and underlining the importance of speculating about it.

This influential philosophical current has its specific moment of birth when, in 2007, four philosophers presented works at Goldsmiths College, University of London, under the banner of what they themselves called speculative realism. Meillassoux, Graham Harman, Ray Brassier, and Iain Hamilton Grant have sometimes been perceived as a relatively cohesive group, despite harboring differences so significant that it cannot be said that they constitute a single school or philosophical movement. However, their works share the same starting point: the notion that the dominance of epistemology over ontology has prevailed in philosophy since Kant confined it to the perpetual scrutiny of the conditions of thought.

While contemporary philosophy, in its various currents, has argued that reality is "constructed" by language, power, or human cultural practices, speculative realism is presented as a more realistic philosophy. This means, among other things, that this current asserts the existence of the external world independently of human consciousness. As mild and sensible as this point may sound, it diverges from the essence of the last century of continental philosophy and leads us in directions surprisingly foreign to common sense.

The resurgence of philosophical speculation in the twenty-first century is an attempt to liberate itself from this dilemma. It aims to challenge the Kantian dominance in epistemology and steer clear of both logocentrism and ethnocentrism on one hand, and ceaseless deconstruction and self-criticism on the other. Kant criticized speculation for exceeding the boundaries of all possible knowledge. For today's emerging speculative thinkers, speculation is essential precisely because of the limits of knowledge. There are many things that are real that I can never know. Reality is much stranger than I can imagine. Things are never in line with the ideas I have about them; there is always something beyond what I can understand. That is why speculation is necessary.

This path, which is becoming increasingly clear to me, although only outlined here, leads me to be more prepared and open to a cinema that seems more of an exploration of what it means to think about reality, without placing concerns about the human being's ability to know the world at the center of the entire discussion. It describes a world populated not by active subjects and passive objects but by animated and interactive materials, essentially comprising human and non-human bodies. Apichatpong seems dedicated to what Salvador Dalí called "the poetic autonomy of things."[124] Objects are not important because of their effect on the human subject but in themselves. Apichatpong insists on the ontological persistence of things beyond human subjectivity.

So, I feel closer and closer to an author who, little by little, almost impercepti-bly, has been insinuating himself since the beginning of this book: Alfred North Whitehead. It is not up to me to provide further explanations about his immense work. What is important to me is to emphasize its place in the genealogy of what we call speculative realism. For Whitehead, "Man" is not the measure of all things. He is one of the few thinkers of the 20th century who dared to "venture beyond the human sphere"[125] and puts all entities on an equal footing. Whitehead dismisses the notion that the divide between humans and the world is of utmost importance. Quite the opposite. For the philosopher, all existing entities in the universe are on an ontological equal footing. As Whitehead explains, no special ontological privileges that can distinguish God from "the most trivial puff of existence in far-off empty space" in spite of all "gradations of importance, and diversities of function, yet in the principles which actuality exemplifies all are on the same level."[126] And what is true for God can also be said for human sub-jectivity. What he envisions, therefore, is a world in which all things perceive each other rather than just being perceived by us. Steven Shaviro, one of the most interesting commentators on Whitehead's work, summarizes:

> *Causal and perceptual interactions are no longer held hostage to human-centric categories. For Whitehead and Harman alike, there is therefore no hierarchy of being. No particular entity — not even the human subject — can claim metaphysical preeminence or serve as a favored mediator. All entities, of all sizes and scales, have the same degree of reality. They all interact with each other in the same ways, and they all exhibit the same sorts of properties.*[127]

The basic aim of Whitehead's philosophy is always to overcome what he referred to as "the bifurcation of nature," or the absolute division between "the nature apprehended in awareness and nature which is the cause of aware-ness."[128] There is the world's phenomenal appearance to us: "the greenness

---

[124.] Dalí (1998, 80).

[125.] Harman (2011, 190).

[126.] Whitehead (1978, 18).

[127.] Shaviro (2014, 34).

[128.] Whitehead (1994, 30–31).

of the trees, the song of the birds, the warmth of the sun, the hardness of the chairs, and the feel of the velvet."[129] And there is the hidden physical reality: "the conjectured system of molecules and electrons which so affects the mind as to produce the awareness of apparent nature."[130] Modern thought is widely founded on this bifurcation (primary and secondary qualities, noumena and phenomena, "the manifest image" and "the scientific image" etc.). Whitehead intends to overcome the bifurcation altogether:

> *We may not pick and choose. For us, the red glow of the sunset should be as much part of nature as are the molecules and electric waves by which men of science would explain the phenomenon. It is for natural philosophy to analyze how these various elements of nature are connected. In making this demand I conceive myself as adopting our immediate instinctive attitude towards perceptual knowledge which is only abandoned under the influence of theory.*[131]

Whitehead's desire to end the bifurcation of nature plunged him into a long process of metaphysical speculation. In the end, in works such as *Process and Reality* and *Adventures of Ideas*, he delineates a vision of cosmological scope. For Whitehead, the being of a thing is constituted by its becoming. In fact, if we are to be rigorous, there are no things. The world is made of processes. And each thing must first become what it is. Nothing is given in advance. Concepts such as "becoming" and "creativity" are quite generic. They do not bond with humans in particular. They can refer to all events in the cosmos. There are, of course, differences in degree. In *Process and Reality*, Whitehead warns us at least twice that a human being is more original than a stone. However, these variations in degree are never translated into gender distinctions. All things are active and transforming. In this manner, Whitehead undermines the inveterate anthropocentrism of Western philosophy and encompasses both aspects of the bifurcation of nature. I am not a subject facing a world beyond me, because subject and object "are themselves processes of becoming, and all actual things are alike objects [and] subjects."[132]

For Whitehead, echoing William James, and in absolute affinity with the experience of seeing a film like *Cemetery of Splendour* "we find ourselves in a

---

[129] Ibid., 31.

[130] Ibid.

[131] Whitehead (1994, 37).

[132] Whitehead (1978, 56–57).

vibrant world, in the midst of a democracy of creatures."[133] I experience my finite being and my physical senses in the presence of a universe whose possibilities are infinite, and even if I cannot apprehend them, these infinite possibilities are there, as possible realities. I am led to believe, in a very serene manner, that matter is not inert and passive but immanently active, productive, and formative. I do not come to know a world of things outside of me. I feel, along with things that go beyond my knowledge of them, that we are all equal, inhabitants of a "common world."

Apichatpong, for his part, describes his work as "open cinema": "Sometimes you don't need to understand everything to appreciate a certain beauty. And I think the film operates in the same way. It's like tapping into someone's mind. The thinking pattern is quite random, jumping here and there like a monkey."[134] Now, what would it mean to think like a monkey, jumping here and there? This is a delightful question that Apichatpong's cinema, akin to Whitehead's thought, encourages me to explore. I am talking about a speculative gesture that touches the limits of what the image can do. Apichatpong and Whitehead have led me to this crossroads, prompting me to investigate, in an ongoing process, how this threshold carries an incipient form, from image to experience and from experience to image.

I recall a moment in the basement of a modern hospital when the moving camera of *Syndromes and a Century* slowly zoomed in on the entrance to a ventilation tube, positioned right in the middle of the screen, until it began to resemble a large, round black hole drawing in smoke. The vent pipe seems to capture not only the essence of the film but also my intellect, vision, and senses. I am then taken to an ontological terrain, an empty, raw, and excessive space-time. An abrupt cut leaves me in a typical cityscape. We see a sunny day in a park, with people dating, talking, playing, and exercising. We see an aerobics class in the open air. The class is accompanied by pop-electronic music. A solitary boy walks in and out of the frame in the left corner. He tries to keep up with the professor in the background of the frame. The vent now seems to belch the entire world, granting us access the impossible depth of objects. And I feel good, on the verge of a smile, enjoying the mystery around me, aware of my loneliness, and energized by my universality.

Feeling itself is a process of selection and determination. Apichatpong, like Whitehead, rejects the notion that truth already exists in the world or in the

---

[133.] Ibid., 50.

[134.] Rose (2011).

mind, independent of all experience, just waiting to be discovered. Rather, we are invited or required to observe how truths are produced within experience through various processes and practices. This does not mean that nothing is true or that truth is merely subjective; rather, it suggests that truth is always embodied in a real process and cannot be disengaged from that process. Truth involves the practices and processes of an infinite variety of "actors," such as animals, viruses, rocks, weather systems, neutrinos, and human beings.

As Erin Manning describes it,[135] Apichatpong's films turn us into visionaries, requiring us to engage in a thought that does not retreat in the face of this uncertain and ambivalent experience that connects us, esthetically, emotionally, and sensually with the world. This connection allow us to live not only with what we have seen or are seeing but also with what we have yet to see. It invites us to see with different eyes, beyond what we understand as real and human.

That is what the last shot of *Cemetery of Splendour* summarizes so beautifully. Jen is sitting motionless on a park bench, her eyes wide open and wearing an expression that is a blend of wonder and ecstasy. It is a close-up—one of the few dedicated to humans. The shot lasts for a few minutes. She looks at the soil-digging machine. She looks at the boys playing soccer. But she sees more than that. She feels more than that. She notices more than that. She seems to experience the total and irreducible existence of all things. The shot gives voice to a type of non-human knowledge, older than humanity itself, capable of seeing that, beyond all conquests and hypotheses, the universe belongs to what is given.

---

[135] Bordeleau and Rose-Antoinette (2017, 16).

CONCLUSION

The full stop is simply a matter of formal necessity. The scope of the questions explored in this book remains uncertain. This has always been my intention—not to institutionalize a certain perspective to replace others but rather to maintain an ongoing interrogation; not merely an exercise in methodical and deliberate doubt but a continuous exploration; not a direct refutation of theories but a return to their origins to uncover what was left unexplored. It is science understood as an adventure—something I may have grasped belatedly from an author who only caught my attention at the end of this book, Alfred North Whitehead. There is no adventure without risks. Every environment has the potential to complicate the adventure or even condemn it to failure.

To those who have accompanied me here, I earnestly ask for a few more pages of your attention. I propose a game to you, a montage. I attempt to re-enact something I've learned from Adrian Martin (2012), who, in turn, got it from Gayatri Chakravorty Spivak. The idea is to open the way to this brief conclusion through three fragments: a film, a story, a poem. I will follow, like Martin and Spivak, the same order in which these passages reached me, in which they found me. In a dialectic of contingent and transient synthesis, I aim to explore not only what unites these fragments together but also what separates them. I hope that we will reach the end together, still amazed.

I start with Jean-Luc Godard and his urgent gesture to reclaim the sky in *Lettre à Freddy Buache* (1982), a film commissioned by the City of Lausanne to celebrate the 500th anniversary of the city's founding and the opening of its Cinematheque's new headquarters. The order, however, will not be fulfilled as expected. "They will be furious," anticipates Godard off-camera. *Lettre à Freddy Buache* is not a film about Lausanne but rather a curious kind of video letter addressed to the critic, historian, and director of the Swiss Cinematheque, Freddy Buache. In a confessional and hesitant tone, Godard talks about cinema, language, the creative process, reality and fiction.

It is a typical work of a certain phase of the filmmaker, increasingly leaning toward the essay, in which the eternal dilemma of cinema, between showing and allowing to be seen, is updated. Godard is seeking nothing less than a new way of seeing,[1] a way of examining bodies, nature, love, and work. The filmmaker knows that what he presents only exists through his gaze, although he desires everything to be seen in that manner, without having to show it. This is the insurmountable yet urgent impasse that Godard is attempting to overcome. This is the question that drives the filmmaker's speculative search for what Alain Bergala refers to as "the visual," a rare quality of the image in which a person or an object ceases to have a merely filmic existence and is remembered as having "once pulsed on this earth, belonging to this planet and this species that is so temporarily ours."[2]

It was Daniele Rugo (2016), in his insightful book on Stanley Cavell and Jean-Luc Nancy, who brought my attention to a specific and revealing passage in this brief film. Godard is stopped by the police as he urgently tries to capture the sky. It is a matter of urgency and of a sky whose light quickly dissipates: "These days, the police stopped us many times while we were filming. We pulled over on the side of the road and they said, 'You can't stop there unless it's an emergency.' We replied: 'It's an emergency, the light, it's only going to last ten seconds.' " It is a matter of recapturing the fleeting nature of this pass-ing sky, of a light that endures for just a few seconds. What is required of us is an equally urgent attention. Our thoughts must grasp the measure of those ten seconds and the urgency they require. It is not urgent to fix those ten seconds but to follow their passage. Godard teaches me that the world, as Nancy says, "is always a creation."[3]

Throughout this book, I found myself encountering filmmakers who, like Godard, seek to reclaim the sense of urgency in the presence of things. They are interested in capturing the movement of a world to which they belong and the only possible way to do so is from a certain point of view or instant, always passing. What is at stake is thinking of images as critical acts, analyzing them for the issues they create and in which they participate. The image would be more like a process rather than a reflection or reproduction of something that already exists. It would be more like the emergence of a visionary critical activity. This implies an eternal return to the same questions: What is a body? How is a body constituted or composed? How do gestures convey openness

---

[1] Jacques Aumont referred to this period as "a new apprenticeship in the look: how, little by little, to look better, and then let others see" (2004, 231).

[2] Bergala (1999, 122).

[3] Nancy (1997, 41).

or constraint? What kind of relationships does it establish? What is cinema? What is the cinema for?

Cave of Forgotten Dreams (2010), by Werner Herzog, found me shortly afterward. It is a typical film-essay by the German filmmaker on the mysteries of the Chauvet cave in the south of France, where the oldest known cave drawings are in perfect condition. *Cave of Forgotten Dreams* is a 3D film about "fluidity" and "permeability," both crucial for understanding primitive man, says one of the anthropologists interviewed. An essay that, like few others, makes me recognize how we are the result of an entire history. It is also, above all, a film about the potential for transcendence within immanence.

This is exactly what a short story told by French archaeologist Julien Monney has me wondering. It refuses to leave my mind and sometimes, like some kind of undesirable tenant, takes me by storm. Monney takes us to Australia in the 1970s. He talks about an anthropologist and an aboriginal guide who traveled to research cave painting, a practice that was still common among Australian natives at that time. They enter a cave. They spot a worn drawing of an animal. The guide is saddened. He cries and shortly afterward he begins to touch up the drawing. The anthropologist, intrigued, asks the question that any Westerner would ask: "Why do you paint?" "But it's not my hand that paints," replies the Aboriginal, astonished by the anthropologist's ignorance: "It's the hand of the spirit."

Beyond the mystical and religious charge of the Aboriginal's response, a different look at art in its origin emerges: art as a donation, bringing material life to something immaterial, making the absent present; art as an expression of oneself without ever being outside oneself; as an ebb and flow between the work, the artist, and, later, the spectator. Art is always the possibility of a new history. It is a speculative gesture that throws us into an enigma, prompting us to decipher it and compelling us to recognize the impossibility of this task. Art is not born as an appreciation or judgment of the world but rather as a dynamic and perpetual process of creation, recreation and experimentation of a world. A process that implies a simultaneity of presence and absence, visibility and invisibility, perfection and incompleteness, totality and openness, connective and differentiated tissue of the world.

Like cave paintings, cinema is not simply an external view of the world or a detailed account of the events that take place within it. Cinema is evidence that the world is no longer placed before us as an externality. This is what the authors of phenomenological inspiration evoke between the lines or through crooked ones: the search for a "feeling of being" in the phenomenal vibration of the world, which does not simply refer to something prior to the image, but delineates and animates, represents and narrates, figures and sets in motion, at the same time, in a coming and going constitutive of our imagination. Cinema as an animation, marked by the malleable nature of its elements and procedures, where bodies, characters, objects, landscape, emotions, and dramas are always in formation, in a continuous birth of matter, form, and meaning.

I conclude this montage with a poem, "The Keeper of Sheep," by Alberto Caeiro:

> *My gaze is clear like a sunflower.*
> *It is my custom to walk the roads*
> *Looking right and left*
> *And sometimes looking behind me,*
> *And what I see at each moment*
> *Is what I never saw before,*
> *And I'm very good at noticing things.*
> *I'm capable of feeling the same wonder*
> *A newborn child would feel*
> *If he noticed that he'd really and truly been born.*
> *I feel at each moment that I've just been born*
> *Into a completely new world...*
> *I believe in the world as in a daisy,*
> *Because I see it. But I don't think about it,*
> *Because to think is to not understand.*
> *The world wasn't made for us to think about it*
> *(To think is to have eyes that aren't well)*
> *But to look at it and to be in agreement.*
> *I have no philosophy, I have senses...*
> *If I speak of Nature it's not because I know what it is*
> *But because I love it, and for that very reason,*
> *Because those who love never know what they love*
> *Or why they love, or what love is.*
> *To love is eternal innocence,*
> *And the only innocence is not to think...* [4]

[4.] Pessoa (2006, 11–12).

Caeiro, heteronym of Fernando Pessoa,[5] is a pagan and pantheistic poet, freed from religion and a radical follower of the most spontaneous sensation. He introduces himself here as "a keeper of the flock" who wanders through the countryside, who only cares about seeing reality objectively and naturally. With each verse, the poet makes an unyielding apology for the senses. It is through them that the world presents and constitutes itself. Caeiro believes that "to feel" is equivalent to "to know": things are sensations. Art is the conversion of a sensation into an object, the conversion of one sensation into another. His poetry embodies a specific pedagogical project: a "learning of unlearning." This project leads him to a certain scientific, philosophical, and religious skepticism.

Caeiro invites us to reconsider the assumed nature of truth that would be linked to words, to unlearn the presumed intimate connection between words and things, and to recognize that there is no necessarily a direct link between the world and metaphysical reality. Keep being curious. The poet seeks a direct contact with nature; his aim is to be natural. However, if, on the one hand, Caeiro's work intends to strip man of his thoughts, on the other hand, his poetry presupposes a complete engagement with language, as well as an inherently reflective nature. The main theme of this poem is the expression and appreciation of the mystery of things. But where do the mysteries of things ultimately reside? Well, they are in the language. It is through language that, in an imaginative and speculative leap, I not only dress what I feel with words but also recognize the boundaries around.

As in Caeiro, I see in the theory of phenomenological inspiration and in Merleau-Ponty and Deleuze, the same distrust regarding the idea of a starting point, the philosopher's sovereignty, and the concept of thought as self-foundation and intellectual possession of the world. Caeiro, like the contemporary cinema that interests me, highlights the world as that which resists worldviews, as that

---

[5.] Pessoa began writing under Alberto Caeiro in 1912, according to the statement expressed in a letter sent by the Portuguese author to Adolfo Casais Monteiro:

Around 1912, if I'm not mistaken (not greatly anyway), the idea came to me to write poems of a pagan nature. So I scribbled something down in irregular verse (different to the style of Álvaro de Campos, more irregular), and abandoned the idea. It was a badly woven twilight, a blurred portrait of the person who was composing it. (I hadn't realized it yet, but that was when Ricardo Reis was born). One and a half or two years later, I decided to play a trick on Sá-Carneiro — to invent a bucolic poet, of a complicated kind, and introduce him, I don't remember how, in some kind of reality. I spent a few days trying in vain to envision this poet. One day when I'd finally given up — it was March 8, 1914 — I walked over to a high chest of drawers, took a sheet of paper, and began to write standing up, as I do whenever I can. And I wrote thirty-some poems at one go, in a kind of ecstasy I'm unable to describe. It was the triumphal day of my life, and I can never have another one like it. I began with a title, *The Keeper of Sheep*. This was followed by the appearance in me of someone whom I instantly named Alberto Caeiro. Excuse the absurdity of this statement: my master had appeared in me. It was my immediate sensation. So much so that, with those thirty-odd poems written, I immediately took up another sheet of paper and wrote as well, in a row, the six poems that make up 'Oblique Rain' by Fernando Pessoa. Immediately and totally…It was the return from Fernando Pessoa/Alberto Caeiro to Fernando Pessoa alone. Or better still, it was Fernando Pessoa's reaction to his own inexistence as Alberto Caeiro. (Pessoa 1986, 199)

which distances itself from any attempt to represent it as this or that, enclosing it in a certain gaze, idea, theory, and investigation. Art makes the state of the world evident, and actively engages with it. That is to say, art creates the world in order to show it.

The eternal novelty of the world. Its never ending wonder. In fact, this is perhaps the promise that all the arts hold on the horizon. Godard's sky in *Lettre à Freddy Buache*, the cave paintings in *Cave of Forgotten Dreams*, and Caeiro's "The Keeper of Sheep" elevate art to an experience that cannot be reduced to generalization. An experience that, precisely because it defies our capabilities, compels us to think from an apparently paradoxical unity. These three fragments, collected in this way, over the years, have nurtured my relationship with a certain contemporary cinema. They invite me to set aside the descriptions and names we assign to things, and they challenge me to revisit each film, each sequence, and each shot, in an eternal cycle of restart. A restart filled with question marks and exclamation points. Godard's sky in *Lettre à Freddy Buache*, the cave paintings in *Cave of Forgotten Dreams*, and Caeiro's "The Keeper of Sheep" teach me that engaging with mystery is not exactly deciphering but rather experiencing it.

Art does not simply represent, copy, or reproduce reality. It opens up a posture toward the world, a gesture at once ontological, aesthetic, and ethical, collapsing the distinction between the three. It is not a question, therefore, of producing a copy of what is, but of revealing what remains distant in "what is." It is the unknown being sought within the known. Art implies this effort to embed itself in the formative principle of the world, which never fully reveals itself, and strengthens a relationship that always needs to be restarted.

Cinema, the seventh art, came to complicate all of this. That's what all the authors I've researched in this book tell me, each in their own way. It's always noon in a film, when the day splits in two, when matter is free and unencumbered. Cinema is a finite and infinite mess, substance and accident, soul and body, sensitive and intelligible. It is an intimate relationship between artifice and reality. It is the likeness of an icon and the impression of an index. It is the physical light of the photograph and the magical and spiritual light of the projector. A scientific invention and a circus attraction. Cinema is the possibility of the presence of pure duration within the temporal construction, of new relationships between continuity and discontinuity. It works on a new connection between appearance and reality, between a thing and its double, between the virtual and the real. "Film is a paradox,"[6] says Alain Badiou.

[6.] Badiou (2013, 207).

In other words, cinema transforms the very notion of an idea. It consists precisely in creating new ideas about what an idea is. Cinema illuminates the question of the meaning of the world without referring to anything beyond this world. Cinema is a way of articulating an original thought of the world, rather than simply providing an outline, a "picture" of its development. Cinema thinking must be able to resist being absorbed into a more original gesture and must be seen as an opportunity to think differently. A film, therefore, is not a matter of representation or meaning but rather of ontology.

Living up to this ontological imperative is no easy task. How can one approach a film without being invaded by the words that judge and distribute what belongs to the subject and what belongs to the object? That's what I tried to do here — and it is up to you, dear reader, to say whether I succeeded — with the assistance of Maurice Merleau-Ponty, André Bazin, Amédée Ayfre, Michel Mourlet, Roger Munier, Jean Mitry, and Gilles Deleuze. To think of cinema as a movement between the instituted and the instituting, which cannot be reduced, in any way, neither to the artistic will of an author, nor to the effect obtained on the spectator, nor to an intrinsic charge within the work, out of context. Thinking about what tradition (of cinema and its theory) has offered us, not to deny or refute it but to open it up in still unthought paths, as if by speculative leaps, in a movement that is itself creative.

This notion of speculation has gained ground in recent chapters. It is present in the three fragments quoted at the beginning of this conclusion. It is in the title of this book. Speculation is the term that sets Whitehead in motion, turning to what he himself calls "the elucidation of immediate experience."[7] It is a philosophy that treats the experience as something yet to be built and continually remade. Its task is to install itself in the terrain of experience in its multiplicity, preserving what it makes important, intensifying the sense of the possible it contains, making us recognize that our "immediate instinctive attitude" irresistibly exceeds the limits assigned to it by thought.

His work is speculative in the common sense of the word, speculating about a possibility. Whitehead is betting that his system, which flaunts its affiliations with the rationalist tradition, is capable of exposing that tradition to adventure. He bets that he will be able to remove from tradition the power of classification and/or exclusion. Whitehead does not aim to create a system of general categories capable of accounting for experience in a coherent, necessary, and logical manner. It seems to me, more and more, as years, films, and readings go by,

---

[7.] Whitehead (1978, 4).

that coherence, logic, and necessity are perhaps "methodical constraints," as definitions of what must satisfy rational interpretation, rather than an imperative to be always followed.

Whitehead suggests that philosophy begins and ends in wonder and fascination. I can say the same thing about any critical or theoretical approach to cinema. To think with Whitehead is to say that the success of a philosophical proposition is not to resist objections but rather to inspire what he refers to as a "leap of imagination."[8] His philosophy has the mission to make us experience that leap. These speculative leaps and gestures, plural by definition, have the truth of the relative, of something always situated. "We did not decide to execute a speculative gesture," comment Didier Debaise and Isabelle Stengers, "we risked this gesture insofar as we feel 'linked' to a situation, obliged to respond to virtualities made perceptible only by the way in which we feel linked."[9]

It is curious. In this book, I went to different authors to better resist the imposition of an idea of experience which usually comes with limits established a priori. No wonder the concept of experience is "one of the most deceitful in philosophy."[10] It is always limited, intertwined with other problems—those of perception, intentionality, or consciousness—as if we could look elsewhere for its conditions and justifications. Whitehead's path, however, is quite different from phenomenology—perhaps, in a sense, its exact opposite. "Philosophy cannot exclude anything."[11] It is still a strange proposition, but one that denotes a deliberately polemical and violent position. Whitehead aims to maximize the friction with the most immediate experience, refusing the right that all thought in general grants: to explain, while eliminating anything that cannot be framed by its explanation. Every statement that causes nature to bifurcate will be a defeat.

I feel, dear reader, in the midst of a seductive digression, absolutely identified with the notion of speculation that, little by little, forced its place into the title of this book. I then find myself, unexpectedly, starting perhaps another adventure. Whitehead is now unavoidable. Despite being important to me, decisive in the unforeseen paths this book ended up taking, I will have to return to him. I will need to deal with his work. Not here. Not now. I like it, I must say. The adventure continues, in an interrogative and fascinating way, as a meticulous, serious undertaking, and always to be resumed.

[8.] Ibid.

[9.] Debaise and Stengers (2016, 89).

[10.] Whitehead (1927, 16).

[11.] Whitehead (1966, 2).

It is an adventure that, like this one coming to an end, does not aim to bring about any form of awakening. Whitehead and the filmmakers who have accompanied me throughout this book don't seem genuinely interested in leading us out of the cave. Their work is itself a dream, a narrative: learning "inside" the Platonic cave, alongside those who reside in it. Not in the hope that false apparitions will gradually reveal their secrets but in the hope that appearances, when appreciated and articulated, can generate striking contrasts, as Stengers (2014) insists. Denis, Costa, Tsai, and Apichatpong films want me to be a visionary. They want the inconclusive, "the profound organic disaster that nevertheless hints at an underlying order. The great potency of potentiality."[12] And if, wanting the inconclusive, we bounce off the edge of thought, it is because we are struggling with the gravity of our finitude. This particular contemporary cinema that we visited can be seen as a form of futuristic archaeological work, a speculative gesture that touches the limits of what the image can do.

Cinema, my friends, belongs to the future.

It has yet to be invented.

[12.] Lispector (1998, 31).

BIBLIOGRAPHY

Abel, Richard, ed. *French Film Theory and Criticism, 1907–1939: Volume 1, 1907–1929*. Princeton University Press, 1988.

Abel, Richard, ed. *French Film Theory and Criticism, 1907–1939: Volume 2, 1929–1939*. Princeton University Press, 1993.

Amiel, V. *Le corps au cinéma*. PUF, 1998.

Andrew, Dudley. *The Major Film Theories—An Introduction*. Oxford University Press, 1976.

Andrew, Dudley. "The Neglected Tradition of Phenomenology in Film Theory." *Wide Angle* 2, no. 2 (1978): 44–49.

Andrew, Dudley. *What Cinema Is! Bazin's Quest and Its Charge*. John Wiley & Sons, 2010.

Agel, Henri. *Esthétique du cinéma*. Presses Universitaires de France, 1957.

Agel, Henri. *Poetique du cinema*. Signe, 1973.

Appadurai, Arjun. *Modernity at Large: Cultural Dimensions of Globalization*. University of Minnesota Press, 1998.

Appadurai, Arjun. *Dimensões culturais da globalização*. Teorema, 2004.

Astruc, Alexandre. *Du stylo à la caméra et de la caméra au stylo*. Ed. L'archipel, 1992.

Aumont, Jacques, ed. *La mise en scène*. De Boeck, 2000.

Aumont, Jacques, and Michel Marie. *Dicionário teórico e crítico do cinema*. Papirus, 2003.

Aumont, Jacques, ed. *As teorias dos cineastas*. Papirus, 2004a.

Aumont, Jacques, ed. *O olho interminável*. Cosac & Naify, 2004b.

Aumont, Jacques, ed. *O cinema e a encenação*. Edições 70, 2006.

Aumont, Jacques, ed. *Moderno? Por que o cinema se tornou a mais singular das artes*. Papirus, 2008.

Ayfre, Amédéé. "Cinéma et présence du prochain." *Esprit*, no. 249 (1957): 624–40.

Ayfre, Amédéé. *Le cinéma et la foi Chretienne*. Librarie Artheme Fayard, 1960.

Ayfre, Amédéé. *Conversion Aux Images?* Éditions du Cerf Bourges, 1964.

Ayfre, Amédéé. "Neo-Realism and Phenomenology." In *Cahiers du Cinema: The 19505: Neo-Realism, Hollywood, New Wave*, edited by Jim Hiller. Harvard University Press, 1985.

Badiou, Alain. *Cinema*. Polity Press, 2013.

Baecque, Antoine. *Les Cahiers du cinema: Histoire d'une Revue—Tome II : Cinéma, tours detours 1959–1981*. Cahiers du Cinéma, 1991.

Baecque, Antoine. "O corpo no cinema." In *História do Corpo 3—As mutações do olhar,* edited by by Jean-Jacques Courtine. Vozes, 2008.

Baecque, Antoine. "Mister Hou e a experiência do olhar." In *Hou Hsiao-Hsien e o cinema de memórias fragmentadas,* edited by by Luísa Marques. CCBB, 2011.

Barbaras, Renaud. *The Being of the Phenomenon: Merleau-Ponty's Ontology*. Indiana University Press, 2014.

Barker, Jennifer. *The Tactile Eye: Touch and the Cinematic Experience*. University of California Press, 2009.

Bazin, André. *What Is Cinema?* Vol. I. University of California Press, 2005a.

Bazin, André. *What Is Cinema?* Vol. II. University of California Press, 2005b.

Bazin, André. *Orson Welles*. Ed. Jorge Zahar, 2005c.

Bazin, André, and François Truffaut. "Entretien avec Jacques Tati." *Cahiers du Cinéma*, no. 83 (1958): 2–18.

Bello, Angela Ales. *Introdução à fenomenologia*. Bauru, 2006.

Bellos, D. *Jacques Tati: His Life and Art*. The Harvill Press, 2001.

Bellour, Raymond. *L'analyse du film*. Bronché, 1975.

Bergala, Alain. "D'une certaine manière." *Cahiers du Cinéma*, n0. 370 (1985).

Bergala, Alain. *Nul mieux que Godard*. Cahiers du Cinéma, 1999.

Bergson, Henri. *Matéria e memória: ensaio sobre a relação do corpo com o espírito*. Martins Fontes, 2006.

Bérnard da Costa, João. "No quarto de Vanda." In *O cinema de Pedro Costa*, edited by Daniel Ribeiro Duarte. CCBB, 2010.

Berry, Chris. "Where Is the Love? The Paradox of Performing Loneliness in Tsai Ming-Liang's Vive l'amour." In *Falling for You—Essays on Cinema and Performance*, edited by Lesley Stern and George Kouvaros. Power Publications, 1999.

Beugnet, Martine. *Claire Denis*. Manchester University Press, 2004.

Beugnet, Martine. *Cinema and Sensation: French Film and the Art of Transgression*. Edinburgh University Press, 2007.

Bonitzer, Pascal. "The Disappearance (on Antonioni)." In *L'avventura: Michelangelo Antonioni*, edited by by Seymour Chatman and Guido Fink. Rutgers University Press, 1989.

Bonitzer, Pascal. *Le champ aveugle*. Gallimard, 1999.

Bordeleau, Érik, Toni Pape, Ronald Rose-Antoinette, and Adam Szymanski. *Nocturnal Fabulations—Ecology, Vitality and Opacity in the Cinema of Apichatpong Weerasethakul*. Open Humanities Press, 2017.

Bouquet, Stephane. "Plan contre flux." *Cahiérs du Cinema*, no. 566 (2002): 46–47.

Bouquet, Stephane. "Des films et des gestes." *Cahiers du Cinéma*, no. 578 (2003): 52–53.

Bouquet, Stephane. "De manera que todo comunica." In *Teoría y crítica de cine*, edited by Antoine de Baecque. Paidós, 2005.

Bragança, F. "Seis perguntas para Apichatpong Weerasethakul." *Revista Cinética*, December 2006. http://www.revistacinetica.com.br/entrevistajoe.htm.

Bragança, F. "Filmar, hoje, um corpo (em alguns atos)." *Revista Cinética*, 2007a. http://www.revistacinetica.com.br/filmarumcorpo.htm.

Bragança, F. "O real como milagre." *Revista Cinética*, October 2007b. http://www.revistacinetica.com.br/kawase.htm.

Brenez, Nicole. "The Ultimate Journey: Remarks on Contemporary Theory." *Screening the Past*, December 1997. http://www.latrobe.edu.au/screeningthepast/reruns/brenez.html.

Brenez, Nicole. "The Body's Night: An Interview with Philippe Grandrieux." *Rouge*, no. 1 (2003). http://www.rouge.com.au/1/grandrieux.html.

Brenez, Nicole. *Abel Ferrara*. University of Illinois Press, 2006.

Brenez, Nicole. *On the Figure in General and the Body in Particular—Figurative Invention in Cinema*. Anthem Press, 2023.

Bresson, Robert. "S'isoler des arts existants." *Nouvelle revue française*, no. 226 (1971): 153–54.

Bresson, Robert. *Notes on Cinematography*. Urizen Books, 1977.

Butcher, Pedro. "Documentar uma sensibilidade humana." *Revista Cinética*, 2010. http://www.revistacinetica.com.br/entpedrocosta.htm.

Cabo, Matos Ricardo, ed. *Cem mil cigarros*. Orfeu Negro, 2009.

Carbone, Mauro. "Merleau-Ponty e o pensamento do cinema." *Cinema: Journal of Philosophy and the Moving Image*, no. 2 (2011). http://cjpmi.ifl.pt/2-carbone/.

Carbone, Mauro. *The Flesh of Images Merleau-Ponty Between Painting and Cinema*. State University of New York, 2015.

Carlin, S., S. Delorme, and M. Levin. "Jacques Rancière." *Balthazar*, July 2000. http://dicionariosdecinema.blogspot.com/2009/09/entrevista-jacques-ranciere.html.

Carrol, Noël, and Jinhee Choi. *Philosophy of Film and Motion Pictures*. Blackwell Publishing, 2006.

Cavell, Stanley. *The World Viewed*. Harvard University Press, 1979.

Cerisuelo, Marc. *Hollywood a L'Ecran*. Presses de la Sorbonne Nouvelle, 2001.

Cerisuelo, Marc. "Le Mac-Mahon: histoire et légende." In *Les salles de cinéma: Enjeux, défis et perspectives (Hors Collection)*, edited by Laurent Creaton and Kira Kitsopanidou. Armand Colin, 2013.

Cesarino, Flávia Costa. *O primeiro cinema: espetáculo, narração, domesticação*. Scritta, 1995.

Chakali, Saad. "À corps ouvert(s)." *Cahiers du Cinéma*, 2005. http://www.cahiersducinema.com/article398.html.

Chauí, Marilena. *Da realidade sem mistérios ao mistério do mundo*. Brasiliense, 1999.

Chauí, Marilena. *Experiência do pensamento*. Martins Fontes, 2002.

Chauvin, Jean-Sébastien. "Au-delà des genres." *Cahiers du Cinéma*, no. 559 (2001): 77–78.

Ciment, Michel. "The State of Cinema." *Unspoken Cinema*, October 2003. http://unspokencinema.blogspot.com/2006/10/state-of-cinema-m-ciment.html.

Comolli, Jean-Louis. *Ver e poder—A inocência perdida: cinema, televisão, ficção, documentário*. Ed. UFMG, 2008.

Costa, Cláudio. "O Rio." In *O Cinema dos anos 90*, edited by Denilson Lopes. Argos, 2005.

Costa, Pedro. "Uma porta fechada que nos deixa a imaginar." In *O cinema de Pedro Costa*, edited by Daniel Ribeiro Duarte. CCBB, 2010.

Dalí, Salvador. *The Collected Writings of Salvador Dalí*. Cambridge University Press, 1998.

Daney, Serge. "O cinema e a memória da água." *Libération*, December, 1989. http://dicionariosdecinema.blogspot.com.br/2008/12/o-cinema-e-memria-da-gua-le-grand-bleu.html.

Daney, Serge. *L'exercice a été profitable, Monsieur.* Pol, 1993.

Daney, Serge. *A rampa*. Cosac & Naif, 2007.

da Silva, Camila Vieira. "O sensível da imagem: sensorialidade, corpo e narra-tiva no cinema contemporâneo da Ásia." Dissertação de Mestrado, UFC, 2010.

Davies, Robert. "Intruding Beauty: An Interview with Claire Denis." *Pas-temagazine*, 2004. http://pastemagazine.com/action/article?article_id=1325.

de Baecque, Antoine. *La Cinéphilie: Invention d'un regard, histoire d'une culture (1944–1968)*. Fayard, 2003.

Debaise, Didier, and Isabelle Stengers. "L'insistance des possibles: Pour un pragmatisme spéculatif." *Multitudes* no. 65 (2016/4): 82–89.

de Beauvoir, S. *A Força da Idade*. Nova Fronteira, 1984.

Deleuze, Gilles. *Kafka: Toward a Minor Literature*. University of Minnesota Press, 1986.

Deleuze, Gilles. *Spinoza: Practical Philosophy*. City Lights Books, 1988.

Deleuze, Gilles. *Cinema 2: The Time-Image*. University of Minnesota Press, 1989.

Deleuze, Gilles. *The Logic of Sense*. Columbia University Press, 1993.

Deleuze, Gilles. *Negotiations, 1972–1990*. Columbia University Pres, 1995.

Deleuze, Gilles. *Cinema 1: The Movement-Image*. University of Minnesota Press, 1997.

Deleuze, Gilles. *Essays Critical and Clinical*. Verso, 1998.

Deleuze, Gilles. *Francis Bacon: The Logic of Sensation*. Continuum, 2003.

Deleuze, Gilles. *Foucault*. University of Minnesota Press, 2006.

Delluc, Louis. *Écrits cinématographiques, Tome I: Le Cinéma et les Cinéastes*. Cinémathèque française/Cahiers du cinéma, 1985.

Delorme, Stéphane. "Les lois d l'affection." *Cahiers du Cinéma*, no. 609 (2006): 78.

Denorme, Vincent, and Emmanuel Douin. "Travelling Light." *Modam* I (2001): 20–27.

Descartes, R. *Meditations and Other Metaphysical Writings*. Penguin, 1999.

Douchet, Jean. "Mizoguchi e a apreensão do real." In *Mestre Mizoguchi: uma lição de cinema*, edited by Lúcia Nagib. Navegar Editora, 1990.

Douchet, Jean. "O corpo." In *Nouvelle Vague*, edited by Luís Miguel Oliveira. Cinemateca Portuguesa, 1999.

Duarte, Daniel Ribeiro. *O cinema de Pedro Costa*. CCBB, 2010.

During, Lisabeth, and Lisa Trahair. "Belief in Cinema: Revisiting Themes from Bazin." *Angelaki* 17, no. 4 (2012): 2–8.

Eisenstein, Sergei. *Film Form, Essays in Film Theory*. A Harvest Book, 1977.

Elsaesser, Thomas. "A Bazinian Half-Century." In *Opening Bazin*, edited by Dudley Andrew and Hervé Joubert-Laurencin. Oxford University Press, 2011.

Eno, Brian. "Music for Airports Liner Notes." *Music for Airports / Ambient 1* (Álbum), September 1978. http://music.hyperreal.org/artists/brian_eno/MFA-txt.html.

Epstein, Jean. "Le Cinematographe Vu de l'Etna." In *Écrits sur le Cinéma, Tome I, 1927–1947*. Cinéma Club / Seghers, 1974.

Espinosa, B. *Ética*. Relógio D'água, 1992.

Fabris, Mariarosaria. "Neo-realismo: novo em relação a qual realismo?" In *Olhares neo-realistas*, edited by G. C. Franco. CCBB, 2007.

Fairfax, Daniel. " 'Yes, We Were Utopians; in a Way, I Still Am…': An Interview with Jean-Louis Comolli." *Senses of Cinema*, no. 62 (2012). http://sensesofcinema.com/2012/feature-articles/yes-we-were-utopians-in-a-way-i-still-am-an-interview-with-jean-louis-comolli-part-1/.

Faria, Tiago, and Yale Gontijo. "Premiado em Cannes, cineasta português critica modelo hollywoodiano." *Correio Brasiliense*, September 18, 2009. http://pedrocosta-heroi.blogspot.com.br/2010/09/premiado-em-cannes-cineasta-por-tugues.html.

Ferraz, Marcus Sacrini. *A Fenomenologia e a ontologia em Merleau-Ponty*. Papirus, 2009.

Ferreira, Francisco, "Entrevista a Pedro Costa." *Expresso*, 2001. www.atalantafilmes.pt/2001/quartovanda/entrevista.htm.

Fiant, Antony. "Apichatpong Weerasethakul: des films qui muent." *Trafic*, no. 53 (2005): 27–38.

Filho, Luiz Rezende. "Realismo e neorrealismo em André Bazin." *Revista Contracampo*. 1991. http://www.contracampo.com.br/01-10/andrebazin.html.

Flanagan, Matthew. "Towards an Aesthetic of Slow in Contemporary Cinema." In *16:9 in English: Towards an Aesthetic of Slow in Contemporary Cinema*, 6, no. 29, 2008. http://www.16-9.dk/2008-11/side11_inenglish.htm.

Foucault, Michel. "Theatrum Philosophicum." In *Language, Counter-Memory, Practice* Bouchard, edited by F. Donald. Cornell University Press, 1977.

Foucault, Michel. *A arqueologia do saber*. Forense Universitária, 1995.

Foucault, Michel. *As palavras e as coisas*. Martins Fontes, 2002.

Frazão, Joana de Souza. "Entre ver a doença e narrá-la: os casos de Safe (Todd haynes) e The River (tsai Ming-Liang)." Dissertação de Mestrado, Universidade de Lisboa, 2009.

Frodon, Jean-Michel Frodon. *Hou Hsiao-hsien*. Cahiers du Cinéma, 1999.

Frodon, Jean-Michel Frodon. "Il s'agit de s'aventurer au-devant d'une forme." *Le Monde*, July 11, 2001.

Frodon, Jean-Michel Frodon. *Le cinéma chinois*. Cahiers du cinema, 2006.

Gallagher, Tag. *The Adventures of Roberto Rossellini*. Da Capo Press, 1998.

Gallagher, Tag. "Reading, Culture, and Auteurs." *Screening the Past*, March 2001. http://www.latrobe.edu.au/screeningthepast/firstrelease/fr0301/tgbfr12a.htm.

Gardnier, Ruy, Luiz C. Oliveira Jr., et al. "Cinema contemporâneo em debate." *Contracampo*, no. 78 (2005). http://www.contracampo.com.br/78/debatecine-macontemporaneo.htm.

Gardnier, Ruy. "Mal dos trópicos." *Contracampo*, no. 64, 2004. http://www.contracampo.com.br/64/tropicalmalady.htm.

Gil, José. *Metamorfoses do corpo*. Relógio D'água, 1997.

Gil, José. *Movimento total—O corpo e a dança*. Relógio D'água, 2001.

Gil, José. *A imagem-nua e as pequenas percepções: Estética e Fenomenologia*. Relógio d'Água, 2005.

Guimarães, Pedro Maciel, and Daniel Ribeiro. "Entrevista a Pedro Costa." October 2007. http://pedrocosta-heroi.blogspot.com/2008/02/mais-uma.html.

Gunning, Tom. "The World in Its Own Image: The Myth of Total Cinema." In *Opening Bazin*, edited by Dudley Andrew and Hervé Joubert-Laurencin. Oxford University Press, 2011.

Hagin, Boaz. "Inverted Identification: Bergson and Phenomenology in Deleuze's Cinema Books." *New Review of Film and Television Studies* 11, no. 3 (2011): 262–87.

Harman, Graham. "I Am Also of the Opinion That Materialism Must Be Destroyed." *Society and Space*, 28, no. 5 (2010): 772–90.

Harman, Graham. *Guerrilla Metaphysics: Phenomenology and the Carpentry of Things*. Open Court, 2011.

Harman, Graham. *Bells and Whistles: More Speculative Realism*. Zero Books, 2013.

Hasumi, Shigehiko. "Eloquence of the Taciturn: An Essay on Hou Hsiao-hsien." *Inter-Asia Cultural Studies*, 9, no. 2 (2008): 184–94.

Heidegger, Martin. *Discourse on Thinking*. Harper & Row, 1959.

Heidegger, Martin. *Philosophical and Political Writings*. Continuum, 2003.

Hu, Brian. "The Unprofessional: An Interview with Lee Kang-sheng." 2005. https://international.ucla.edu/institute/article/27006.

Husserl, Edmund. *Cartesian Meditations: An Introduction to Phenomenology*. Kluwer Academic Publishers, 1982.

Husserl, Edmund. *The Idea of Phenomenology*. Kluwer Academic Publishers, 1999.

Jarvie, Ian. *Philosophy of the Film: Epistemology, Ontology, Aesthetics*. Routledge, 1987.

JGC. " 'Vive l'amour': Cineasta malaio Tsai Ming-Liang retrata deserto das cidades." *Folha de São Paulo*, June 30, 2000.

Jones, Kent. *L'Argent*. British Film Institute, 1999.

Jones, Kent. "The Dance of the Unknown Soldier." *Film Comment* 36 (2000): 26–27.

Jones, Kent. "Here and There: The Films of Tsai Ming-Liang." In *Movie Mutations: The Changing Face of World Cinephilia*, edited by J. Rosenbaum. British Film Institute, 2008.

Joyard, Olivier. "C'est quoi ce plan? (La suite)." *Cahiérs du Cinema*, no. 580 (2003): 26–27.

Joyard, Olivier, Jean-Pierre Rehm, and Danièle Rivière. *Tsai Ming-liang*. Dis Voir, 1999.

Kennedy, Barbara. *Deleuze and Cinema: The Aesthetics of Sensation*. Edinburgh University Press, 2000.

Koresky, Michael. "This World and the Last." *Reverse Shot*, 2016. http://reverseshot.org/reviews/entry/2094/cemetery_of_splendor.

Kracauer, Siegfried. *Theory of Film: The Redemption of Physical Reality*. Oxford University Press, 1960.

Labarthe, André S. "Marienbad ano zero." *Cahiers du Cinéma*, no. 123 (1961): 28–31.

Lalane, Jean Marc. "C'est quoi ce plan?" *Cahiérs du Cinema*, no. 569 (2002): 26–27. http://ladroesdecinema.wordpress.com/furto-critico/que-plano-e-esse/.

Leenhardt, Roger. " 'Cinematic Rhythm' from 'Rythme cinematographique.'" *Esprit*, no. 40 (1936): 627–32.

Leopold, Nanouk. "Confined Space—Interview with Tsai Ming-Liang." *Senses of Cinema*, May 2002. http://sensesofcinema.com/2002/20/tsai_interview.

Lim, Dennis. "Tsai Ming-liang Opens the Floodgates." *Village Voice* 26 (2001). https://www.villagevoice.com/tsai-ming-liang-opens-the-floodgates/.

Lins, Daniel, ed. *Nietzsche e Deleuze—O que pode o corpo*. Relume Dumará, 2002.

Lispector, Clarice. *Água viva*. Rocco, 1998.

Malraux, André. *Esquisse d'une psychologie du cinéma*. Nouveau monde éditions, 2003.

Marks, Laura U. *The Skin of Film*. Duke University Press, 2000.

Marks, Laura U. *Touch: Sensuous Theory and Multisensory Media*. University of Minnesota Press, 2002.

Marques, Luisa, ed. *Hou Hsiao-Hsien e o cinema de memórias fragmentadas*. CCBB, 2010.

Martin, Adrian. *¿Qué es el cine moderno?* Uqbar Editores, 2008.

Martin, Adrian. "A Lyric Space: From Cinema to Media Art." 2011a. http://www.filmcritic.com.au/essays/lyric.html.

Martin, Adrian. "Incursions." In *The Language and Style of Film Criticism*, edited by Alex Clayton and Andrew Kleavan. Routledge, 2011b.

Martin, Adrian. *Last Day Every Day: Figural Thinking from Auerbach and Kracauer to Agamben and Brenez*. Punctum Books, 2012.

Martin, Fran. *Situating Sexualities: Queer Representation in Taiwanese Fiction, Film and Public Culture*. Hong Kong University Press, 2003a.

Martin, Fran. "Vive l'Amour: Eloquent emptiness." In *Chinese Films in Focus*, edited by Chris Berry. BFI, 2003b.

Mayne, Judith. *Claire Denis*. University of Illinois Press, 2005.

McMahon, Laura. "Rhythms of Relationality: Denis and Dance." In *The Films of Claire Denis: Intimacy on the Border*, edited by Marjorie Vecchio. I. B. Tauris, 2014.

Meillassoux, Quentin. *After Finitude: An Essay on the Necessity of Contingency*. Bloomsbury Academic, 2008.

Melville, Herman. *Bartleby the Scrivener*. Simon & Schuster, 1997.

Merleau-Ponty, Maurice. *The Structure of Behavior*. Beacon Press, 1963.

Merleau-Ponty, Maurice. *Signs*. Northwestern University Press, 1964a.

Merleau-Ponty, Maurice. *Sense and Non-Sense*. Northwestern University Press, 1964b.

Merleau-Ponty, Maurice. *The Primacy of Perception*. Northwestern University Press, 1964c.

Merleau-Ponty, Maurice. *The Visible and the Invisible*. Northwestern University Press, 1968a.

Merleau-Ponty, Maurice. *Résumés des cours: Collège de France 1952–1960*. Gallimard, 1968b.

Merleau-Ponty, Maurice. *The Prose of the World*. Northwestern University Press, 1973.

Merleau-Ponty, Maurice. *Notes des cours au Collège de France 1958–1959 et 1960–1961*. Gallimard, 1996.

Merleau-Ponty, Maurice. *Phenomenology of Perception*. Routledge, 2002.

Merleau-Ponty, Maurice. "Le monde sensible et le monde de l'expression." Coeditado por Emmanuel de Saint Aubert, Stefan Kristensen. Mètis Press, 2011.

Metz, Christian. *Essais sur la signification au cinéma*. Editions Klinksieck, 1972.

Mitry, Jean. *Sergei Eisenstein*. Editions Universitaires, 1961.

Mitry, Jean. *The Aesthetics and Psychology of the Cinema*. Indiana University Press, 2000.

Monassa, Tatian. "Cinema mundo." *Contracampo* no. 66, 2004. http://www.contracampo.com.br/66/cinemamundotatiana.htm.

Moriconi, Sérgio. "Sobre todo o líquido e o sólido." In *Catálogo da mostra Tsai Ming-Liang — O homem do tempo*. Centro Cultural Banco do Brasil, 2010.

Morrey, Douglas. "Open Wounds: Body and Image in Jean-Luc Nancy and Claire Denis." *Film-Philosophy* 12, no. 1 (2008): 10–31. http://www.film-philosophy.com/2008v12n1/morrey2.pdf.

Mourlet, Michel. *Sur um art ignore: La mise-en-scène comme langage*. Editions Ramsay, 2008.

Mourlet, Michel. *L'écran éblouissant*. Puf, 2014.

Mourlet, Michel. "On a Misunderstood Art (1959)." *Critical Inquiry* 48, no. 3 (2022): 483–98.

Munier, Roger. "The Fascinating Image." *Diogenes* no. 38, 1962. http://dio.sagepub.com/content/10/38/85.full.pdf.

Munier, Roger. "Le Chant second." *Revue d'Esthétique*, tome XX, 1967.

Munier, Roger. *Contre l'image*. Gallimard, 1989.

Munier, Roger. "La séduction des images." *Le Portique* 12, 2003. http://journals.openedition.org/leportique/569.

Nancy, Jean-Luc. *The Sense of the World.* University of Minnesota Press, 1997.

Nancy, Jean-Luc. *L'Intrus*. Galilée, 2000.

Nancy, Jean-Luc. "L'Intrus selon Claire Denis." *Remue.net*, 2005. http://remue.net/spip.php?article679.

Nancy, Jean-Luc. *The Creation of the World or Globalization*. SUNY Press, 2007.

Oliveira, Luiz Carlos, Jr. "A estética do fluxo no cinema contemporâneo." Monografia de conclusão de curso de graduação em cinema, inédita, UFF, 2006.

Oliveira, Luiz Carlos, Jr. "O Cinema Sob o Paradoxo do Contemporâneo." *Contracampo*, no. 91 (2008). http://www.contracampo.com.br/91/artrotterdam.htm.

Oliveira, Luiz Carlos, Jr. "O cinema de fluxo e a *mise-en-scéne*." Dissertação de Mestrado, ECA/USP, 2010.

Oliveira, Luiz Carlos, Jr. "O que é a *mise-en-scéne*, onde está a *mise-en-scéne*? Entrevista com Luiz Carlos Oliveira Jr." *Aurora*, edição 1, Fall 2012.

Oliveira, Luiz Carlos, Jr. *A mise en scène no cinema: Do clássico ao cinema de fluxo*. Papirus Editora, 2013.

Oliveira, Luiz Carlos, Jr. "Hey Joe." *Contracampo* no. 66, 2014. http://www.contracampo.com.br/66/heyjoejunior.htm.

Ortega Y. Gasset, José. *A desumanização da arte*. Cortez Editora, 2005.

Panozzo, Marcello, and Pablo Schanton. *Una sandía es una sandía—las películas de Tsai Ming Liang.* Festival Internacional de Cine de Gijón, 2004.

Parodi, Ricardo. "Cuerpo y cine: Reporte fragmentario sobre extrañas intensidades y mutaciones de orden corporal." In *Pensar El Cine 2,* edited by by Gerardo yoel. Manantial, 2004.

Peranson, Mark. "Pedro Costa: An Introduction." *CinemaScope* no. 27 (2006).

Peranson, Mark, and Kong Rithdee. "Interview: Ghost in the Machine: Apichatpong Weerasethakul's Letter to Cinema." *CinemaScope* no. 43 (2010). http://cinema-scope.com/spotlight/spotlight-ghost-in-the-machine-apichatpong-weerasethakuls-letter-to-cinema/.

Perez, Gilberto. *The Material Ghost: Films and Their Medium.* The Johns Hopkins University Press, 1998.

Pessoa, Fernando. *Páginas íntimas e de auto-interpretação.* Ática, 1966.

Pessoa, Fernando. *Escritos íntimos, Cartas e Páginas Autobiográficas.* Europa-América, 1986.

Pessoa, Fernando. *A Little Larger Than the Entire Universe: Selected Poems.* Penguin Books, 2006.

Poiares, Marta, and Pedro Dias da Silva. "Pedro Costa: 'Este não é o meu país. O meu país é as Fontaínhas.'" *Revista Rua Larga* no. 29 (2010).

Quandt, James, ed. *Apichatpong Weerasethakul.* Synema, 2009a.

Quandt, James, ed. "Resistant to Bliss: Describing Apichatpong." In *Apichatpong Weerasethakul,* edited by James Quandt. Synema, 2009b.

Ramos, Fernão Pessoa. *A imagem-câmera.* Papirus, 2012.

Rancière, Jacques. "De uma imagem à outra? Deleuze e as eras do cinema." *Intermídias,* Vitória-ES, Ano 4, no. 8 (2000): 1–25. http://www.intermidias.com/txt/ed8/De.pdf.

Rancière, Jacques. *A partilha do sensível: estética e política.* Ed., 2005a.

Rancière, Jacques. "Política da arte." 2005b. http://www.sescsp.org.br/sesc/images/upload/conferencias/206.rtf.

Rancière, Jacques. *Film Fables*. BERG, 2006.

Rancière, Jacques. "Política de Pedro Costa." In *Cem mil cigarros*, edited by Matos Ricardo Cabo. Orfeu Negro, 2009.

Rancière, Jacques. "A carta de Ventura." In *O cinema de Pedro Costa*, edited by Daniel Ribeiro Duarte. CCBB, 2010.

Rayns, Tony. "Touching the Voidnes." In *Apichatpong Weerasethakul*, edited by James Quandt. Synema, 2009.

Renouard, Jean-Philippe, and Lise Wajeman. "The Weight of Here and Now: A Conversation with Claire Denis." *Journal of European Studies* 34, no. 1/2 (2004): 19–33.

Reynaud, Bérénice. "Entretien avec Tsai Ming-Liang." *Cahiers du Cinéma* no. 516: 35–37.

Ricouer, Paul. "Sur La phénoménologie." *Esprit* 21, no. 12 (1953): 821–39.

Riegl, Alois. *Late roman art industry.* Giorgio Bretschneider, 1985.

Rimbaud, Arthur. *Uma estadia no inferno / Poemas escolhidos / A carta do vidente*. Martin Claret, 2002.

Rithdee, Kong. "Cemetery of Splendour." *CinemaScope* 63, no. 48 (2015). https://cinema-scope.com/spotlight/cemetery-of-splendour-apichatpong-weerasethakul-ukfrancegermanymalaysiathailand/.

Rivette, Jacques. "Letter on Rossellini." In *Cahiers du Cinema: The 1950S: Neo-Realism, Hollywood, New Wave*, edited by Jim Hiller. Harvard University Press, 1985.

Rohmer, Éric. "La 'Somme' d'André Bazin." *Cahiers du Cinéma*, 91 (1959): 36–45.

Rohmer, Éric. *Le goÛt de la beauté*. Cahiers du cinéma, 2004.

Romney, Jonathan. "Claire Denis Interviewed." *Guardian*, 2000. http://film.guardian.co.uk/interview/interviewpages/0,,338784,00.html.

Romney, Jonathan. "Unsatisfied Men." *Chicago Reader*, May 26. https://www.jonathanrosenbaum.net/2000/05/unsatisfied-men/.

Rose, Steve. " 'You Don't Have to Understand Everything': Apichatpong Weerasethakul." *Guardian*, November 11, 2011. https://www.theguardian.com/film/2010/nov/11/apichatpong-weerasethakul-director-uncle-boonmee-interview.

Rosenbaum, Jonathan. "City Without Tears." *Chicago Reader*, 2000. Disponível *Online*. https://jonathanrosenbaum.net/2021/04/city-without-tears/.

Roy, Jean. " 'Mon cinéma est immédiatement identifiable': une interview avec Tsai Ming-Liang." *L'humanité*, June 2007. http://www.humanite.fr/journal/2007-06-06/2007-06-06-852529.

Rugo, Daniele. *Philosophy and the Patience of Film in Cavell and Nancy*. Palgrave Macmillan, 2016.

Ruiz, Raúl. *Poetics of cinema 1: Miscellanies*. Dis Voir, 1995.

Russo, Eduardo. "Plano, tiempo y puesta en escena em el cine de Tsai Ming Liang." In *Pensar El Cine 2*, edited by Gerardo Yoel. Manantial, 2004.

Santayana, George. *The Sense of Beauty*. Dover Publications, 2012.

Sartre, Jean-Paul. *Cahiers pour une morale*. Gallimard, 1983.

Sartre, Jean-Paul. *Situações I*. Cosac & Naif, 2005.

Sartre, Jean-Paul. *The Imaginary*. Routledge, 2010.

Schefer, Jean Louis. *L'Homme Ordinaire du Cinéma*. Cahiers du cinéma, 1980.

Schefer, Jean Louis. *Du Monde et du Mouvement des Images*. Cahiers du Cinéma, 1997.

Serguine, Jacques. "Education du spectateur." *Cahiers du Cinéma* no. 111 (1960): 39–45.

Shaviro, Steven. *The Cinematic Body.* University of Minnesota Press, 1993.

Shaviro, Steven. *The Universe of Things: On Speculative Realism*. University of Minnesota Press, 2014.

Simon, Alissa. "Not an Ordinary Joe: An Interview with Apichatpong Weerasethakul." *Facets.org*, 2004. http://www.facets.org/critics/simon/Weerasethakul.htm.

Smith, Damon. "L'Intrus: An Interview with Claire Denis." *Senses of Cinema* no. 35 (2005). http://sensesofcinema.com/2005/35/claire_denis_interview/.

Sobchack, Vivian. *The Address of the Eye: A Phenomenology of Film Experience*. Princeton University Press, 1992.

Sobchack, Vivian. *Carnal Thoughts: Embodiment and Moving Image Culture*. University of California Press, 2004.

Sobchack, Vivian. "Phenomenology." In *The Routledge Companion to Philosophy and Film*, edited by Paisley Livingston and Carl Plantinga. Routledge, 2009.

Son, Luiz Rezende. "Realism and neorealism in André Bazin." *Contracampo Magazine*. 2023. http://www.contracampo.com.br/01-10/andrebazin.html.

Sontag, Susan. *Under the Sign of Saturn*. Vintage Books, 1981.

Spaziani, Paolo. "A alegria terminal: Uma estranha projeção de No quarto de Vanda." In *Cem mil cigarros*, edited by Ricardo Matos Cabo. Orfeu Negro, 2009.

Stengers, Isabelle. *Thinking with Whitehead: A Free and Wild Creation of Concepts*. Harvard University Press, 2014.

Sylvester, David. *Interviews with Francis Bacon*. Thames & Hudson, 1999.

Tarkovski, Andrei. *Esculpir o tempo*. Martins Fontes, 1998.

Tomasulo, Frank P. "The Text-in-the-Spectator: The Role of Phenomenology in an Eclectic Theoretical Methodology." *Journal of Film and Video* 40, no. 2 (1988): 20–32.

Vecchio, Marjorie, ed. *The Films of Claire Denis: Intimacy on the Border*. I. B. Tauris, 2014.

Veríssimo, Fernando. "Tsai Ming-liang: a água e o rio." *Contracampo* no. 23 (2000). http://www.contracampo.com.br/23/tsaieorio.htm.

Vieira, Erly Monteiro, Jr. "Recortes e rasuras no corpo: Sagrado e erotismo no Teorema de Pasolini." Dissertação de Mestrado, UFF, 2004.

Vieira, Erly Monteiro, Jr. "Marcas de um realismo sensório no cinema contemporâneo." Tese de Doutorado, UFRJ, 2012.

Vijn, Ard. "An Interview with Tsai Ming-Liang." *Twitch*, 2010. https://scre-enanarchy.com/2010/12/iffr-2010-an-interview-with-tsai-ming-liang.html.

Virilio, Paul. *Voyage d'hiver*. Parenthèses, 1997.

Wambacq, Judith. *Thinking Between Deleuze and Merleau-Ponty*. Ohio University Press, 2017.

Whitehead, Alfred North. *Symbolism: Its Meaning and Effect*. Fordham University Press, 1927.

Whitehead, Alfred North. *Modes of Thought*. Macmillan, 1966.

Whitehead, Alfred North. *Adventures of Ideas*. The Free Press, 1967.

Whitehead, Alfred North. *Process and Reality*. Free Press, 1978.

Whitehead, Alfred North. *O conceito de natureza*. Martins Fontes, 1994.

Whitehead, Alfred North. *A ciência e o mundo moderno*. Paulus, 2006.

Wittgenstein, Ludwig. *Philosophical Investigations*. Basil Blackwell, 1986.

Xavier, Ismail, ed. *A experiência do cinema*. Edições Graal, 1983.

Xavier, Ismail, ed. *O discurso cinematográfico: a opacidade e a transparência*. Paz e Terra, 2005.

Yacavone, Daniel. "Film and the Phenomenology of Art: Reappraising MerleauPonty on Cinema as Form, Medium, and Expression." *New Literary History* 47, no. 1 (2016): 159–85.

Zavattini, Cesare. *Sequences from a Cinematic Life*. Prentisse-Hall, 1970.

FILMOGRAPHY

Karim Aïnouz

Madame Satã (2002)

Michelangelo Antonioni

The Adventure (*L'Aventura*, 1960)
The Night (*La notte*, 1961)
The Eclipse (*L'eclisse*, 1962)

Alexandre Astruc

Le Rideau Cramoisie (1953)

Robert Bresson

Diary of a Country Priest (*Journal d'un Curé de Campagne*, 1950)
A Man Escaped (*Un condamné à mort s'est échappé*, 1956)
Pickpocket (1959)
The Trial of Joan of Arc (*Le Procès de Jeanne d'Arc*, 1962)
Balthazar (*Au hasard Balthazar*, 1966)
Mouchette (1967)
Money (*L'argent*, 1983)

Tod Browning

L'inconnu (1927)

Jane Campion

The Piano (1993)

Charles Chaplin

Modern Times (1936)

Pedro Costa

Blood (*O sangue*, 1989)

Down to Earth (Casa de lava, 1994)
Bones (Ossos, 1997)
In Vanda's Room (No quarto de Vanda, 2000)
Colossal Youth (Juventude em marcha, 2006)

Claire Denis

Chocolate (Chocolat, 1988)
Man No Run (1989)
Nénette et Boni (1996)
Good Work (Beau travail, 1999)
Trouble Every Day (2001)
Friday Night (Vendredi soir, 2002)
Stars at Noon (2002)
The Intruder (L'intrus, 2004)
35 Shots of Rum (35 rhums, 2008)
White Material (White Material, 2009)
High Life (2018)

Maya Deren

Meshes of the Afternoon (1943)
A Study Choreography for Camera (1945)

Vittorio De Sica

Bicycle Thieves (Ladri di biciclette, 1948)
Umberto D (1952)

Sergei Eisenstein

Battleship Potemkin (Bronenosets Potiokin, 1925)
October (Oktiabr, 1927)

Jean Epstein

The Fall of the House of Usher (La chute de la maison Usher, 1928)
The Tempest (Le tempestaire, 1947)

Paul Gégauff

Le reflux (1965)

Jean-Luc Godard

Breathless (*À bout de souffle*, 1959)
A Woman Is a Woman (*Une femme est une femme*, 1961)
My Life to Live (*Vivre sa vie*, 1962)
The Little Soldier (*Le Petit soldat*, 1963)
Contempt (*Le Mépris*, 1963)
Pierrot le fou (1965)
Ici et Ailleurs (1974), co-directed by Anne-Marie Miéville
Passion (1982)
Lettre à Freddy Buache (1982)

Werner Herzog

Cave of Forgotten Dreams (2010)

Alfred Hitchcock

Foreign Correspondent (1940)
Notorious (1946)
Rear Window (1954)
The Wrong Man (1956)
Vertigo (1958)
North by Northwest (1959)
Psycho (1960)

Hou Hsiao-Hsien

Cute Girl (*Jiu shi liuliu de ta*, 1980)
The Green, Green Grass of Home (*Zai na hepan qigcao qing*, 1982)
The Sandwich Man (*Er zi de da wan'ou*, 1983)
The Boys from Fengkuei (*Fengkuei-lai-te jen*, 1983)
A City of Sadness (*Beiqing chengshi*, 1989)
The Puppetmaster (*Ximeng Chengsheng*, 1993)
Goodbye South, Goodbye (*Zaijian, nanguo, zaijian*, 1996)
Flores de Shangai (*Hai Shang hua*, 1998)
Millennium Mambo (*Qian xi man pó*, 2001)
Flowers of Shanghai (*Kôhî jikô*, 2003)

Kon Ichikawa

The Burmese Harp (*Biruma no Tategoto*, 1956)

Naomi Kawase

Shara (2003)

Buster Keaton

The Scarecrow (1920)
Electric House (1922)
Sherlock Jr. (1924)
The General (1927)

Alberto Lamorisse

White Mane (*Crin-Blanc*, 1953)
The Red Balloon (*Le Ballon Rouge*, 1956)

Irmãos Lumière

Arrival of a Train at La Ciotat (*L'Arrivée d'un train en gare de La Ciotat*, 1895)

Adrian Lyne

9½ Weeks (1986)

Lucrecia Martel

The Swamp (*La Ciénaga*, 2001)

Tsai Ming-Liang

Rebels of the Neon God (*Qing shao nian nuo zha*, 1992)
Vive l'amour (*Ai qing wan sui*, 1994)
My New Friends (1995)
The River (*He Liu*, 1997)
The Hole (*Dong*, 1998)
What Time Is It There? (*Ni na bian ji dian*, 2001)
Fish, Underground (2001)
Goodbye, Dragon Inn (*Bu San*, 2003)
Aquarium (*segmento de Bem-Vindo a São Paulo*, 2004)
The Wayward Cloud (*Tian bian yi duo yun*, 2005)

Journey to the West (*Xi you*, 2014)

Jean Mitry
Pacific 231 (1949)
Images Pour Debussy (1952)

Robert Montgomery
The Lady in the Lake (1947)

Francois Ozon
Sitcom (1998)
Eight Woman (*Huit femmes*, 2002)

Marcello Pagliero
Un homme marche dans la ville (1950)

Maurice Pialat
Naked Childhood (*L'enfance nue*, 1967)
To Our Loves (*À nous amours*, 1983)

Otto Preminger
Bunny Lake Is Missing (1965)
The Human Factor (1979)

Vsevolod Pudovkin
Storm over Asia (*Potomok Chingis-Khana*, 1928)

Satyajit Ray
Pather Panchali (1955)

Jean Renoir
Diary of a Chambermaid (1946)

Alain Resnais
Hiroshima mon amour (1959)
Last Year at Marienbad (*L'année derrière à Marienbad*, 1961)

Muriel (1963)

Leni Riefenstahl

Triumph of the Will (*Triumph des Willens*, 1935)
Olympia (1938)

Roberto Rossellini

Rome, Open City (*Roma, cittá aperta*, 1945)
Paisá (1946)
Germany, Year Zero (*Germania, anno zero*, 1948)
Stromboli (1950)
Europa' 51 (1952)
Voyage to Italy (*Viaggio in Italia*, 1953)

Gus Van Sant

Gerry (2002)

Jacques Tati

Monsieur Hulot's Holiday (*Les Vacances de Monsieur Hulot*, 1953)
My Uncle (*Mon Oncle*, 1958)
Playtime (1967)

Dziga Vertov

Man with a Movie Camera (*Cheloveks Kinoapparatom*, 1929)

Jean Vigo

Zero for Conduct (*Zéro de conduite*, 1933)

Luchino Visconti

Obsession (*Ossessione*, 1943)
La Terra Trema (1948)

Andy Warhol

Sleep (1963)

Empire (1964)

Apichatpong Weerasethakul

Mysterious Object at Noon (Dokfa nai meuman, 2000)
Blissfully Yours (Sud sanaeha, 2002)
Tropical Malady (Sud pralad, 2004)
Syndromes and a Century (Sang sattawat, 2006)
Cemetery of Splendour (Rak ti Khon Kaen, 2015)
Memoria (2021)

Orson Welles

The Magnificent Ambersons (1942)
The Lady from Shanghai (1947)

Index